THE GREAT TYRCONNEL:
A CHAPTER IN ANGLO-IRISH RELATIONS

THE GREAT TYRCONNEL:
A CHAPTER IN ANGLO-IRISH
RELATIONS

by

SIR CHARLES PETRIE

THE MERCIER PRESS
CORK and DUBLIN

The Mercier Press
4 Bridge Street, Cork
25 Lower Abbey Street, Dublin 1

© Sir Charles Petrie 1972

SBN 85342 270 2

Printed in Great Britain by Bristol Typesetting Co. Ltd.
Barton Manor, St. Philips, Bristol

CONTENTS

Resource. The Jacobite Retreat. Estimate of the Casualties. William's Ineffective Pursuit. James and Frances Tyrconnel. The King's Dilemma. He Decides to Leave Ireland. His Nose Bleeds at Shelton Abbey. Reappoints Tyrconnel as Lord Deputy. Sails for France.

PROLOGUE

FOR IRELAND the seventeenth century was a revolutionary age and Richard Talbot, one day to be Duke of Tyrconnel, was the child of his age; so that to understand him it is first of all necessary to understand the Ireland into which he was born, yet the difficulty of doing this is enhanced by the fact that he and the Ireland of his time have rarely been approached with objectivity, least of all by contemporaries. The sixteenth century had proved to be the watershed of Irish history. When it began the country was subject to the rule of Gerald, Eighth Earl of Kildare, generally known as Garret More, who was the real sovereign of Ireland, whether the English throne was occupied by York or Tudor, from 1477 to his death in 1513; during this period, and for some years afterwards, the Anglo-Irish remained in entire possession of the Irish government: even so in 1530 it was reckoned that the chiefs alone could have brought twenty thousand armed men into the field.[1] Home Rule of a sort had been achieved. However, the heavy hand of the Tudors, particularly that of Henry VIII and Elizabeth I, gradually brought this state of affairs to an end, and by the accession of the Stuart dynasty in 1603 Ireland was an English province. It was disarmed from end to end, and revolt against the rule of the foreigner was impossible without aid from the Continent: it is true that this had been given by Spain on more than one occasion, but it was always a case of ' too little and too late ', and in any case it was much easier to send troops across the Irish Sea than the Bay of Biscay.

Had this been merely a military conquest its results would

not have been so far-reaching, but there was a great deal more
to it than that, for it was the definite policy of the English
government to obliterate the old Irish civilization, and to
replace it by what was considered in London to be the superior
culture of England herself. English landlordism took the place
of the older tenures of Brehon and semi-feudal law – a change
that was disastrous to the numerous free tenants of Irish
society; but the chief instrument in effecting the overthrow of
the old order was Protestantism. Professor Curtis is doubtful if
when it was introduced there were ' more than a handful of
Protestants in all Ireland among the Irish and Old English '.[2]
Yet it was pushed down the throats of the people with all the
force of government behind it, and quite regardless of the feelings of those concerned. The wanton destruction of the abbeys
was especially abhorrent to the common people, who entertained
no sort of animosity towards the monks, while the civilization
of the country received a terrible blow by the disappearance of
these centres of learning, religion, and hospitality, especially in
view of the fact that, unlike the sister kingdom across the
Irish Sea, Ireland was lacking in towns, villages, and manor-
houses. The cause of the Reformed Church was, moreover,
represented by men who knew no word of Irish, and had no
educational machinery at their command with which to replace
what they were destroying. It is one of the darkest blots on
English policy in Ireland at this time that out of the wealth
derived from the suppression of the religious houses not a
penny was spent upon the endowment of an Irish school or
university.[3]

In these circumstances it goes without saying that no
attempt was made to temper the wind to the shorn lamb, for
so far as the English government was concerned religious persecution was its primary instrument in a policy of genocide. The
Catholic Church was definitely a church of the people, and if
it could be destroyed the Irish way of life would be obliterated
with it: so we read in the *Annals of the Four Masters* that in
1540, ' The English, throughout every part of Ireland where
they extended their power, were persecuting and banishing the

religious orders, and particularly they destroyed the monastery of Monaghan, and beheaded the guardian and some of the friars.' Foremost in this work was the Archbishop of Dublin, George Browne,[4] who ordered the public burning of the *Baculum Jesu*, the supposed Staff of Christ, which had long been an object of veneration. Another ' Popish idol ' which was destroyed at the same time was the celebrated image of the Virgin at Trim.

It is true that similar barbarities marked the progress of the Reformation in England and Scotland, but there were two important differences. In those countries there was at least a minority, how large or small is admittedly a matter of controversy, favourable to change, while in Ireland there was none at all, although there was a handful of renegade ecclesiastics and avaricious noblemen ready to profit by it. Then, again, in the other two kingdoms, the Reformers were at any rate natives, and they were often quite sincere, whereas in Ireland they were aliens who were actuated not by their consciences but by a desire to serve the interests of the English Court. The ' English Garrison ' struck its first blow for ascendancy with the coming of the Reformation.

It is probable that as Europe passed from the Middle Ages into the modern world the old order in Ireland was doomed in any event, but it need not have passed away in fire and smoke with consequences that have not been wholly effaced even today. Yet perhaps it is possible to be over-censorious where the English government of those days is concerned, for as Hilaire Belloc wrote in our own time, ' No English authority (since the Lancastrian usurpation of the English throne in the Middle Ages) had ever attempted to understand Irish conditions. The Lancastrians let Ireland go. The Tudors returned to it as to another world . . . We have all seen how the ignorance of these modern politicians of ours, even today, with Ireland at twelve hours from London for transport, at a few seconds for information, with overwhelming superiority in wealth and power, has managed to lose Ireland.'[5]

With the coming of the second half of the sixteenth century,

as we shall see, the Anglo-Irish situation was further exacer-
bated by the fact that Ireland became involved in the struggle
between Philip II and Elizabeth I, and to some extent this was
a by-product of the Revolt of the Netherlands, for the position
was admirably summed up by Naunton when he wrote, ' For
as the Queen by way of division had at her coming to the
crown supported the revolted states of Holland, so did the
King of Spain turn the trick upon herself towards her going
out by cherishing the Irish rebellion.'⁶ At this point it is necessary to look closer at those Anglo-Spanish relations which for
many years formed the background against which the struggle
between England and Ireland was set.

Until the Reformation relations between Spain and England
had been friendly, and that for a variety of reasons. It is true
that England was weak in comparison with Spain and France,
and there were very definite limits to what she could do in the
event of war. Contemporaries, however, were in some doubt as
to her capabilities, and it was only natural that this should be
the case, for there was no guarantee that she would not resume
her career of aggression on the mainland of Europe when circumstances allowed, and it was a significant fact that the English monarchs continued to call themselves Kings of France.
The return of the lost provinces of Normandy and Guyenne
was still loudly demanded in London on all and every occasion,
though in retrospect it seems clear that these claims were not
very seriously meant, and that in reality they were put forward
partly to alarm the French, and partly as a sop to the more
bellicose spirits at home. However this may be, English foreign
policy for many years had a Gallophobe basis, and as Spain, too,
had several bones of contention with France, notably in respect
of Italy, it was only natural that England and Spain should tend
to work together, and their co-operation was strengthened by
the marriage of Henry VIII with Catherine of Aragon.

As the twenties of the sixteenth century passed into the
thirties Anglo-Spanish relations began to deteriorate, and the
main reasons for this were the repudiation by Henry of his wife
and his breach with the Pope. Indeed, the two events were

closely connected. Henceforth the English King had to be on his guard against the possibility of a Catholic alliance to overthrow him, so it became a matter of absolute necessity to exacerbate the differences between France and Spain. In pursuit of this policy he carried on a series of intrigues among the Protestant rulers of Germany, and although these were primarily directed against Charles V as Holy Roman Emperor they put an increasing strain upon English relations with Spain, of which he was King. It may thus be said that by the middle of the sixteenth century the bonds which had earlier held England and Spain together had become relaxed. So long as France was still formidable there was from time to time the necessity to combine against her, but she was on the eve of one of those periods of weakness and internal strife which are so prominent a feature of her history, and as her eclipse became pronounced England and Spain began to eye one another with increasing suspicion. The bitterness which was to mark the struggle between Philip II and Elizabeth I was being born, but first of all there was to be a brief interlude when the two countries were closer together than they had ever been before or were ever to be again.

This interlude was the period during which Philip was married to Mary Tudor and when they reigned together as 'Philip and Mary, by the Grace of God, King and Queen of England, France, Naples, Jerusalem, and Ireland, Defenders of the Faith ', for as his father had not yet abdicated Philip was only heir to the Spanish kingdoms. Nevertheless, Ireland was among his titles, and thus began its connection with the Spanish crown, though it can hardly be in doubt that in those early days Ireland was little more than a name to Philip, even though one of its newly-formed counties, and the latter's principal town, were called after him.

With the death of Mary Tudor in 1558 the relations between Spain and England steadily deteriorated, especially as their antagonism in the Americas became more bitter, and from a purely strategic point of view there was much to be said for an immediate Spanish offensive, that is to say for a ' preven-

tive-war' as it would now be termed. There is little doubt
that at that date Spain could easily have overwhelmed England, but political considerations ruled out anything of the
sort. Quite apart from the question of expense, Philip was
exposed to a very serious threat from the Turks in the Mediter-
ranean, while, even if he was successful in dethroning Elizabeth,
her heir was Mary, Queen of Scots, who had been Queen of
France, and would clearly further French, rather than Spanish,
interests if she got to London.

This explains why for so long the Spanish monarch tempor-
ized in spite of the appeals which now began to reach him from
Ireland, and when his ambassador in London forwarded
requests from Shane O'Neill for support he was told ' gently
to cut short his Irish negotiations as they were not desirable '.⁷
During the whole of the sixties the policy of Madrid was to
avoid any serious commitments in Ireland, and when Pope Pius
V excommunicated the English Queen his action was so dis-
pleasing to Philip that he not only refused to allow the publica-
tion of the Bull in his own dominions, but he also did all he
could to prevent it reaching England: indeed, he even went so
far as to tell Elizabeth herself that no act of the Pope had
caused him so much displeasure. This policy may have been in
accordance with Spanish interests, but it did not suit the
Papacy at all, so Rome proceeded to force the pace. Julius III
had created a kingdom of Ireland for the benefit of Mary
Tudor, and what a Pope could grant a Pope could clearly take
away, so on the excommunciation of Elizabeth the Irish throne
became vacant, and in these circumstances contemporary
opinion was in no way surprised when in February 1571 the
Spanish ambassador in London wrote to Philip to say that he
had received news through France to the effect that Pius V had
ceded the kingdom to him. As may be supposed the Irish
leaders were delighted, and they lost no time in trying to persuade Rome to put pressure upon Spain to assist them.

How long it might have taken Philip to comply with the
wishes of the Pope and the Irish in normal circumstances, given
his commitments elsewhere, is a matter for speculation, but his

hand was forced by English intrigues in the Netherlands, and here there is a definite parallel with the age of Louis XIV. It was to distract the attention of the English government from the Low Countries that Louis sent troops to Ireland in 1690, and it was for precisely the same reason that Philip took similar action a hundred and ten years earlier. He was also annoyed that Elizabeth should aid the Dutch, whom he regarded as rebels; so any assistance he could give the Irish was in his eyes merely tit-for-tat.

From this time Philip is found sending representatives to Ireland for the double purpose of keeping in touch with those who were discontented with English rule and of keeping himself informed of the progress of events. Captain Diego Ortiz de Urizar, for instance, was certainly in Ireland in 1574, when he reported to Madrid that nine-tenths of the people were Catholic, and he also reminded his master of the old saying:

> He who would England win,
> With Ireland must begin.

A couplet which, incidentally, exactly expressed the views of James II a century later.

By this time the Pope was Gregory XIII, and like his predecessors he pressed Philip to do something for the Irish, but the King still refused to commit himself to any course of action which might mean an open breach with Elizabeth: after all he was King of Spain, and Spanish interests came first. He was, however, prepared to subsidize what today we should call ' volunteers ' if we sympathized with their aims and ' mercenaries ' if we did not. Accordingly Sir James Fitzmaurice was allowed to recruit a motley force round Ferrol consisting of about eighty Spaniards, a handful of Italians, and some Irish and English refugees from Elizabeth's rule. With them were Nicholas Sanders, as Papal Legate, and Father, subsequently Cardinal, Allen, S. J. The fate of this expedition is extremely important to an understanding of Irish affairs at that time.

The actual dates of the events which immediately followed are not definitely established, but it would appear that the expedition sailed in six ships from – probably – Santander on 17 June 1579 and was off the coast of Kerry a fortnight later. The original intention may have been to put into Dingle, as in the following year, but bad weather rendered this impossible, and Smerwick was chosen instead. Even so, things went wrong from the start, for an English man-of-war – some accounts say several – which happened to be at Kinsale, got wind of what was taking place, and captured at least two of Fitzmaurice's transports, thus cutting him and his followers off from retreat by sea.

In any event Smerwick was a most unsuitable place at which to land. After the expedition had failed the Spanish ambassador in London reported to Philip, ' The Queen is informed that it would have been impossible to have found a worse place to build a fort, since it neither commanded a port nor a land pass, had no natural capabilities of defence, and did not even possess in the neighbourhood wood for fuel.'[8] It is indeed overlooked in every direction, so it is not surprising that what should have been a bridgehead became a death-trap. What the invaders should have done, at any rate after the arrival of the second contingent, and what their Irish allies urged them to do, was to have fanned out immediately, and seized the surrounding hills, when their activities in and round the harbour would have been safe from enemy observation. In effect what they lacked was audacity, and instead, like Stopford at Suvla Bay in the First World War and Lucas at Anzio in the Second, they set about consolidating their bridgehead, which gave time for the enemy to contain them. The result was that the invaders were bunkered until the English were in a position to dispose of them altogether.

Nor was this all, for the prospects of a national rising to shake off the English yoke appeared much more promising in the Vatican and the Escorial than they did in the harbour of Smerwick, for Fitzmaurice had calculated upon being joined by Gerald, Fourteenth Earl of Desmond, as soon as he landed, but that extremely slippery nobleman now hesitated to commit himself, though his two brothers, John and James, took the field. Having waited in Smerwick for a month, Fitzmaurice decided to force Desmond's hand, so he remembered a vow which he had made in Spain to go on a pilgrimage to Holycross in County Tipperary: basically it was a particularly shrewd move for that county was always easy to rouse to arms. Unfortunately, however, Fitzmaurice's ill-luck pursued him inland, for the Irish were divided in their loyalties, and those faithful to the English connection barred his path; there was some severe fighting in County Limerick, but although Fitzmaurice's forces had the better of it he was himself killed, and was succeeded in command of the Hispano-Papal army by John and James of Desmond, brothers of the Earl. How great a misfortune was Fitzmaurice's death it is hard to say, but it is difficult to resist the conclusion that it was probably a very considerable loss for he seems to have possessed the offensive spirit, and to have realized that a rebellion on the defensive had already failed.

We are told that this reverse had the most demoralizing effect upon the Papal soldiers at Smerwick, and that John of Desmond had the greatest difficulty in holding them to their allegiance, which is not surprising considering the type of men they were, for Nicholas Sanders described them as ' so little inflamed with military ardour that they were accustomed to use their swords as spits, and their helmets as pots when cooking their meat'.[9] To give John of Desmond his due, he realized the dangers attendant upon keeping his force shut up in a fort on the coast when command of the sea was in the hands of the enemy, so he distributed his men in small bodies about Kerry, which effectively prevented them being destroyed by the English at one blow.

At this point it must be confessed that the English had leadership while the Irish had not, as was so often to be the case in the following century too; in the present instance the Earl of Desmond continued to hedge with the most fatal consequences. On the other hand, as soon as Sir William Drury, who ruled Ireland with the title of Lord Justice, heard in Dublin of the landing at Smerwick, he marched into Munster

B

with all the troops he could muster, though they amounted to
no more than two hundred horse and four hundred foot. All
the same he had with him some lieutenants experienced in Irish
warfare in the persons of Sir Nicholas Bagenal, the Marshal
of Ireland; Sir Nicholas Malby, who came from his post as
President of Connacht; and James Wingfield, Master of the
Ordnance, who had considerable experience of modern war on
the battlefields of Flanders. Drury's intention was clearly to
dispose of the invaders at one stroke before they could be
reinforced, but John of Desmond's skilful strategy of dispersal
rendered this impossible, while uncertainty concerning the
position of the Earl of Desmond rendered any advance with
a small force into the areas which he controlled highly
dangerous.

The truth is that at this time Ireland was even more dis-
turbed than was usually the case in the closing decades of the
sixteenth century, and if the Pope and the King of Spain
thought that with the very meagre assistance they were giving
there could be brought about a national rising against the English this was an outstanding case of the triumph of hope over
experience. Instead, there was an outbreak of sporadic fighting
in which the various parties played each for his own hand
without paying much attention to the views of their backers
in Rome, Madrid, or London. In September 1579 there was a
change of leadership on the English side, for Drury died at
Waterford shortly after handing over command of the army
to Malby: he was succeeded as governor by Sir William Pelham.
Not long before these events took place the English troops had
been reinforced by six hundred men who had been raised in
Cornwall and Devon and landed at Waterford, while a squadron of six men-of-war under Sir John Perrott had taken up its
station in Cork. For the Irish a Papal Bull had arrived vesting
in Sir John of Desmond the authority previously enjoyed by
James Fitzmaurice.

The next twelve months were marked by some desultory
fighting of an extremely savage nature. The Earl of Desmond
finally came down on the side of the Irish, and captured and

sacked Youghal, having been admitted, so it was said, into the town by the Mayor: whether or not this was the case, when the tenth Earl of Ormonde, the ' Black Earl ', who was fighting for the English, managed to get hold of the unfortunate man he had him hanged before the door of his own house in Youghal. James of Desmond was also so unlucky as to fall into enemy hands, and he was executed as a traitor, his body being quartered and his head set upon the gates of Cork. The Spaniards and Italians were involved in this fighting to the extent that, as has been shown, small detachments of them were scattered about Munster on garrison duty, and when the places they were defending were attacked they were naturally implicated. This was what happened, for instance, at Carrig-a-Foyle which was held by a force of some fifty Irish and nineteen Spaniards under the command of an Italian officer; the castle of which they formed the garrison was, on this occasion, taken by storm, and all inside were either put to the sword or hanged.

In the summer of the following year, 1580, a new Lord Deputy arrived at Howth in the person of Lord Grey of Wilton, who determined that at the earliest possible moment he would strike a notable blow for the Queen. This he attempted to do on 25 August, but all that happened was that he met with a severe reverse at Glenmalure in County Wicklow, and when the news of this battle reached the Irish in Cork and Kerry it naturally had a most exhilarating effect.

Lord Grey was not, however, the only person to seek an intensification of the Irish war, for both the Spanish government and the Vatican had the same idea, and a further expedition was sent to Kerry under the command of an Italian, Sebastian de San Giuseppe, who would appear to have been a most unsuitable choice for the post. Dr Sanders described him as ' a most vile and wicked man, being avaricious and luxurious and effeminate and arrogant '. He seems to have been originally a commissary and paymaster to the adventurer Stucley,[10] and after the disaster at Smerwick one of the survivors, Alessandro Bertone of Faenza, wrote to him, ' Without an order from His Holiness you decided to embark on an enterprise disproportionate to your qualities.' On the other hand San Giuseppe himself seems to have entertained no doubts about his own capabilities.

What was the exact strength of this second expedition is not easy to determine, for the numbers who were massacred are no sure guide, since they were certainly augmented by the survivors of the force which had landed in the previous year, and how many these were it is impossible to conjecture with any accuracy. What may be affirmed with certainty is that the numbers never even approached the minimum considered necessary in Madrid for a successful invasion of either Ireland or England. According to English accounts San Guiseppe brought with him some seven or eight hundred Spaniards and Italians, arms for five thousand recruits, and a considerable sum of money. The newcomers entrenched themselves in the fort which had been thrown up by Fitzmaurice, which they strengthened and completed. Ormonde marched against them as soon as he heard of their landing, but he was worsted in some skirmishing which ensued, and fell back on Rathkeale, in County Limerick, to await the decision of the Lord Deputy.

Smarting as he was under his reverse at Glenmalure, Lord Grey of Wilton was under no illusions about the seriousness of these latest developments, for it must have seemed to him that the Spanish net was closing around Elizabeth and her dominions. Alba had annexed Portugal, a few weeks before, and as this gave Philip the Azores and Madeira it immensely enhanced his position in the Atlantic, while in another theatre Parma was going on from strength to strength in the Netherlands. If in these circumstances the Spaniards were to be allowed to establish themselves in Kerry, it would only be a question of time before Ireland would be lost to the English Crown. The Lord Deputy, like Kesselring at Anzio, determined at any rate to contain the invaders, so he at once set out from Dublin with about eight hundred men, and joined up with Ormonde at Rathkeale, whence he marched on Smerwick. How strong this combined force was it is impossible to say, for San Giuseppe certainly exaggerated it in a report to the Vatican when he placed Grey's strength at two thousand and Ormonde's at fifteen hundred.

Whether the Papal commander was guilty of treachery as well as of incompetence, there can be no doubt that he was incompetent, while the Lord Deputy displayed generalship of a very high order. He realized that everything depended on frustrating the invaders at Smerwick, so he ignored the threatening situation in the rest of the country and concentrated on this one object; he also realized the importance of 'combined operations', for by bringing up a number of British warships he invested the so-called Fort del Oro on all sides. None of this would have been possible had San Giuseppe fanned out as soon as he landed, occupied the surrounding hills, and so kept in touch with his Irish allies. Peter Lombard, who was Archbishop of Armagh from 1601 to 1625, notes that the Geraldines 'advised the Captain of the Fort that it was not safe to remain there, and that it would be much better to take everything there away and come out to their camp, so that joining forces they might oppose the advancing English'.[11] This advice, however, was rejected.

The next step was the unexpected surrender of the fort after very little attempt at defence, and naturally grave suspicion has ever since attached to San Giuseppe. The Earl of Desmond had no doubts where the blame lay, for writing to the Pope a year later he said that San Giuseppe had 'wickedly and treacherously surrendered the Fort he had built to the English, and forced his soldiers to lay down their arms so as to give access to the English who entered'. He then continues, 'Only the Colonel, with his men, is to blame for the surrender of the Fort. For I myself, with Sir John and the Bishop of Killaloe and Dr Saunders, were ready with large forces to attack the enemy on the other side, but the Colonel by his surrender of the Fort lost everything'.[12]

The surrender was followed by a massacre which has made the Smerwick landing one of the outstanding events in Irish history and of which the memory was undoubtedly responsible

for much of the savagery that characterized the fighting
between English and Irish in the following century; first of all,
however, the events in question must be regarded in their proper
perspective. Spain and England were not officially at war, and
in consequence Philip's soldiers could not claim the rights of
ordinary prisoners of war when they were taken in arms
against Elizabeth. That was the rule of the time, and that it
was rigidly enforced two examples will serve to show. Fadrique
de Toledo, the son of the Duke of Alba, had not hesitated to
put to the sword a force of French mercenaries who had been
trying to raise the siege of Mons a few years earlier on the
ground that France and Spain were nominally at peace, and the
same reason was later to be given by the Marqués de Santa
Cruz when he hanged from the yard-arm all the prisoners he
took from a French squadron off the Azores which had come
to the aid of the Portuguese Pretender. Whether England was
at war with the Papacy is a more difficult problem upon which
it is not easy to pronounce, but she certainly did not recognize
the Pope as suzerain of Ireland, and Elizabeth would have none
of his Irish kingdom: anyhow, Grey had already refused to
regard the Papal troops as soldiers at all, so it was clear enough
what their fate would be if they fell into his hands. What is
not in question is the fact that a victor had no right whatsoever to put non-combatants to death, and this was the usual
practice of Elizabeth's lieutenants in Ireland.

Were, however, the vanquished at Smerwick just mercenaries
who had surrendered unconditionally? All the evidence would
seem to show that such was not the case. Mendoza reported to
Philip that ' they surendered on condition of their lives being
spared ',[13] and it would be safe to assume that he got his
information from English sources as his direct contacts with
Ireland were few. In the *Annals of the Four Masters* we read
that before the surrender ' many communications mutually
took place on both sides, and a promise of protection was made
to them ',[14] while Peter Lombard, writing not later than 1600
says that ' the English offered the besieged such favourable
terms of escape that they accepted them, and surrendered the

Fort'. Most of the early seventeenth-century writers take the same view, and the latest authority, Dr O'Rahilly, who has examined all the evidence most carefully,[15] has no doubts, and he states without qualification that 'Grey did really make terms which he afterwards violated, while San Giuseppe was an accomplice in the treachery'. Grey was clearly a bloody-minded fellow anyhow, and he was later to be one of the commissioners for the trial of Mary, Queen of Scots, a task in which he revelled. According to *The Complete Peerage* he was called to account in the Star Chamber for his part in the Smerwick massacre, but it is at least as likely that this was because he had spared the lives of San Giuseppe and a few other traitors than on account of the butchery of the rest of the Papal expeditionary force.

The contemporary English authorities do not admit the fact that the surrender was on terms, but the transparent uneasiness of Spenser, Fynes Morison, and others can only lead to the conclusion that they suspected that Grey had broken his word. In the next generation, Thomas Russell, writing in County Clare in the reign of Charles I, had no doubt that he did, and his testimony is particularly valuable for he did not only rely for his information on books and manuscripts, but wrote down events as narrated to him by men who had taken part in them.

Treachery of this sort was bad enough, but the massacre of the Irish women and children who had taken refuge in the Golden Fort was worse, and worst of all was the torture of three of the prisoners, namely Oliver Plunkett, an Irishman from the neighbourhood of Drogheda; an English servant of Saunders by the name of Walsh; and a priest called Laurence Moore. These three were first of all told that their lives would be spared if they would take the oath of allegiance to Elizabeth and acknowledge her as Head of the Church; when they refused they were taken to a blacksmith's forge where their joints were broken with a hammer: in addition Father Moore had his thumbs and fore-fingers cut off. In this mutilated condition the three victims were left for a day and a night, after which their bodies were used for target practice by the English soldiers.

In effect, the Smerwick episode reflected no credit upon either party concerned – the English on the score of common humanity and the invaders on that of military competence. The only man of real ability connected with it on the Papal side was Fitzmaurice, and he was killed before he was able to bring his influence to bear upon the contending Irish factions. San Giuseppe was disaster, and the only doubt that arises concerning him is whether he was a traitor from the start, or whether he was suborned by Grey after the commencement of the attack on the Golden Fort; that he was utterly incompetent admits of no question. Smerwick would have been the grave of English dominion in Ireland had the invaders displayed the most elementary knowledge of strategy in a situation where the Lord Deputy's forces were caught between those of the Pope and Desmond like a nut in the crackers. Thug as he was, Grey of Wilton's strategy deserves the highest praise, though his methods of warfare would have been more suited to a general of Genghis Khan than to one of a Christian Queen.

The threat from the Continent to their security rendered the English deaf to all pleas on the score of humanity, just as was to be the case in 1798 and 1916, and the massacre at Smerwick was typical rather than exceptional. Even Froude made no attempt to defend what was done, for he wrote, ' The English nation was shuddering over the atrocities of the Duke of Alba. The children in the nurseries were being inflamed to patriotic rage and madness by tales of Spanish tyranny. Yet Alba's bloody sword never touched the young, the defenceless, or those whose sex even dogs can recognize and respect.'[16] Froude had plenty of evidence with which to support this statement, as one or two examples will testify. For instance, in April 1580 we find Sir Nicholas Malby writing to Walsingham, ' This day the forces which I have entertained took the strong castle of Ownemere from Shane MacHubert, and put the ward – both men, women, and children – to the sword '; while six years later Sir Richard Bingham wrote of the battle of Ardnaree,

' The number of fighting men slain and drowned that day we estimated and numbered to be fourteen or fifteen hundred – besides boys, women, churls and children, which could not be so few as so many more and upwards.'[17] It is true that Bingham was a particularly merciless scoundrel, but it is to be feared that he was typical not exceptional. The cruelties perpetrated on the shipwrecked soldiers and sailors from the Spanish Armada and on such of the Irish as were so ill-advised as to help them is further proof of the same terrorist policy.[18]

What the contemporary Irish possibly found more irritating than English barbarity – it was a rough age anyhow – was English hypocrisy, from which the Queen herself was by no means exempt, as she showed in the matter of the independence of the Low Countries. In 1581 the Dutch insurgents declared that ' God did not create the people slaves to their prince to obey his commands whether right or wrong, but rather the prince for the sake of the subjects ':[19] this was rather strong meat for the Tudor taste, so four years later Elizabeth published *A Declaration of the Causes moving the Queen of England to give aid to the Defence of the People afflicted and oppressed in the Low Countries;* in this she declared that ' Kings and princes sovereign are not bound to yield account or render the reasons of their actions to any others but to God '. This doctrine of Passive Obedience was officially held by the Church of England for the next hundred years until in 1688 it became highly inconvenient and was accordingly dropped; it is, however, by no means easy to reconcile with the Queen's complaint that Philip had begun ' to appoint Spaniards, foreigners, and strangers of strange blood – men more exercised in wars than in peaceable government, and some of them notably delighted in blood as hath appeared by their actions – to be the chiefest governors of all his said Low Countries, contrary to the ancient laws and customs thereof '. Presumably what the King of Spain should have done in the Netherlands was what his ex-sister-in-law did in Ireland, wither she sent as governors such peaceable non-military men of pure native blood such as Pelham, Grey, Raleigh and Bingham. Hypocrisy could go no further.

It would appear that the Queen was not wholly satisfied with her own arguments for later that same year she instructed Thomas Bilson, who was in due course rewarded with the sees successively of Worcester and Winchester, to return to the fray with *The True Difference between Christian Subjection and Unchristian Rebellion*, which purported to prove that rebellion was all right in Germany, Flanders, Scotland, and France — Ireland was not even mentioned, it may be added. During the Civil War the Roundheads made considerable play with the Queen's arguments to justify their attitude towards Charles I.

The consequences of this genocidal policy were not long in making themselves felt, and they have been admirably described by Alice Stopford Green:

> Torturers and hangmen went out with the soldiers. There was no protection for any soul: the old, the sick, infants, women, scholars: any one might be a landowner, or a carrier-on of the tradition of the tribal owners, and was in any case a rebel appointed to death. No quarter was allowed, no faith kept, and no truce given . . . It lasted for some seventy years. The Irish were inexhaustible in defence, prodigious in courage, and endured hardships that Englishmen could not survive. The most powerful governors that England could supply were sent over, and furnished with England's armies and stores. Fleets held the harbours, and across all the seas from Newfoundland to Dantzig gathered in provisions for the soldiers. Armies fed from the seaports chased the Irish through the winter months, when the trees were bare and naked and the kine without milk, killing every living thing and burning every granary of corn, so that famine should slay what the sword had lost. Out of the woods the famishing Irish came creeping on their hands, for their legs would not bear them, speaking like ghosts crying out of their graves, if they found a few water-cresses flocking as to a feast; so that in a short space there were almost none left, and a most populous and splendid country suddenly left void of man and beast.[20]

It was not until 1601 that Spanish commitments elsewhere allowed her government to give a hand once more in what it was hoped might prove to be the liberation of Ireland: by this

time England and Spain were officially at war, and Philip III
and his minister, the Duke of Lerma, determined to strike one
more blow. Messages kept on arriving in Madrid to the effect
that now was the time to act, and that unless the Irish leaders
were supported by Spain with men and money the chance of
expelling the English from Ireland would be lost for ever.
Lerma agreed with this argument, and he induced the Cortes
to vote an extra-ordinary tax of twenty-four million ducats
spread over six years. The resulting expedition was of some size
for those days, since it consisted of thirty-three ships carrying
4,500 men and a large quantity of war material. Bad weather,
however, drove many of the vessels back into port, and
although reinforcements were sent, the expedition never really
looked like being successful. The Spaniards took possession of
several places on the South Coast, notably Kinsale, but not
having command of the sea they were promptly blockaded in
them by the English forces, who pursued the same strategy as
Grey of Wilton at Smerwick, and in no case were their Irish
allies strong enough to raise the siege. In 1602, therefore, the
Spanish commander came to terms with the English authorities
and evacuated Ireland.[21]

The last Spanish army had landed on Irish shores, and belied
the hope expressed in Costello's great Gaelic poem, so beautifully rendered into English by James Clarence Mongan:

> There's wine from the royal Pope
> Upon the ocean green;
> And Spanish ale shall give you hope,
> My dark Rosaleen.

Unfortunately the Pope's wine was never sent in sufficient
quantities, nor was the Spanish ale strong enough.

The withdrawal of foreign aid consequent upon the Spanish
evacuation of Kinsale marked the beginning of the end of
Irish resistance to English domination and was followed in due
course by what is known as ' The Flight of the Earls '. The earls
in question were Hugh O'Neill, Earl of Tyrone, and Rory
O'Donnell, Earl of Tyrconnel of an earlier creation; they sailed

from Lough Swilly for the continent in September 1607, and with them went a number of lesser Celtic magnates who felt that life would no longer be safe for them in their own country. The departure of their natural leaders in these circumstances created the most profound impression upon the Irish people, in whose history it henceforth formed one of the outstanding landmarks, and, as always, they expressed their feelings best in song, of which the following, translated by Dr Robin Flower, is an admirable example.

TONIGHT IRELAND IS DESOLATE

This night sees Eire desolate,
Her chiefs are cast out of their state,
Her men, her maidens weep to see
Her desolate that should peopled be.

How desolate is Connla's plain
Though aliens swarm in her domain;
Her rich bright soil had joy in these
That now are scattered overseas.

Man after man, day after day,
Her noblest princes pass away
And leave to all the rabble rest
A land dispeopled of her best.

Men smile at childhood's play no more,
Music and song, their day is o'er;
At wine, at Mass the kingdom's heirs
Are seen no more; changed hearts are theirs.

Her chiefs are gone. There's none to bear
Her cross, or lift her long despair;
The grieving lords take ship. With these
Our very souls pass overseas.

The Flight of the Earls left a large portion of Ulster at the disposal of the Crown, and this proved to be the first step in its plantation. The Lord Deputy from 1605 to 1616 was Sir Arthur Chichester, a good enough man according to his lights, and certainly an improvement upon most of those by whom the English Crown was represented in Ireland. He seems earnestly to have desired to end the rule of the sword, and to make English law popular by making it beneficial, but it clearly never occurred to him that the Irish might prefer to abide by the old ways, or that it was after all their own country. However excellent his intentions, he acquiesced in a settlement that was wholly inequitable. The commissioners appointed to draw up a scheme paid no regard to vested interests and treated the whole territory as something which might be freely apportioned between natives and settlers. There were three classes of grantees, namely English and Scottish settlers; servitors, that is to say old servants of the Crown, civil and military; and native Irish. The land was to be divided into portions of 2,000, 1,500 and 1,000 acres apiece, and the greater and better part was assigned to the settlers, who were each to build a castle or a walled enclosure containing a stone house. The existing Irish cultivators were to be removed to such lands as had been assigned to their countrymen, or to other desolate parts of Ireland.

The estimates of the total acreage forfeited, and of the proportions assigned to English and Scottish settlers, servitors, and natives, differ in the most bewildering fashion, but the fact remains beyond dispute that a large proportion of the most fertile land in Ulster was torn from the native proprietors, who had mostly committed no overt act of rebellion, and given to foreign colonists. At the same time the designs of the government were imperfectly executed, for some of the undertakers who received lands never came near them, and the native peasantry in most places remained on the soil as labourers under new masters. Yet the Ulster plantation was in one sense successful in that it grew into a large and prosperous colony big enough to keep its distinctive character – and to form an English advance-post in Ireland. The natives who had no share in its opulence remembered with implacable hatred how they had been robbed of their lands, and their victimization under James was the direct cause of rebellion and massacre under Charles. The lesser plantations elsewhere were undertaken in the later years of Chichester's government with as little regard for justice and humanity as the policy of civilizing the people was more and more abandoned for that of turning them off the land. The Irish remained in a constant fear of attack upon their religion and their property which kept alive all the bitter memories of the past as well as prompting hunger for revenge and freedom in the future.

David Rothe, the Catholic Bishop of Ossory from 1618 to 1650, well described contemporary opinion of these happenings.

> The Viceroy should have considered more carefully before he put forward a title, flimsy and imperfect, to these lands, on behalf of the King, and expelled from their ancient possessions harmless poor people who have many children and no friends to take their parts. They have nothing but flocks and herds, no trade but agriculture, no learning. They are unarmed, but so active in mind and body that it is dangerous to drive them from the homes of their ancestors, making the desperate seek revenge and even the more moderate think of taking to arms. Their weapons have been taken from them, but they are in a mood to fight with fists and feet, and to tear their oppressors with their teeth. Despair is a sharp spur. These Leinstermen and others like them now see no hope of restitution or compensation. It is their nature that they would rather live on husks at home than feast richly anywhere else, and they will fight for their altars and hearths, and seek a bloody death near the graves of their fathers rather than be buried as exiles in foreign earth and alien sands.

In these circumstances it is not surprising that when a French traveller, La Boullaye le Gouz, visited Ireland in the seventeenth century, he found that while a warm reception always awaited his own fellow-countrymen and the Spaniards, the English and Scots were universally regarded as ' irreconcilable enemies '.[22]

It has been necessary to relate these unhappy events at some length as otherwise it would be impossible to understand the background against which Richard Talbot's life was set. They also explain the savagery which, it must be confessed, only too often marked the conduct of the Irish themselves in their rising against their oppressors in the middle of the seventeenth century: they had many wrongs to avenge, and it was only natural that they should follow the example of barbarity which had been set them. In any event, they were fighting on their own soil against an alien aggressor, so much may surely be forgiven. Elsewhere in the British Isles the conduct of warfare was becoming increasingly humane, and the contest between King Charles I and the Parliament was a very gentlemanly affair compared with the Wars of the Roses; even in Scotland the English in Cromwell's time behaved with a restraint which had not marked their activities there in the past, or was to mark them again a century later. Only in Germany during the Thirty Years' War was there a ferocity comparable with the fighting in Ireland in which Richard Talbot was to spend so large a part of his life.

NOTES

[1] *Cf.* Curtis, Edmund: *A History of Ireland*, p. 220. London. 1936.

[2] *Ibid.* p. 165.

[3] *Cf. The Political History of England*, Vol. V, p. 473. London. 1910.

[4] He was deprived under Philip and Mary, and died in 1556.

[5] *James the Second*, p. 241. London. 1928.

[6] *Fragmenta Regalia*, pp. 101-102. London. 1641.

[7] *Spanish Calendar*, Vol. I, p. 370.

[8] *Cal. S. P. Spanish*, 1580-86, p. 70.

[9] *Cf.* Moran, *History of the Catholic Archbishops of Dublin*, Vol. I, p. 201. Dublin. 1864.

[10] For Stucley's career, cf. Petrie, Sir Charles: *Don John of Austria*, pp. 244 *et seq.*, London, 1967.

[11] *Cf.* Byrne, M.: *The Irish War of Defence*, p. 11. Cork. 1930.

[12] *Archivium Hibernicum*, Vol. VII, p. 300.

[13] *Cal. S. P., Spanish*, 1580-86, p. 70.

[14] P. 1741, O'Donovan, A. D. 1580.

[15] *Cf.* his *The Massacre at Smerwick, passim*. Cork. 1938.

[16] *History of England,* Vol. X, p. 508. London. 1866.

[17] Quoted by O'Rahilly, Prof. Alfred: *The Massacre at Smerwick,* pp. 25-26. Cork. 1938.

[18] *Cf.* Danaher, Capt. Kevin, in *The Irish Sword,* Vol. II, pp. 321-31. Dublin. 1956.

[19] Somers, *Tracts,* Vol. I, p. 323.

[20] *Irish Nationality,* pp. 131-3. London. 1911.

[21] *Cf.* Jones, F. M.: *Mountjoy, 1563-1606,* pp. 109 *et seq.* Dublin. 1958.

[22] *Tour,* ed. by T. Crofton Croker, p. 43. London. 1837.

CHAPTER I

Family and Early Years

SUCH WAS the land in which Richard Talbot, the future Duke of Tyrconnel, was born in 1630. His great detractor, Macaulay, says that 'he was descended from an old Norman family which had long been settled in Leinster, which had there sunk into degeneracy, which had adopted the manners of the Celts, which had like the Celts adhered to the old religion, and which had taken part with the Celts in the rebellion of 1641'.[1] There is plenty to be said against Richard Talbot without having to resort to the denigration of his family, which was one of the most ancient in the British Isles, for an ancestor, also called Richard, is mentioned in Domesday Book, while the castle and lordship of Malahide were conferred upon the Talbots by Henry II. Of this family, which was related to the Earls of Shrewsbury, Richard was the member of a cadet branch.

What, if anything, Macaulay meant by the phrases 'sunk into degeneracy' and 'adopted the manners of the Celts' is not easy to discover. He surely cannot intend to imply that the Talbots made undesirable marriages, for Richard's mother was Alison Netterville, of Castleton, Co. Meath, a member of an old Pale family with whom the Talbots seem to have been closely associated for some time, since in a list of nobility and gentry of the Pale who, in the reign of Elizabeth I, had complained of the 'cess' as contrary to law and justice, and who refused to subscribe, are to be found side by side the names of William Talbot and John Netterville, and on 7 February 1578 they were fined £100 and £75 respectively.[2] Richard's grandfather married a Luttrell, also from the Pale. Richard himself

C

had not a drop of Celtic blood in his veins; indeed the lack of it was the chief argument used by his fellow-countrymen against him, and the first member of the family to marry into the old Irish was his own sister. On the other hand it is true that the Talbots had remained Catholic.

Nevertheless the fact that the Talbots were a Pale family of Anglo-Irish stock cut them off effectively from the native Irish in spite of the religious tie. Contrary to what is often supposed a Pale was neither more nor less than a medieval area of jurisdiction,[3] and the Irish one was subject to the royal government in Dublin. The Statute of Kilkenny in 1367 set up very definite barriers between what may be described as the new Irish inside the Pale and the old Irish outside it, but in the following century there was a gradual shrinkage of the Pale until it comprised nothing but the county of Dublin and parts of Louth, Meath, and Kildare – an area extending approximately from Dundalk southward to Dublin and Kilcullen, and westward as far as Kells and Trim: a statute of Edward IV actually used the word 'Pale', and ordered it to be fortified with a double ditch and a wall.

Richard's father, William Talbot, had played quite a conspicuous part in the stormy politics of the day. By profession a lawyer, he had become Recorder of Dublin, but on the accession of James I he had refused to take the Oath of Supremacy and had in consequence been removed from his post. He then turned to politics, which afforded an equal scope for his talents, since in 1613 the only Irish Parliament summoned during the reign of James duly met: to it Talbot was elected for County Kildare. It had been convoked for the purpose of confirming the Ulster and other Plantations, to vote supplies, and to legalize the introduction of English law into the country. Catholics were not barred from sitting, as in England, so in order to secure a Protestant majority the Government had to have recourse to a certain amount of gerrymandering. Pressure was accordingly brought to bear on the sheriffs, and thirty-nine new boroughs, calculated to return Protestant members, were created, which brought the numbers of the Commons up to 232. The Upper

House, though not numerically strong, was mainly composed of peers from the Pale and the neighbouring counties, who, although English by descent, were Catholic by religion. This Parliament, therefore, clearly required careful handling.

There was an initial tussle over the election of the Speaker, in which Talbot was well to the fore, but the Government got their man elected by a small majority; thereafter all went well for Dublin Castle where political business was concerned. On such matters as the Plantations and the confirmation of the attainder of the Earl of Tyrone there was little opposition, while the King's title was duly acknowledged, a generous subsidy was granted, the Statutes of Kilkenny were pronounced obsolete, and all Irishmen without distinction were declared subject to one common law. Apart from their Catholicism, there was as yet no community of interest, still less of co-operation, between the families of the Pale and the Celtic population.

Where religion was concerned, the Government found no such docility. In fact as soon as it became known that a Parliament was to be summoned Catholics all over the country saw in the decision a determination to pass penal measures against their faith. The Lords of the Pale claimed under Poynings' Law, enacted in the reign of Henry VII, the right to be consulted as to new legislation, and on the eve of the meeting of Parliament eleven of them petitioned the Lord Deputy, Sir Arthur Chichester, in person, protesting against 'miserable villages by whose votes extreme penal laws shall be imposed on the King's subjects'. As these Recusants were mainly composed of possessors of such names as Talbot, Roche, Barry, Butler, and Nugent they clearly could not be just ignored.

The Commons went even further, and at this point William Talbot appeared upon the scene, for they placed him at the head of a deputation which was appointed to represent their views to the King in London. So across the sea he and his colleagues went, claiming to represent twenty-one counties and twenty-one ancient boroughs. James received them on 12 April 1614 and treated them to what Professor Curtis calls 'one of his usual pawky lectures '.[4] He asked them, ' What if I create forty noblemen and four hundred boroughs?', and then remarked, ' The more the merrier '. There were a number of other pleasantries of like nature. Talbot and his colleagues were told that as Catholics they were but half-subjects and therefore deserved only half-privileges. The King further charged them with believing in the doctrine that heretic monarchs, deposed by the Pope, might be lawfully murdered.[5] In the end, however, the Royal bark proved to be worse than the Royal bite, and James agreed that eleven boroughs should be abolished; no open toleration was promised, but no new measures against Catholics were enacted and compulsory attendance at Protestant services was dropped. Parliament itself was dissolved in October 1615, and it did not meet again for eighteen years.

Talbot himself did not fare so well, though whether he suffered because he was an Irish patriot, or because of his alleged views as a Catholic on the assassination of kings, is not easy to decide. Anyhow, instead of being allowed to return to Ireland he was lodged in the Tower, and in due course he made his appearance before the Star Chamber, with Francis Bacon, then Attorney-General, leading for the prosecution. Talbot still declined to take the oath, but he acknowledged that James was lawful and undoubted King, to whom he would bear true faith and allegiance during his own life. This, however, was not good enough, and the unhappy man was fined the enormous sum of ten thousand pounds; in the meantime he was returned to the Tower to ' attend on His Majesty's pleasure '.

At this point either he was bought off or his luck turned, for he does not appear to have had to pay the fine, while he was allowed to go home before the end of 1614. Nor was this all, for he received a pardon for his offences, whatever they may have been, and that without any change of religion. From this moment Talbot went out of Irish politics – certainly he never again criticized the Government; eight years later, in February 1622, he received a baronetcy, and this was followed by various gifts of land, so that when he died on 16 March 1634 he left a considerable estate. In all the circumstances it is

difficult to resist the conclusion that he gave himself a
' nuisance value ', duly received his price, and thereafter became
a loyal subject of the King of England, though without any
compromise on his part where religion was concerned.

Sir William Talbot and his wife had in all sixteen children,
eight sons and eight daughters, of whom Richard was the
youngest. The dates of their birth are uncertain, and about
some of them all that is known is their names, which according to Burke's *Dormant and Extinct Peerages* were, of the sons,
Robert, John, Garrett, James, Thomas, Peter, Gilbert, and
Richard, and, of the daughters, Mary, Bridget, Margaret,
Frances, Elizabeth, Jane, Catherine, and Eleanor. Robert, who
succeeded his father as second baronet of Carton, afterwards
Talbotstown, in County Kildare, seems to have been born
in 1608, for Dalton says that he was twenty-six when he came
into the title,[6] by which time he was married to Grace Calvert,
whose father was created Lord Baltimore by Charles I. Robert,
who died in 1678, is described by Clarendon as ' much the best;
that is the rest were much worse men ',[7] while Carte goes even
further and admits that he was ' a gentleman of very good
sense, strict honour, and great bravery '.[8]

None of the other sons and daughters of Sir William Talbot
and Alison Netterville played any great part in Irish annals
except Peter, who in due course became Archbishop of Dublin.
Of the daughters, Mary, the eldest, married Sir John Dongan;
she must have been a good deal older than her brother, Richard,
since at the age of seventeen we find him serving under her
son. Another daughter, Eleanor, became the wife of Sir Henry
O'Neill, and mother of Niall O'Neill whose dragoons at the
Battle of the Boyne vainly tried to hold the ford at Rosnaree
against Meinhart Schomberg, when he was himself mortally
wounded.

Little or nothing is known of Richard Talbot's early life: he
was not more than four when his father died, and he was
brought up at Carton, which was now the property of his
eldest brother, Robert. If these years of childhood were peaceful, and there is no reason to assume that such was not the

case, they represented the only peaceful period of his life, for in 1641 the Irish insurrection broke out, and with its repercussions he was to be involved until his dying day.

As so often during the period of English rule the main problems were religion and the land, and where both were concerned there had been relative quiescence under the first two Stuart sovereigns. The genocidal policy of Elizabeth I had erased the Celtic Irish as a factor in the political life of their own country,[9] and many of their natural leaders had taken refuge on the Continent, while the Plantation of Ulster had completely changed the situation in that province. In all this the Government had been able to rely upon the support of what for want of a better word may be described as the Old English, to whom the Talbots belonged. Religious persecution might have united all Catholics irrespective of racial origin, and as early as 1611 Lord Carew, who had been sent by James I to Ireland on what today would be termed a fact-finding mission, foresaw a drawing together, through community of faith, of the Old English settlers and the native Irish, and he prophesied that they would rebel ' under the veil of religion and liberty '. For a generation this state of affairs did not materialize owing to what Professor Dudley Edwards has described as 'the relative toleration enjoyed since the beginning of Charles's reign '.[10]

While Strafford ruled in Ireland, the discontented were afraid to lift their heads, but in 1640 he was recalled and lesser men took his place. Before long it became obvious that there was really no government in the country at all, while Britain herself was distracted by quarrels which might at any moment end in civil war. Such being the case, Irishmen might well hope that a general uprising would shake off the foreign yoke, regain the lost lands, and ensure full freedom for the Catholic religion.[11] The elements of this rising existed both at home and abroad. In Ireland it found its leaders among the surviving members of the Celtic aristocracy, such as Sir Phelim O'Neill, who regarded himself as head of the great house which had so long ruled in Ulster; Lord Maguire; and Rory

O'More, whose family had been deprived of their lands in Leix. Abroad there was a whole army of soldiers in the service of Spain and the Empire, not least among them being Owen Roe O'Neill, and large numbers of priests and friars in the Irish colleges of Spain, Italy, and the Low Countries. A union was now formed between these different elements, and while Rory O'More championed the cause at home Father Luke Wadding organized it abroad and sought the help of the Pope and of Cardinal Richelieu.

In Ireland itself there was a certain lack of co-ordination among the conspirators, and an attempt to capture Dublin Castle by a *coup de main* failed to materialize, but by the end of October 1641 the North was in flames as the result of what was definitely a popular movement, at the head of which were the chiefs of the old Irish septs, such as The O'Conor Don. So rapidly did the rising spread that within a week the insurgents were absolute masters of Tyrone, Monaghan, Longford, Leitrim, Fermanagh, Cavan, Donegal, and Londonderry, with a part of Armagh and Down; and only a few forts, as well as the towns of Derry, Coleraine, Enniskillen, Lisburn, and Carrickfergus remained in the hands of the English settlers.

It would be idle to pretend that the rising was not accompanied by a number of revolting atrocities, but there was much to avenge, and what horrors did take place were the work of downtrodden and enraged peasants, and not of the organized policy of a civilized government as in the case of Elizabeth's commanders in the previous century. It is, too, often stated that in more than one instance the Catholic clergy encouraged their flocks in the perpetration of these excesses, and it is to be feared that sometimes they did, for toleration of the opinions of others was not an outstanding characteristic of seventeenth-century clerics of any denomination; on the other hand there were priests who at the peril of their lives gave shelter to fugitive Protestants, and the names of the Rev. James Saul, S.J., and the Revs J. Everard and R. English, O.S.F., deserve to be rescued from oblivion in this connection. The actual number of people killed was probably not considerable – some three

or four thousand slaughtered at the outbreak of the rebellion,
and twice as many may have perished in ways less direct. What
admits of no doubt is the effect upon contemporary English
and Scottish opinion: neither the number of the victims nor
the manner of their deaths lost anything in the telling, while
the blame was unanimously placed upon the Catholic Church,
and both then, and for years afterwards, it became almost a
dogma of the Protestant faith that the Catholics were plotting
a general massacre of their opponents in all three kingdoms,
the provocation which the Irish had so long received being
conveniently forgotten.

At first there was no co-operation between the insurgents
and the Catholic lords of the Pale, who even offered if provided
with arms to reduce the rebels, but it was not long before the
two parties came together. There was throughout Ireland a
genuine fear of Puritan ascendancy, and a belief that the English Parliamentarians intended to eradicate Catholicism in all
three kingdoms. In the spring of 1642 the Catholic hierarchy
examined the whole situation and expressed themselves as
satisfied that the war had been undertaken in defence of religion. This view, however, was not unanimous, for the Bishop
of Meath was of the opinion that the Church should dissociate
itself from the militant movement. Nevertheless, the rest of the
bishops went ahead, and it was through their endeavours that
there was established at Kilkenny the Confederation of the
Irish Catholics with which the lords of the Pale proceeded to
associate themselves.

Kilkenny has always been an attractive town, and in those
days had also long been an important one. Writing some
twenty-five years earlier Justice Luke Gernon, who was second
Justice of Munster, said that it was ' an inland town situate in
a pleasant valley, and upon a fresh river. It is praised for the
wholesome air, and delightful orchards and gardens, which are
somewhat rare in Ireland. The houses are of grey marble
fayrely built, the fronts of theyr houses are supported (most
of them) with pillars or arches upon which there is an open
pavement to walk on. At one end of the town is a large

cathedral, at the other end, a high mounted Castle appertaining to the Earls of Ormond.'[12]

Meanwhile, as on so many occasions, Irish politics were becoming inextricably entangled with those of England, and the progress of events in Ulster considerably diminished the possibility of adjusting religious differences in any of the three kingdoms in a reasonable manner, while it also made the political dispute between Charles and the Parliament irreconcilable. There was general agreement in London that Ireland must be reconquered, but this would involve the raising of an army, and as the full proportions of the rising became known it was obvious that this army must be a strong one, while its task would not be rapidly achieved. The King of England was captain-general of his people, and the raising and commanding of armies were among his most undoubted prerogatives; but the times were not normal, and if Charles were to raise, and still more to command, the army destined for Ireland and if he were to return at its head after it had been victorious, it was clear that his enemies in England would get short shrift. In effect, the Irish rebellion rendered certain that English civil war which had hitherto been only probable, and not for the last time the injustice of the English towards the Irish recoiled upon their own heads.

As soon as the magnates of the Pale decided to throw in their lot with their Celtic fellow-countrymen Richard Talbot's brother, Sir Robert, came to the fore among the Confederates, but rather as an exponent of their cause in negotiation than as a fighting man, and Carte pays a tribute to him in this connection when he says, ' Sir Robert . . . having been driven by the lords justices' treatment unwillingly into the rebellion, and retaining always a true affection to his country, and good inclinations to the King's service, had constantly laboured to dispose his countrymen to peace, and persuade them to submission to His Majesty's authority. He was very active in promoting this end, whenever an opportunity offered.[13]

With every month that passed the situation became increasingly complicated, and Irish politics were a mass of intrigue.

It would be impossible to exaggerate the influence of all this upon young Richard Talbot who was in his formative years; if in his later days his ways were often devious and his methods downright dishonest it was because he had been brought up in a world where few made any effort to distinguish between right and wrong. The Royal commander-in-chief, the Marquess of Ormonde, was in a particularly hopeless position, for the forces that were supposed to be engaged in the suppression of the rebellion were also fighting against one another. In the North there was a Scottish Presbyterian army under a general called Monro, which was ' distinguishing itself by appalling atrocities '[14] and was just as ready to attack the King's garrisons as it was to fight the Irish. In Munster there was not only Lord Inchiquin, a nobleman of somewhat fickle political allegiance, though at the moment favouring the Parliament in spite of his Gaelic origins, but also Lord Broghill who was trying with a high degree of ruthlessness ' to carry out the plan of the Parliamentary leaders of making the war pay for itself by becoming a gigantic speculation in land robbery, coupled with the expulsion or extermination of the peasant owners '.[15] Lastly, there were the Lords Justices in Dublin, who relayed the orders of the English Parliament to such as were willing to obey them.

In these very difficult circumstances Sir Robert Talbot showed himself remarkably circumspect, and he would not appear to have taken any part in the warfare against Ormonde, either before or after the latter was made Lord-Lieutenant in 1643, but when it came to negotiation he was very much to the fore. In January 1643 the King authorized Ormonde to confer with the Irish leaders, and to report on their demands; accordingly a meeting of commissioners from both sides was held at Trim on 17 March, and Talbot was one of the representatives of the Confederates. The Irish tendered a remonstrance of grievances, closing with a demand for a free Parliament unfettered by the provisions of Poynings' Act: if this was granted they would send an army of ten thousand men to assist the Royal cause. In view of the unfavourable reaction which was a certainty in England and Scotland, the King realized that it was impossible for him to go so far, but in April he gave authority to Ormonde to treat for one year's cessation of hostilities, while in July he went even further, and agreed to a free Parliament.

Talbot and his colleagues were uncertain what line to adopt. Among the Old English many felt that the best game to play would be to support the monarchy, with whose fate they felt that their own was bound up, while the Old Irish, particularly those from the North, took a different view, in which they were largely supported by the clergy. After all, they had suffered most by confiscation and plantation, quite apart from the fact that they felt that Charles would never be allowed to grant their full demands; as so often, ' England's extremity was Ireland's opportunity ', and their best hope surely lay in recovering the whole country, so that which ever party emerged victorious in England would be compelled to acknowledge an independence which it could not undo. In this they were un-questionably right, but so general was the desire to bring the fighting to an end that the ' Cessation ' was signed on 15 September, and among the ten signatories was Robert Talbot. By this arrangement Charles and the Confederates respectively were to keep what they actually held, while the Scots under Monro were to have the benefit of the armistice if they chose to come in; but if they stood aloof Ormonde was to remain neutral while they were attacked, or even, if the King agreed, was to help in attacking them. Finally, the terms of a definite peace were to be discussed between Charles and the represent-atives of the Confederates, of whom Robert Talbot was one, and he went to Oxford for that purpose. The immediate upshot was that the question of terms was referred to Ormonde, who was by now Lord-Lieutenant.

Thus closed the first period of the Irish rising, and the years which immediately followed witnessed a decline in the influence of Talbot and the other magnates of the Pale for a variety of reasons. In the first place, the King's cause began to go down in England and Scotland, and with it they were closely identified. Secondly, an outstanding victory was won by Owen Roe O'Neill over Monro at Benburb, and this was very definitely a triumph for the Old Irish. Thirdly, and most important of all, was the arrival of Giovanni Battista Rinuccini, Archbishop of Fermo, as the nuncio of Pope Innocent X, with a supply of money, arms, and ammunition which heightened the influence of his sacred character.

His secretary, Dr Massari, Dean of Fermo, was an exceedingly intelligent visitor to Ireland, and he was found writing to his brother in Florence:

> The country through which we passed from Kenmare to Kilkenny, though mountainous, is very agreeable, and, since the richest pastures are found everywhere, it abounds in herds of every kind. One also came frequently upon long valleys, studded with groves and woods – not very big or dense – a pleasant rather than a fearsome feature of the landscape. For seventy miles the prospect was of this kind, but, having crossed the mountains, we entered upon a broad plain, varied with hills and valleys, delightful to look at, well cultivated, and rich in an infinite number of herds, especially cows and sheep. From the sheep the people get a very fine wool, known amongst us in Italy as *English* wool.
>
> The men are fine-looking and of incredible strength, swift runners, and ready to bear every kind of hardship with cheerfulness. They are all trained in arms, especially now that they are at war. Those who apply themselves to letters are very learned, and well fitted to the professions and sciences.
>
> The women are distinguished by their grace and beauty, and they are as modest as they are lovely. Their manners are marked by extreme simplicity, and they mix freely in conversation on all occasions without suspicion or jealousy. Their dress differs from ours, and is somewhat like the French. They also wear cloaks reaching to their heels and tufted locks of hair, and they go without any head-dress, content with linen bands bound up in the Greek fashion, which display their natural beauty to much advantage. Their families are very large. Some have as many as thirty children, all living; not a few have fifteen or twenty, and all these children are handsome, tall and strong, the majority being fair-haired, white-skinned and red-complexioned.

Food is abundant, and the inhabitants eat and entertain very well. They are constantly pledging healths, the usual drinks being Spanish wines, French claret, very good beer and excellent milk. Butter is used abundantly with all kinds of food . . . There is also plenty of fruit – apples, pears, plums, artichokes. All eatables are cheap. A fat ox costs sixteen shillings, a sheep fifteen pence, a pair of capons or fowls, five pence; eggs a farthing each, and other things in proportion. A good-sized fish costs a penny, and they don't bother about selling game. They kill birds almost with sticks. Both salt and fresh-water fish are cheap, abundant, and of excellent flavour . . . We bought a thousand pilchards and oysters for twenty-five *baiocchi*. The horses are numerous, strong, well-built, and swift. For £5 you can buy a nag which in Italy could not be got for a hundred gold pieces.

The nuncio was not concerned with politics but with the interests of the Catholic Church, and he was by no means disposed to let a heretical prince have orthodox help at a low rate. This brought him into conflict with Ormonde, who therefore decided to surrender Dublin to the Parliament forces which were on their way to Ireland, preferring, as he said, ' English rebels to Irish rebels ': accordingly when Colonel Michael Jones arrived with several thousand Roundheads he put this plan into execution on 28 July 1647, and himself left the country.

It was at this moment that Richard Talbot made his first appearance on the stage of history, for now aged about seventeen he is heard of, little more than a week after Ormonde's departure, serving as a cornet of horse in the army of Thomas Preston, who, with Owen Roe O'Neill, was one of the outstanding Confederate generals.

NOTES

[1] *History of England*, Vol. I.

[2] *Cf. H.M.C. Reports, Egmont MSS*, Vol. I. London. 1905.

[3] Prior to 1558 there was also one at Calais.

[4] *A History of Ireland*, p. 235. London. 1936.

[5] The whole subject of regicide was decidedly topical as Henry IV of France had been murdered four years previously.

[6] *King James's Irish Army List*, Vol. I, p. 47.

[7] *Continuation of the Life of Edward, Earl of Clarendon*, Vol. III, p. 117. London. 1827.

[8] Quoted by Sergeant, P. W.: *Little Jennings and Fighting Dick Talbot*, Vol. I, p. 22. London. 1913.

[9] ' The Elizabethan conquest of Ireland had been so destructive as to hinder a fresh appeal to arms by the children of the soil.' Montague, F. C.: *The Political History of England*, Vol. VII, p. 251. London. 1911.

[10] *Father Luke Wadding Commemorative Volume*, p. 95. Dublin. 1957.

[11] *Cf.* Carte, T.: *Life of Ormonde*, Vol. I, pp. 105-168. London. 1739.

[12] *Discourse*: Stowe Papers, B.M.

[13] *History of the Duke of Ormonde*, Vol. IV, p. 67. London. 1739.

[14] Wingfield-Stratford, Esme: *King Charles and King Pym*, 1637-1643, p. 366. London. 1949.

[15] *Ibid.*

CHAPTER II

Dungan's Hill and Drogheda

ENOUGH HAS been said to demonstrate the confused nature of the fighting in Ireland in which Richard Talbot was now to be involved, and being an observant youth, what he saw was to be of the greatest value to him in later years when the chaos of the middle of the century bade fair to be repeated. Apart from the shifting pattern of alliances, to which allusion has already been made, the map was never divided neatly into compact parts, for there were both Royalist and Parliamentary enclaves within the territory controlled by the Confederates. In Connacht, for example, the Earl of Clanricard retained control of Loughrea, Portuma, and Athenry, while other magnates, such as the Earl of Thomond, were virtually neutral for much of the period, though from time to time one side or the other made temporarily effective raids into the neighbouring territory.[1] In actual fact, with Ormonde's departure the Royalist cause visibly collapsed, and the Parliamentarians began to play a decisive military rôle, though there was mounting friction between them and the Scots who were now veering round towards the King.

Furthermore an 'outstanding feature of these wars is that none of the combatants seemed capable of exploiting a favourable situation or a major victory '.[2] Perhaps the most outstanding example of this was the failure of the Confederates to follow up O'Neill's great victory at Benburb, but Ormonde, too, won several battles from which he extracted little profit. The war lasted off and on for roughly a decade, but there was remarkably little actual fighting and there were few pitched battles. All this, of course, was to be radically altered with the arrival of Cromwell, but at the beginning of 1647 the distribution of territory was to all intents and purposes what it had been at the end of 1642, and in the whole period from 1642 to 1649 the Confederates registered practically no gains. One reason for this may well have been the jealousy which existed between their leading generals, Thomas Preston and Owen Roe O'Neill, a position which has been admirably summed up by Clarendon:

> They of the more moderate party, and whose main end was to obtain liberty for the exercise of their religion, without any thought of declining their subjection to the King, or of invading his prerogative, put themselves under the command of General Preston: the other, of the fiercer and more savage party, and who never meant to return to their obedience to the crown of England, and looked upon all the estates which had ever been in the possession of any of their ancestors, though forfeited by their treason and rebellion, as justly due to them, and ravished from them by the tyranny of the crown, marched under the conduct of Owen Roe O'Neill; both generals of the Irish nation; the one descended of English extraction through many descents; the other purely Irish, and of the family of Tyrone; both bred in the wars of Flanders, and both eminent commanders there, and of perpetual jealousy of each other; the one of the more frank and open nature; the other darker, less polite, and the wiser man.[3]

Rinuccini saw the situation in the same light, but naturally from a somewhat different angle.

> The Catholics of Ireland have from time immemorial been divided into two adverse factions. One under the name of the Old Irish, although dispersed over the four provinces of the Kingdom, are yet more numerous in that of Ulster, which seems to be in a manner their headquarters, since it was there the Earl of Tyrone placed himself at their head and carried on a long war on their behalf against Queen Elizabeth. The other faction may be called the old English, a race introduced into Ireland at the time of Henry II, and so called to distinguish them from the new English who came over with the Protestant heresy . . .

The discord between these two factions may be attributed to the following causes: the old Irish averse to heresy are also averse to the dominion of England, and refused to accept of the ecclesiastical property offered to them when the Kings of England apostatized from the Church. The new Irish on the contrary enriched with the monastic possessions, and bound to the King no less by obligation than interest, desire nothing better than the increase of the royal prerogative; acknowledge no laws save those of that Kingdom, are completely English in their prejudices, and in consequence of their connection with the heretics, less jealous of the difference of religion. Nature even seems to widen the breach by difference of character and qualities, the new party being for the most part of low stature, quick-witted and of subtle understanding, while the old Irish are tall, simple-minded, unrefined in their manner of living, generally slow of comprehension and quite unskilled in negotiation. They regard each other with mutual distrust . . .

At the time of my arrival the greater part of the Catholic troops were under the command of two generals, Owen O'Neill and Thomas Preston, the latter of the new Irish, the former of the old, who were not only rivals by nature, and from party spirit, but embittered by jealousy from having both served in the Flemish wars, and from having even then shown signs of mutual aversion . . . These two chiefs, so different in their aims, so opposite in their management of affairs, were still more different in their nature. The O'Neill, a man of few words, cautious and phlegmatic in his operations, a great adept in concealing his feelings; the other very subject to fits of anger in which he was so rash and outspoken.

Thomas Preston, under whom young Talbot was to serve his apprenticeship to arms, had been born in 1585, the fourth son of the Fourth Viscount Gormanston. His family had originally had Yorkist tendencies, and he had himself been educated in the Spanish Netherlands. Adopting a military career, he held a commission in Henry O'Neill's Regiment in the Spanish service, and from early days, as Clarendon and the rumours testify, he was on the worst terms with Owen Roe. Dr Lowe has a poor opinion of his generalship, and will give him no more than 'a modest reputation for competence' in

D

Flanders. Preston arrived in Ireland in July or August 1642, but he did nothing of note in the next few years, when, again according to Dr Lowe, he ' floundered from mishap to mishap': he captured Birr Castle and Duncannon Fort it is true, but he allowed himself to be beaten by Ormonde at New Ross. It may be noted that through the Nettervilles there was a family connection between Preston and Richard Talbot.

It would, too, appear to be family reasons that brought Talbot to serve under Preston, for Carte wrote that Sir Robert Talbot's ' prudence, credit, and influence first brought his youngest brother into the world, where the favour and eminent worth of their sister's son, Sir Walter Dongan, contributed to advance him '. Richard's sister, Mary, had, as we have seen, married Sir John Dongan, and several of their sons were in the Confederate army with their father. The most prominent of those was Walter, and in his troop of horse Richard was now serving as a standard-bearer, for although he was Walter's uncle he was his junior in years. According to Carte, two years earlier Walter had come to Ormonde with letters from the King recommending him for employment on account of the services of his father and himself to the Royal cause; he was accordingly given a commission to raise men, and told to join Preston's forces.

The strategy of the campaign in the summer of 1647 centred round Dublin which Ormonde had surrendered to the Round-heads and which could almost certainly have been wrested from them had the Confederate leaders not been torn by jealousy and personal rivalries. For these reasons the opportunity was allowed to pass, and in June, as we have seen, Colonel Michael Jones, who had already distinguished himself in the fighting in England, arrived in Dublin with a force of Parliamentary troops. He was, however, outnumbered by Preston, who was at the head of a thousand horse and seven thousand foot, and who – now that it was too late – proceeded to take the offensive. Accordingly he captured Naas, and then moved on to Trim, preparatory to a final advance on Dublin, for the idea of masking these places while he made a dash at the capital never seems to have occurred to him. At this point Jones marched out to relieve Trim, whereupon Preston conceived the plan of cutting his opponent off from his base, and reaching Dublin before the enemy could re-occupy it: he was, however, forestalled, and the armies met on 8 August 1647 at a place called Dungan's Hill.

The battle that ensued was a very confused affair. The offensive was at once taken by the Parliamentarians, and Preston's men proved unable to resist their onset; the result was that the Confederates were routed with heavy loss. Preston himself, and some of his cavalry, escaped to Carlow, where he had the mortification to receive orders to hand over most of his remaining forces to Owen Roe.[4] In the contest Richard Talbot was taken prisoner, but whether he was released, exchanged or escaped is uncertain: at any rate before long he is found fighting against the Roundheads once more.

In the high politics of the next two years he naturally played no part, so it will suffice to say that Ormonde returned to Ireland, that Rinuccini left it, and that the Confederation of Kilkenny came to an end with the signing of the second Ormonde Peace on 17 January 1649, after which the Irish Catholics were at any rate in theory subject to the King's Viceroy, Ormonde. The incredible military incapacity of the Confederation survived it, and Ormonde's forces proved no match for the ruthlessly efficient army, led by Oliver Cromwell in person, which landed at Dublin in August 1649.

He came to Ireland with an inexorable determination to break the Royalist power there, to beat down the national resistance, and to avenge the events of 1641 which, in his mind, as in that of so many others, had assumed gigantic and fabulous proportions. He shared the Puritan loathing for the Church of Rome, and in Ireland in particular he pursued it with remorseless hate, for he believed that the priests had promoted the rising, and would always stimulate revolt against English rule. It need hardly be said that of the Irish character and of Irish grievances he knew nothing, and cared less.

In this connection mention must be made of the activities

of the Puritan printing-press in the exacerbation of Anglo-Irish relations. The middle years of the century were marked by a spate of sectarian propagandist pamphlets such as *A Sermon Preached to the Protestants of Ireland in and about the City of London,* which were mainly responsible for rousing English public opinion against Ireland. Pym and his associates in particular by thus creating the legends of the ' bloody Massacre and Rebellion begun by the Irish Papists ' set the stage for the savage Cromwellian retribution, for Cromwell was able to justify such atrocities as the sack of Drogheda and Wexford on these grounds.

On landing in Dublin he made a speech to the people in which he spoke of his purpose as ' the great work against the barbarous and bloodthirsty Irish, and all their adherents and confederates, for the propagating of the Gospel of Christ, the establishing of truth and peace, and restoring that bleeding nation to its former happiness and tranquillity '. His first act was to remodel the local Parliamentary forces, making ' a huge purge of the army which we found there: it was an army made up of dissolute and debauched men '; and to give Cromwell his due, he issued a procalamation against swearing and drunkenness and another against the ' wickedness ' that had been taken by the soldiery ' to abuse, rob, and pillage, and too often to execute cruelties upon the country people ', promising to protect all peaceable inhabitants and to pay them in ready money for all requisitioned goods: two soldiers were in fact hanged shortly afterwards for disobeying these orders. Cromwell then ordered a general review of his troops to the number of 15,000 horse and foot, of which he selected 10,000 for an immediate advance on Drogheda.[5]

Ormonde had not sufficient troops to face this formidable force. Originally he had intended to garrison Drogheda with his whole army, but he now realized that to do this would probably merely mean that he would be bottled up in the town to no purpose. He therefore changed his mind, and ' put into that place, which was looked upon, besides the strength of the situation, to be in a good degree fortified, the flower of his

army, both of officers and soldiers, most of them English, to
the number of three thousand foot, and two or three good
troops of horse, provided with all things '. At their head was
Sir Arthur Aston, an officer of great experience who had little
doubt of his ability to hold out against Cromwell for a month,
at the end of which time he reckoned to be relieved by
Ormonde; serving under him was Richard Talbot. In the meantime Ormonde withdrew into the interior with his field-army
which was being strengthened by reinforcements from all over
the country. It was sound strategy, but it did not allow for the
rapidity of Cromwell's movements.

The Roundhead cavalry reached the town on 3 September,
their general's lucky day; some skirmishes followed, and on 10
September the besiegers' batteries opened in earnest after the
usual formal summons to surrender. On the first day a steeple
and a tower were beaten down, and all through the following
day the firing continued until at length there had been effected
' two reasonable breaches '[6] on the south, and about five that
evening ' after some hot dispute we entered, about seven or
eight hundred men; the enemy disputing it very stiffly with
us '. The defenders, however, rallied, and drove out the assault-
ing column with heavy loss, and Cromwell realized that with
autumn approaching he might be held up before Drogheda
indefinitely, which was exactly what Ormonde wanted, unless
he could take the place by storm. ' Resolved,' writes Ludlow,
' to put all upon it, he went down to the breach; and calling
out a fresh reserve of Colonel Ewer's men, he put himself at
their head, and with the word "our Lord God ", led them up
again with courage and resolution, though they met with a hot
dispute.'

Thus encouraged his men finally burst into the town, but
Aston with a select band fell back on the Millmount which
' was exceedingly high and strongly palisaded ', but the Roundheads had now got the bit between their teeth, and nothing
would stop them: they burst in on the heels of their adversaries, and on Cromwell's orders put all the Royalists to the
sword. The rest of the garrison fled over the Boyne to the

northern side where they were closely pursued by their trium-
phant enemies; many of them took refuge in St Peter's Church,
which was then set on fire by the instructions of their general,
who wrote to the Speaker of the House of Commons, ' Indeed,
being in the heat of the action, I forbade them to spare any
that were in arms in the town; and I think that night they
put to the sword about two thousand men.' Next day the
various parties of defenders who were still holding out were
forced to surrender and were duly butchered; the slaughter
went on for another twenty-four hours even after that and
Cromwell is found writing, ' Their friars were knocked on the
head promiscuously.'

The slaughter was indeed prodigious, and he who was
primarily responsible for it made no secret of the fact for he
wrote, ' I believe we put to the sword the whole number of the
defendants. I do not think thirty of the whole number escaped
with their lives. . . I do not believe, neither do I hear, that any
officer escaped with his life, save only one lieutenant.'[7] Hugh
Peters, Cromwell's chaplain, confirms this butchery when he
reported, ' Sir, the truth is, Drogheda is taken, 3,552 of the
enemy slain, and 64 of ours. Aston, the governor, killed, none
spared.' All this was bad enough, but what made it worse was
that Cromwell positively exulted in what he had done. ' It had
pleased God to bless our endeavours. . . This had been a mar-
vellous great mercy. . . I am persuaded that this is a righteous
judgment of God upon these barbarous wretches, who have
imbued their hands in so much innocent blood and that it will
tend to prevent the effusion of blood for the future. Which are
the satisfactory grounds to such actions, which otherwise cannot but work remorse and regret. . . It was set upon some of
our hearts, that a great thing should be done, not by power or
might, but by the Spirit of God.' All of which was in marked
contrast with the attitude of Charles I after the first battle
of Newbury six years before when he gave instructions that the
Roundhead sick and wounded should be carefully looked after,
' though they be rebels, and deserve the punishment of
traitors '.[8]

A more personal account of what took place was given in 1663 by Anthony Wood, the Oxford historian, on the authority of his brother, Thomas, who was serving under Cromwell on the occasion.

> In 1650 . . . being often with his mother and brethren, he would tell them of the most terrible assaulting and storming of Tredagh,[9] wherein he himself had been engaged. He told them that 3,000 at least, besides some women and children, were, after the assailants had taken part, and afterwards all the town, put to the sword on the 11 and 12 Sept. 1649; at which time Sir Arthur Aston, the governor, had his brains beat out, and his body hack'd and chop'd to pieces.
>
> He told them, that when they were to make their way up to the lofts and galleries in the church and up to the tower where the enemy had fled each of the assailants would take up a child and use it as a buckler of defence, when they ascended the steps, to keep themselves from being shot or brain'd. After they had killed all in the church, they went into the vaults underneath where all the flower and choicest of the women and ladies had hid themselves.
>
> One of these, a most handsome virgin and arrayed in costly and gorgeous apparel, kneeled down to Thomas Wood with tears and prayers to save her life: and being stricken with a profound pity, took her under his arm, went with her out of the church, with intention to put her over the works and to let her shift for herself; but then a soldier perceiving his intentions, ran his sword . . . Whereupon Mr Wood seeing her gasping, took away her money, jewels, etc., and flung her down over the works.

As we have seen, the English Civil War in England itself was on the whole a gentlemanly affair, and very unlike the contemporary Thirty Years' War on the mainland of Europe; almost the only exception was the behaviour of Cromwell. Total victory had always been his policy, and at Marston Moor, Naseby, and Preston he had ' taken execution of the enemy ' over miles and miles of country, while at Basing and elsewhere, after a summons and a storm, he had slaughtered hundreds without mercy; but the killing of hundreds in hot blood is very different from the butchering of thousands spread over days, to say nothing of the promiscuous slaughter of priests and women. A historian, the late Frederic Harrison, who certainly could not be suspected of bias against Cromwell, whom he described as ' the greatest ruler ' Britain has ever had, well summed up the tragedy of Drogheda when he wrote, ' No admiration for Cromwell, for his genius, courage, and earnestness – no sympathy with the cause that he upheld in England – can blind us to the truth, that the lurid light of this great crime burns still after centuries across the history of England and of Ireland; and it is one of those damning charges which the Puritan theology has yet to answer at the bar of humanity.'[10]

Whether there was also duplicity on Cromwell's part is a moot point, and the accusation rests on the authority of Ormonde, who wrote to Lord Byron:

> Having made a breach which he judged assaultable, he assaulted it, and being twice beaten off, the third time he carried it; all his officers and soldiers promising quarter to such as would lay down their arms, and performing it, as long as any place held out, which encouraged others to yield. But when they had once all in their power, and feared no hurt that could be done them, then the word ' no quarter ' went round, and the soldiers were many of them forced against their will to kill their prisoners. Sir Edm. Verney, Colonel Warren, Colonel Wall, and Colonel Byrne, were all killed in cold blood, as also was the Governor, and indeed all the officers, except some few of least consideration, that escaped by miracle. The cruelty exercised there for five days after the town was taken would make as many several pictures of inhumanity as are to be found in the book of Martyrs, or in the relation of Amboyna.[11]

Richard Talbot's escape was indeed miraculous. He was seriously wounded and was considered to be dead when he fell into the hands of Commissary-General John Reynolds who spared his life and seems also to have connived at his escape; anyhow, Richard managed to disguise himself as a woman, and so reached safety.[12]

While he was being cured of his wounds the campaign continued. The Roundheads reduced Dundalk and the other strong places in the North, so that there was no longer any fear that their adversaries would take the offensive from that quarter. His rear thus secure, Cromwell then turned south to attack Wexford and open a way into Munster. He captured in turn Wicklow, Arklow, and Enniscorthy, and appeared before Wexford on 1 October: he then mounted what a later age would have termed a 'combined operation'. The place was a strong one, with a rampart fifteen feet wide, a garrison of over two thousand with fifty-four guns, and in the harbour were two men-of-war armed with the same number of guns. Cromwell brought up his fleet, which took Rosslare and thus cut Wexford off from any hope of relief by sea; he then landed his siege-train, and summoned the Governor, Colonel Sinnott, to surrender. It may not be out of place to quote the correspondence which ensued between them, for although Richard Talbot was in no way implicated, it helps to paint in the Irish background against which his whole career was to be set.

Cromwell to Colonel Sinnott

Sir,

Having brought the army belonging to the Parliament of England before this place, to reduce it to its due obedience, to the end effusion of blood may be prevented, and the town and country about it preserved from ruin, I thought fit to summon you to deliver the same to me, to the use of the state of England. By this offer, I hope it will clearly appear where the guilt will lie, if innocent persons should come to suffer with the nocent. I expect your speedy answer; and rest,

Sir, your servant.

October 3, 1649.   O. Cromwell.

Colonel Sinnott to Cromwell

Sir,

I have received your letters of summons for the delivery up of this town into your hands, which standeth not with my honour to do of myself; neither will I take it upon me, without the advice of the officers and mayor of this corporation (this town being of so great consequence to all Ireland), whom I will call together and confer with, and return my resolution unto you to-morrow by twelve of the clock. In the mean time, if you be so pleased, I am content to forbear all acts of hostility, so you permit no approach to be made: expecting your answer in that particular, I remain,

My lord, your lordship's servant,

Wexford, Oct. 3, 1649.   Da. Sinnott.

Cromwell to Colonel Sinnott

Sir,

Having summoned you to deliver the town of Wexford into my hands, I might well expect the delivery thereof, and not a formal treaty, which is seldom granted, but where the things stand upon a more equal foot. If therefore yourself or the town have any desires to offer, upon which you will surrender the place to me, I shall be able to judge of the reasonableness of them when they are made known to me. To which end, if you shall think fit to send the persons named in your last, entrusted by yourself and the town, by whom I may understand your desires, I shall give you a speedy and fitting answer. And I do hereby engage myself, that they shall return in safety to you. I expect your answer hereunto within an hour; and rest

Your servant,

October 4, 1649   O. Cromwell.

Colonel Sinnott to Cromwell

Sir,

I have returned you a civil answer, to the best of my judgment; and thereby I find you undervalue me and this place so much, as you think to have it surrendered without capitulation or honourable terms, as appears by the hour's limitation in your last.

Sir, had I never a man in this town but the townsmen and artillery here planted, I should conceive myself in a very befitting condition to make honourable conditions; and having a considerable party with them in the place, I am resolved to die honourably, or make such conditions as may secure my honour and life in the eyes of my own party. To which reasonable terms, if you hearken not, or give me time to send my agents till eight of the clock in the forenoon to-morrow, with my propositions, with a further safe-conduct, I leave you to your better judgment, and myself to the assistance of the Almighty; and so conclude,

Your servant,

Wexford, Oct. 4, 1649.   Da. Sinnott.

Colonel Sinnott to Cromwell

Sir,

I have advised with the mayor and officers, as I promised, and thereupon am content that four, whom I shall employ, may have a conference and treaty with four of yours, to see if any agreement may be begot between us. To this purpose I desire you to send mine a safe-conduct, as I do hereby promise to send unto yours when you send me the names. And I pray that the meeting may be had to-morrow at eight of the clock in the forenoon, that they may have sufficient time to confer and debate together, and determine and compose the matter; and that the meeting and place may be agreed upon, and the safe-conduct mutually sent for the said meeting this afternoon. Expecting your answer hereto, I rest,

My lord, your servant,

Wexford, Oct. 4, 1649.   Da. Sinnott.

Send me the names of your agents, their qualities, and degrees. Those I fix upon are Major James Byrne, Major Theobald Dillon, Alderman Nicholas Chevers, Mr William Stafford.

Colonel Sinnott to Cromwell

Sir,

My propositions being now prepared, I am ready to send my agents with them unto you; and for their safe return, I pray you to send a safe-conduct by the bearer unto me; in the hope an honourable agreement may thereupon arise between your lordship and,

My lord, your lordship's servant,

Wexford, Oct. 5, 1649.   Da. Sinnott.

Colonel Sinnott to Cromwell

My Lord,

Even as I was ready to send out my agents unto you, the lord general of the horse[13] came hither with a relief, unto whom I communicated the proceedings between your lordship and me, and delivered him the propositions I intended to dispatch to your lordship; who have desired a small time to consider of them and to speed them unto me; which my lord, I could not deny, he having a commanding power over me. Pray, my lord, believe that I do not do this to trifle out time, but for his present consent; and if I find any long delay in his lordship's returning them back to me, I will proceed of myself, according to my first intention: to which I beseech your lordship give credit, at the request, my lord, of your lordship's ready servant,

Wexford, Oct. 5, 1649   Da. Sinnott.

Cromwell to Colonel Sinnott

Sir,

You might have spared your trouble in the account you give me of your transaction with the lord general of your horse, and of your resolution in case he answer not your expectation in point of time. These are your own concernments, and it behoves you to improve the relief to your best advantage. All that I have to say is, to desire you to take notice, that I do hereby revoke my safe-conduct from the persons mentioned therein. When you shall see cause to treat, you may send for another.

I rest, Sir, your servant,

October 6, 1649.   Oliver Cromwell.

Colonel Sinnott to Cromwell

Sir,

In performance of my last, I desire your lordship to send me a safe-conduct for Major Theobald Dillon, Alderman Nicholas Chevers, and Captain James Stafford, whom I will send to your lordship instructed with my desires; and so I rest,

My lord, your servant,

Wexford, Oct. 11, 1649.   Da. Sinnott.[14]

The Third Earl of Castlehaven, whose arrival at Wexford had caused this suspension in the negotiations between Oliver Cromwell and Colonel Sinnott, was one of the more considerable minor military figures of the seventeenth century. He was a very capable and active soldier, and throughout his career he proved that he was able to do a good deal with indifferent material. He was very much a professional: that is to say that when the Stuarts required his services his sword was at their disposal, but at other times he was to be found participating in the wars on the Continent. Castlehaven had been born about 1617, and his home life had been unhappy, for when he was fourteen his father was beheaded for felony, that is to say for sodomy with his page, and for the rape of his own wife, or rather for assisting one Giles Browning to rape her: for this his English earldom, but not his Irish one, was forfeited. The Third Earl's wife was also a disappointment to him, for in open court she admitted that while in her early teens she had committed adultery with her mother's paramour, and in later years her morals were not rated very high. When she died her husband married a connection of the Earl of Derby, who seems to have proved a more satisfactory consort.

Cromwell had not allowed these negotiations to interrupt his preparations for the capture of Wexford, but at this point Captain James Stafford turned traitor, and thus confounded the plans of Castlehaven and Sinnott. What actually took place is best recorded in Cromwell's own words.

> Whilst I was preparing for it; studying to preserve the town from plunder, that it might be of the more use to you and your army, the Captain, who was one of the commissioners, being fairly treated, yielded up the Castle to us. Upon the top of which our men no sooner appeared, but the enemy quitted the walls of the town; which our men perceiving, ran violently upon the town with their ladders, and stormed it. And when they were come into the market-place, the enemy making a stiff resistance, our forces broke them; and then put all to the sword that came in their way. Two boatfuls of the enemy attempting to escape, being overprest with numbers, sank; whereby were

drowned near three hundred of them. I believe in all, there was lost of the enemy not many less than two thousand; and I believe not twenty of yours from first to last of the siege.

And indeed it hath, not without cause, been deeply set upon our hearts, that, we intending better to this place than so great a ruin, hoping the town might be of more use to you and your army, yet God would not have it so; but by an unexpected providence, in His righteous justice, brought a just judgment upon them; causing them to become a prey to the soldier, who in their piracies had made preys of so many families, and now with their bloods to answer the cruelties which they have exercised upon the lives of divers poor Protestants . . .

This town is now so in your power, that of the former inhabitants, I believe scarce one in twenty can challenge any property in their houses. Most of them are run away, and many of them killed in this service. And it were to be wished that an honest people would come and plant here.[15]

Whether this was the whole truth is another matter, for a further letter from Cromwell to Sinnott is preserved in the Library of the Royal Irish Academy, and it certainly gives the impression that after the terms of surrender had been agreed upon and signed the English general took advantage of the treachery of Stafford to go back on his word.

Sir,

I have had the patience to peruse your propositions, to which I might have returned an answeare with some disdaine. But (to bee short) I shall give the soldiers and noncommissioned officers quarter for life and leave to go to their severall habitations, with their wearing cloathes. They ingaginge themselves to live quietly there and to take upp arms no more against the Parliament of England And the commissioned officers quarter for their lives, but to render themselves prisoners And as for the inhabitants, I shall ingage myselfe that noe violence shall be offered to their goods, and that I shall protect the towne from plunder.

I expect your possetive answeare instantly and if you will upon these termes surrender and quitt in one houre shall send forth to mee four officers of the quality of feild officers and two

Aldermen for the performance thereof I shall thereupon forbear all acts of hostility.

Your servant,

O. Cromwell.

Cromwell unquestionably owed his success to the treachery of Stafford, and it was followed by the same butchery as that which had marked the fall of Drogheda. All priests were put to the sword, and there can be little doubt that many non-combatants also perished; after this had been done Wexford was sacked. To have taken the place so quickly and with so small a loss was of the utmost advantage to Cromwell, for the autumnal rains had set in and sickness was thinning his ranks.

No general was ever more adept in taking advantage of his opportunities, and his next step was to summon New Ross which surrendered on 19 October. The rot had, in fact, already set in amongst the English soldiers in the King's service, for those in New Ross declared for the Parliament, and the troops in Cork and Youghal followed their example. In face of the widespread defection, Prince Rupert, who was with the Royal fleet at Kinsale, put to sea, and Ormonde purchased O'Neill's assistance by a treaty which restored all the forfeited lands in Ulster and secured the Catholic clergy in the possession of the churches which they had held before the Plantation; but O'Neill died on 6 November, and with him the Irish lost the one leader who might have made head against Cromwell, who was going on from strength to strength. It is true that before the campaigning season of 1649 terminated he had received a check before Waterford, but early in the following year he obtained possession of Kilkenny and Clonmel. Cromwell returned to England at the beginning of May 1650 with the satisfaction of having decided the issue of the Irish war, although one half of Ireland still remained to be conquered; he had also gained a reputation for brutality which has never been effaced.

It has been considered advisable to discuss at some length the part played in the Confederate War by the kinsmen and connections of Richard Talbot, for it would be impossible to understand his attitude in later life towards the politics and politicians of the day without a close acquaintance with the influences which worked upon him in boyhood and youth, thereby moulding his opinions. He was brought up with men of aristocratic traditions who found themselves called upon to solve the problem of how to combine loyalty to the religion of their ancestors, to the land of their birth, and to the King whose right to the throne they never questioned.

Where religion was concerned the Talbots were loyal to their Church, but they were not ultramontane in their religious views and they were certainly not prepared to accept the extreme Papal claims as stated by Rinuccini and his like. In the matter of patriotism they never ceased to uphold what they considered to be the rights of Ireland, but coming from a different race it is not surprising if they were regarded with some suspicion by the Celts, more particularly when it is remembered for how long and to what extent the Old English of the Pale had kept themselves to themselves. As for the Crown, they had an ingrained attachment to it which their Celtic neighbours could not be expected to share, and they were careful to distinguish between what the King said and what he really thought. For example, when Charles II at Dunfermline in August 1650 at the dictation of the Scots, classed all those implicated in the rising as ‘ bloody Irish rebels, who treacherously shed the blood of so many of his faithful and loyal subjects ’, they knew perfectly well that he meant no such thing.

On the other side young Richard became familiar with a nauseating cant and hypocrisy almost without parallel in modern history. He saw men with the name of God ever on their lips commit atrocities which resembled the worst of those taking place in the contemporary Thirty Years’ War. The forties of the seventeenth century were Richard’s formative years, and it would have been remarkable had they formed him in any other way.

NOTES

[1] The best recent account of the conditions prevailing at this time is Lowe, John: 'Some aspects of the Wars in Ireland, 1641-1649' in *The Irish Sword*, Vol. IV, pp. 81-87. Dublin. 1959.

[2] *Ibid.*

[3] *History of the Rebellion*, Book VI. Oxford. 1839.

[4] He was subsequently compensated by Charles II, who created him Viscount Tara.

[5] *Cf.* Harrison, Frederic: *Oliver Cromwell*, p. 136. London. 1912.

[6] The quotations are from Cromwell's own despatches.

[7] Presumably Richard Talbot.

[8] *The Letters of King Charles I*, p. 136. London. 1935.

[9] Drogheda.

[10] *Oliver Cromwell*, p. 140. London. 1912.

[11] Carte, T.: *Original Letters found among the Duke of Ormonde's Papers*, Vol. II, p. 412.

[12] *Cf.* Bagwell, R.: *Ireland under the Stuarts*, Vol. II, p. 195. London. 1909. Reynolds subsequently married Henry Cromwell's sister-in-law, was knighted by the Protector, and commanded the English troops who assisted Turenne against the Spaniards.

[13] Lord Castlehaven.

[14] Wright, T.: *The History of Ireland*, Book V, pp. 79-80. London. 1853.

[15] Carlyle, T.: *Letters and Speeches of Oliver Cromwell*, Letter cvii. London. 1904.

E

CHAPTER III

A Prisoner of Cromwell

WHAT PART, if any, Richard Talbot played in the later stages of the Irish resistance is uncertain, and he seems to have been a prisoner of Sir Charles Coote until October 1651, when his exchange was ordered by the English Commissioners. In March 1655 he arrived in Madrid with his brother, Peter, and his nephew, Sir Walter Dongan, having probably taken advantage of the Kilkenny Articles which his other brother, Robert, and Dongan had, *inter alios*, signed. By transferring himself to Spain young Richard was merely following the example of no inconsiderable number of his fellow-countrymen who had also emigrated – no less than twenty-five thousand according to Clarendon.[1] This movement overseas was definitely encouraged by Cromwell, for he realized that his genocidal Irish policy had no chance of success while there were large bodies of fighting men still in the country, so, to quote Clarendon, ' He declared a full liberty and authority to all the officers with the Irish, and to all other persons whatsoever, to raise what men they would, and to transport them for the service of any foreign princes with whom they could make the best conditions; and gave notice to the Spanish and French ministers, and agents at London, of the liberty he had granted.[2] For historic reasons the Irish preferred the Spanish to the French service, but all the same Cardinal Mazarin managed to entice a number of them into the army of Louis XIV.

Those who, like Richard Talbot, preferred Spain to France found a somewhat paradoxical situation awaiting them when they arrived in Madrid. The King was Philip IV, a man in middle life, and his letters to the nun Maria de Agreda, have enabled posterity to form a better estimate of his character than was possible for his contemporaries, for they reveal a passionate man whose outward impassivity was but a mask to hide his real feelings. Indolent and self-indulgent Philip might be, but he was very far from being a fool, and his great failing was not a lack of ability, but a want of application. Unfortunately for Spain, Philip II had devised a system of government which imposed a life of unremitting toil upon the occupant of the throne, and neither his son nor his grandson had the will to shoulder this burden.

Even if this had not been the case, it is doubtful whether Spain could have maintained the position which she had held under Philip the Prudent in the previous century. The value of money was steadily falling, and uncontrolled inflation was the order of the day. Contemporary statesmen were woefully ignorant of economics, and though Olivares was an abler man than he is often depicted as being, he did not possess the talents necessary to rescue his country from the slough into which she was sinking. Edicts against luxury were issued, and the King set an example by a reduction in the expenses of his court; but all this was to no purpose, for prices were steadily rising, while the whole financial and economic system was antiquated. The cost of collecting the taxes was not infrequently in excess of the amount obtained, and every monopoly, of which there were many, had its own officials. Owing to the *alcabalas* or taxes on sales, tolls, inland customs-dues, and *octrois* to which goods in transit were subject, it was quite out of the question for them to compete with those of foreign origin, except at first-hand in the place where they were produced.

If Spain was in a state of decadence the fact left her inhabitants profoundly indifferent. If the national finances were in disorder; if poverty was increasing with the rise in the cost of living; and if the population was declining, as often happens after a period of great prosperity; it does not appear that the Spanish people were particularly unhappy in the reign of Philip

IV. In Madrid, at any rate, leisure was general. With sword and dagger at their sides, the members of the lower orders jostled those of the upper classes in the streets, and by their swagger maintained their pretension to be treated on the same footing as the aristocracy. It is true that there was no longer any industry worth the name, but one went very elegantly dressed in cloth and linen that came from Holland and Flanders. Most professions were in the hands of foreigners, and the few ships that plied between the Spanish ports were Dutch. There were already forty thousand French in the capital, which proves there was still money to be made there, or they would not have come. As in Britain in not dissimilar circumstances three hundred years later, moralists might groan about the public depravity, the frivolity of all classes, and the increasing looseness of the women, but it made little difference, for the pleasure-resorts were always full.

In spite, too, of the decline of Spanish power at this time, both Philip IV and his predecessor, Philip III, were patrons of literature and art, in which Spain continued to lead the world. The Spanish theatre was the pattern upon which the European stage still modelled itself, and the great Lope de Vega did not die until 1635, or Tirso de Molina until 1648, while Calderón was at the zenith of his fame in the last years of Philip IV. The reverses suffered by the Spanish arms at the hands of the French, and the growing poverty of the country, were entirely without influence upon its literature and art, so that the seventeenth century may justly be described as the golden age of Spanish civilization: during the course of it Cervantes published both *Don Quixote* and the *Novelas Ejemplares*; there flourished the great satirist Quevedo; and in art the period was distinguished by Ribera, Zurbarán, Murillo, and, above all, Valazquez.

Such being the case it is in no way surprising that beneath the superficial light-heartedness there remained the conviction that Spain was the greatest country in the world; so great, in fact, that — again the comparison with Britain in the nineteen fifties and sixties obtrudes itself — the loss of an outlying province or two passed as an accident of no importance.

The Elizabethan persecution had resulted in many Irish exiles finding a home in Spain or the Spanish Netherlands, and the armies of the Catholic King abounded in Irishmen, who were always welcome and soon made to feel at home. Such had been the normal state of affairs for many years, but the situation now was not normal, and the Spanish government was endeavouring to steer its way between the shoals of the Civil War — or at any rate not to get itself committed to the losing side. Soon after the execution of his father Charles II had sent an embassy to Madrid consisting of Lord Cottington and Edward Hyde, later Lord Clarendon,[3] in the hope of obtaining pecuniary or other assistance from Philip IV, but it proved abortive. In his *History of the Rebellion* the future Chancellor has much to say about life in contemporary Spain, and he had every opportunity of observing it for he had little else to do. The two men remained in the Spanish capital for fifteen months, when it was intimated to them, though in the most courteous manner, that their presence was no longer agreeable to King Philip and his ministers; on their way to the coast Cottington, who was nearer eighty than seventy, died at Valladolid.

There can be little doubt that in acting in this way the Spanish government was primarily impressed by Cromwell's victories, but it is more than likely that Philip also had reasons of his own; he had recently bought a number of pictures from the collection of Charles I, which the Commonwealth was dispersing, and he did not wish them to arrive in Madrid under the eyes of Cottington and Hyde.

Then there was the murder of Anthony Ascham, which had taken place in the spring of 1650, at which time the republican government in London was more favourable to Spain than to France. In spite of the protests of Cottington and Hyde, it was decided in Madrid to receive an ambassador from the Commonwealth, and Anthony Ascham was selected for the post. He would appear to have been in an advanced stage of consumption; for when he was first appointed in October 1649 he was doubtful if he could go, and he wrote to Lord President Bradshaw saying that the haemorrhage of the lungs from which he suffered was so bad that he must go to his father's house at Boston to recover before he would be fit to travel.[4] Even had he been in the best of health he would appear to have been an unsatisfactory emissary, and Clarendon described him as ' unacquainted with business, and unskilled in language, attended by three others, the one a renegade Franciscan friar who had been bred in Spain, and was well versed in the language; another, who was to serve in the condition of a secretary; and the third, an inferior fellow for any service '.[5]

When Ascham reached Madrid he put up at an inn while suitable lodgings were being found for him, but no guard was provided by the Spanish authorities, and this proved to be his downfall. Soon after his arrival he was lunching in his quarters with the renegade friar, and close at hand in a hostelry in the Calle de Caballero de Gracia a party of Royalist exiles was participating in what appears to have been something of a carouse. The drink went round, toasts to Charles the Martyr were doubtless drunk, and it was decided to avenge his murder upon the representative of his murderers. The drinkers accordingly made their way to Ascham's quarters, where one of them seized him by the hair, crying out ' Traitor ', while another thrust him through the arm with a dagger, and a third stabbed him in the temples; the rest of the party then finished him off with their swords. At this point the unhappy friar made a rush for the door, but he was cut down before he could reach it, and was just able to stagger into an adjoining room where he fell dead.

The assassins then fled, as they had arranged to do, to the Church of St Andrés where they claimed sanctuary before the high altar. In a few minutes the whole quarter was in an uproar, and when the *alguaciles* entered the inn in which Ascham had met his end they found him and the friar lying dead, with an English serving-man uninjured, but almost beside himself with fright. So scandalous was the whole affair that the civil authorities ordered the murderers to be taken from sanctuary and transferred to prison, which was a very unusual procedure.

Philip was extremely annoyed when the news of the crime reached him, for it rendered his position with the English republican government extremely tricky. At the same time he found himself at issue with the ecclesiastical authorities who were peremptorily demanding the restoration of the prisoners to sanctuary, while public opinion among all classes in Madrid was overwhelmingly on the side of the murderers, who were, in fact, the heroes of the hour. As we have seen, the King was no fool, in spite of being subject to many other weaknesses, and he handled this difficult situation with consummate skill by indulging in a piece of adroit political expediency. Balancing the anger of Cromwell against that of the Church, he came to the conclusion that he could the more easily contain the latter, so he decided to let the murderers remain in prison until the affair blew over and circumstances had changed: this was what happened, when all but one of them, who had died, were quietly released and disappeared into obscurity.[6]

In fact Ascham's fate was not unique among English republican envoys, for his colleague, Dr Dorislaus, had been murdered in The Hague in similar circumstances in the previous year. It was, in short, an age when political assassination was not considered in any way reprehensible, and this fact must be taken into account in any estimate of Richard Talbot's later involvement in a plot to murder Cromwell. Had not Oliver St John said at the trail of Strafford, ' It was never accounted either cruelty or foul play to knock foxes and wolves on the head because they be beasts of prey '?

To return to Richard who, while serving with his nephew, seems also to have been seeing a good deal of his clerical brother, Peter, a natural intriguer, and one who appears to have had an unfortunate facility for inspiring mistrust in those with whom he came in contact; certainly this was the case with Ormonde, although the priests had endeavoured to keep on good terms with him, having been, like most of the members of the Society of Jesus, very suspicious of the claims of Rinuccini. He was destined to die as Archbishop of Dublin of an agonizing disease – a prisoner in the Castle on a charge of complicity in the so-called Popish Plot – but though his death was that of a martyr, his character and reputation were not such as to encourage his Irish contemporaries to enthuse over him in that capacity. With the Spaniards he seems to have been more successful, for in 1654 he left Madrid for London on a mission from Philip to his ambassador in the English capital, and there is a letter extant dated 3 July from Antwerp to the Bishop of Clonmacnois, Anthony MacGeoghegan, in which he says that he and his brother, presumably Richard, had cause to be grateful to an Irish bishop in Madrid for kindness to them in that city.[7]

Meanwhile the ties between Ireland and Spain were weakening, for although there was plenty of fighting to be had in the Spanish service there was little else, so empty were the Catholic King's coffers at this time. Then in 1652 the Duke of York had commenced to serve in the armies of Louis XIV, and many Royalists, though not Richard Talbot, proceeded to follow his example. This state of affairs, however, did not last for long, for Mazarin made an alliance with Cromwell, firm in the conviction that the Stuarts would never be restored, and Charles and his followers had to resume their wanderings. In the autumn of 1654 they settled at Cologne, where they met with an enthusiastic reception from the local authorities, but were cold-shouldered by the Elector – ' a melancholy and peevish man ' according to Hyde – who in any event resided at Bonn.

Richard Talbot now makes his appearance upon the stage of history, and in connection with a plot to murder Cromwell. That there was such a plot, and that he was concerned in it, are clear, but the rest of the story is more than a little obscure. According to Clarendon's *Continuation*,[8] he was brought by Daniel O'Neill, a nephew of Owen Roe, to Flanders,[9] ' as one who was willing to assassinate Cromwell; and he made a journey into England with that resolution not long before his death, and after it returned to Flanders ready to do all he should be required '. This statement is the evidence which Macaulay felt justified him in writing that Richard ' was introduced to Charles and James when they were exiles in Flanders as a man fit and ready for the infamous service of assassinating the Protector '.[10] Clarendon, it may be added, was writing from memory, and although it is possible, though not very probable, that Richard may have met Charles at this time, James he almost certainly did not meet, for that prince did not leave the French service until 1656, and the plot to murder Cromwell took place in the previous year.

To understand why the Royalists should have been driven to such desperation it is necessary to picture the state of the country under the Protectorate. Fear was spreading all over England, and the oldest of friends were becoming shy of one another. A hasty word, or the spite of a discharged servant, and one day there would be a clatter of hooves in the lane or up the drive, and the master of the house would be haled off to prison; there he might stay for years, only to be released on the payment of a crushing fine which would reduce him and his to poverty. It was little wonder that men prayed for ' a speedy deliverance out of the power of the Major-Generals, and restore us to the protection of the Common Law '.

The defeated party was treated with severity, though not, it must be admitted, with the harshness that was meted out to the wretched Irish. Royalists who had participated in any plot or rising after the overthrow of the monarchy were banished and their property was sequestrated. Those who by word or act recognized Charles II were banished or imprisoned, though in this case their property was not confiscated. Those who had fought against the Parliament or suffered sequestration in the past had to pay ten per cent of their income from land, and if that fell below a hundred pounds a year, a proportion of their personal property. No Royalist might be elected on any local body. The use of the Prayer Book was forbidden, and care was taken – by means of drastic purges – to ensure that the universities did not become centres of hostility to the new regime.

Every rising was made the excuse for further severities. In 1655 there was a very half-hearted affair in Wiltshire, which came to an inglorious end at South Molton, in Devonshire. Less than two hundred people were concerned in it, but of these two were beheaded, ten were hanged, and seventy were transported to the West Indies – the last without even the form of a trial. One similarity there was between the procedure in England and Ireland, and that was the tendency to put to death men who had surrendered on terms: in this Salisbury rising such a one was John Penruddock, who had also saved several Roundhead lives. Terror begets terror, and in these circumstances it was not surprising that the Royalists should seek to be avenged upon the man to whom they attributed all their sufferings, namely the Lord Protector himself, quite apart from the fact that the sixteenth and seventeenth centuries were very definitely an age of political murder.

The beginning of the plot in which Richard Talbot was concerned may be dated from the departure from Cologne early in July 1655, of one James Halsall, who was described by the spy, Henry Manning, to Thurloe as ' a little black man ' of ' about thirty-five years of age, round face, in short hair or a periwig, and a round man '; he was further stated to be ' one of our chiefest agents '. Halsall had been implicated in Penruddock's rising, but had managed to escape overseas after a period of hiding in London, and his zeal was in no way abated. On the journey to England he was preceded by Colonel John Stephens and by Richard Rose, a servant to Lord Rochester. News of these events was duly passed on by Manning to Thurloe in the words, ' Captain Talbot, a tall young man and an Irish, and Rob. Dongan, who was Ormonde's page . . . are in England, by way of Dover, their business to assist Stephens.' A week later he added, ' If I had a cypher with the Governor of Dover, Talbot, Dongan, and Halsall, whom I have called Holsey, should not have escaped him.'[11] Robin Dongan was Richard Talbot's nephew, being the son of his sister, Mary, and Sir John Dongan; he, too, had had a varied career, for he had been a page to Ormonde, and had more recently accompanied Edward Wogan to Scotland.

All five conspirators got safely into England by way of

Dover, but it was not long before they were made aware of the risks they were running, for Stephens and Richard were arrested on their arrival in London.[12] Stephens was soon released, and went to Dunkirk, where he fell seriously ill, and Richard was set at liberty shortly afterwards. In view of the information which had been laid against them it is difficult to understand why they were treated in this lenient fashion – unless, of course, they were released to act as unconscious decoys to incriminate their fellow-conspirators.

Halsall had in the meantime remained hidden in his lodgings in London, and to him Richard repaired as soon as he was free, attended by a confidential servant of the name of William Masten, in whom he trusted, as he was later to put on record, ' to the letting him know all his business '. As Rose had by now dropped out of the plot Halsall was left alone with the two Irishmen, who kept on urging him that further delay would be dangerous; he continued, however, to put them off, and in this dilatory attitude he would appear to have been supported from Cologne. He delayed too long, for unknown to him he was being watched by Cromwell's agents. On 16 November 1655, he was arrested outside his lodgings, and when he was searched all sorts of damning evidence came to light to prove what he was doing in England. Among other documents a list of names was discovered, and on the strength of it Richard and his nephew were seized the following day.

Two informers had been responsible for these arrests: one was William Masten and the other Henry Manning. The former's part seems to have been the betrayal of his master's and Halsall's lodgings; Halsall guessed what had happened, but as he was himself a prisoner he had no means of putting his friends on their guard, with the result that Masten was able for a time to continue to betray them while protesting his devotion to Charles. He seems to have avoided detection until 1657, when he fell into Spanish hands, but all the same he somehow managed to avoid being punished for his misdeeds.

Henry Manning was not so fortunate. He was a particularly despicable character, for he had been brought up to know a great deal better than to betray his friends for gain.[13] Clarendon says of him that he was ' a proper young gentleman, bred a Roman Catholic in the family of the Marquess of Worcester, whose page he had been. His father, of that religion likewise, had been a colonel in the King's army, and was slain at the battle of Alresford; where this young man, being then a youth, was hurt, and maimed in the left arm and shoulder.' He arrived in Cologne shortly after Charles. ' He was a handsome man, had store of good clothes, and plenty of money; which, with the memory of his father, easily introduced him, and made him acceptable to the company that was there. . . He associated most with the good fellows, and eat in their company, being well provided for the expense.'[14] Manning's downfall seems to have been due to the Spanish ambassador in London, Don Alonso de Cardenas, who left England in October 1655, when Cromwell made his treaty with France. As soon as Cardenas reached Brussels he told the English Royalists how the Protector obtained his information regarding their movements, and from that moment the noose was round Manning's neck.

His correspondence was searched by the Spanish authorities at Antwerp, with the result that no doubt was left concerning his guilt – in fact he was actually writing a letter to Thurloe on 5 December when he was arrested in his lodgings at Cologne. He was then examined by Lord Culpepper, Ormonde, and Secretary Nicholas, and condemned to death. At this point there was a hitch in the proceedings because the Elector of Cologne strongly objected to the execution taking place on his territory; however, Philip William, who ruled the neighbouring duchy of Julich, had no such scruples, so Manning was taken across the border by Sir James Hamilton and Major Nicholas Armorer and pistolled in a wood.[15]

Meanwhile, Halsall, Talbot, and Dongan were taken to Whitehall so that they might be examined by the Protector himself. Halsall was brought up first, and there could be no doubt about the importance of his captured papers, but there was nothing in them about the assassination plot, and he steadfastly asserted that his business in England was the collection of money for the King. This was true, but it was not the whole truth; anyhow there was nothing more to be got out of him, and he refused to reveal the names of any of his associates except in the case of those whom he knew to be out of reach.

This was highly unsatisfactory from Cromwell's point-of-view, so he next had Richard Talbot brought before him. He seems to have begun the interview with an attempt to win him over by promising preferment, and even going so far as to try snob-appeal by claiming kinship on the ground that he was himself related to the Shrewsbury Talbots; he also made the usual promise of secrecy in the case of any confession that his prisoner might see fit to make. These tactics had no effect upon Richard, so the Protector brusquely changed them, and asked why Richard should think of murdering him seeing that he had never done him any harm. Richard might have instanced Drogheda, but either courtesy or discretion caused him to refrain, and he contented himself with denying all knowledge of a plot.

Cromwell thereupon produced a cipher which had been taken from Halsall, but though it contained the names of Dongan, Wogan, and others, Richard was not mentioned. On the latter pointing this out, the Protector said that Halsall had betrayed it to him, whereupon Richard requested to be confronted with his alleged accuser. Cromwell then ordered Halsall to be fetched, but on reflection countermanded the order as he realized that the confrontation would not get him anywhere, and he appears to have lost his temper. Anyhow he threatened his prisoner with the rack, and declared that he would spin the truth out of Richard's bones. 'Spin me to a thread if you please,' was all the answer he got, 'I having nothing to confess, and can only invent lies.' On this the baffled dictator ordered him to be taken away.

All the same it was clear to Richard that the Protector knew too much for his safety and that it behoved him to get out of Cromwell's clutches at the earliest opportunity; in this resolve he was strengthened by the information that he was to be transferred from Whitehall to the Tower. In the meantime he was visited by Thurloe – according to some accounts by Lambert as well – who tried to bribe him once more, but to all such offers he replied that he only desired the return of £240 of which he had been robbed on his arrest; twenty pounds, however, was all he received, though of that he made very good use. ' That night,' his brother Peter wrote, ' he bestowed much wine upon Cromwell's soldiers, who waited on him and served him like a Prince; slipped down to the Thames by a cord, where he had a boat prepared; and in that little thing was ten days at sea; landed at last at Callis (Calais), still nayled and shut up between some boards of the boate.'[16] Richard had many failings, but a lack of resourcefulness was not among them.

From Calais he made his way to the Low Countries; on 27 December he was at Brussels, and on 3 January 1656 we find him at Antwerp. At the earliest opportunity he wrote a letter to Ormonde, in which he gave some details about his examination by Cromwell and his escape from Whitehall. In respect of the failure of the plot he expressed confidence that if Halsall had the good luck to get away he would confess that it was not through him that ' the business ' was not attempted. As for Dongan and the others who were still in prison there was no great danger to be apprehended provided they did not by their confessions destroy one another; for when Richard got away Cromwell ' had no other ground to proceed upon than bare suspicions, and, consequently, for the safety of theyr lives, it's necessary that nothing be said of it '.[17] With Richard at Antwerp were his brothers Peter and Gilbert, and there they all remained until the arrival of Ormonde. While they were waiting Richard received a letter signed ' Donna Francisca ', who was probably Lady Isabella Thynne, with the information that she had managed to get Dongan out of prison; this was good news so far as it went, but he had not succeeded in leaving England, and in the meantime events were happening which were by no means in the interests of his uncle Richard.

Ormonde arrived in Antwerp in the second week of January, and immediately found himself involved in a mass of intrigue, of which the three Talbot brothers were the centre. Peter was working on a fatuous scheme to combine the Levellers in

England with the Spanish authorities in the Low Countries to restore Charles, but he was not getting very far with it, for the dissident republicans had no use for those by whom the exiled King was surrounded. ' The Cavaliers ', one of them told Talbot, ' are a generation that God cannot prosper; but for their swearing, drinking, and whoring – and little secrecy – Cromwell had been down before.'[18] The Jesuit's optimism was considerable where the Spaniards were concerned, and he wrote to Charles that General Fuensaldaña had said, ' Tell the King that he shall find among us secrecy, honour and fair dealing. . . If he will do what we desire, we will live and die together. Let him make no capitulations, for that will be suspicious. The more he trusts the King of Spain and the Pope, the better it is.' His Holiness, Talbot added, would then help to finance Charles, ' and therefore before six months, the business shall be done '.[19]

Ormonde was not impressed by Peter's diplomacy, so he went to Brussels on 11 January 1656 to check these statements with Fuensaldaña, and found the Spanish commander-in-chief a good deal less enthusiastic than he had been represented, so he wrote to Nicholas in Cologne, ' You will finde that ether the Father is a most exquisite forger or the Counte[20] a great desembler; but I am led to beleeve the former, out of the unhappy experience I have had of the Irish cleargy, and for other reasons.' If Ormonde was sceptical, Hyde was downright suspicious, for on 7 January he had written to Ormonde:

The Jesuite . . . writ in his letter to Mr Harding the story of his brother's escape, contrary to what we had heard before; and that he was taken the next day after Halsey (Halsall); whereas you remember the letter from Will (Masten) that says they were taken together. I have likewise a letter from the Colonel to you inclosed in Mr Lane's letter; which I think it is no matter for sending. . . He seems to fear that making his escape may lose his brother's credit, and make that matter miscarry: whereas I have some reason to be very confident that he and his brother had spoke with each other on this side of the sea, before he came hither; and I am more confirmed than I was when we parted, that they are all in the pack of knavery. I had forgot to tell you that the last night, Mr Raney came to me in some trouble, and asked me whether one Gilbert Talbot had been lately here, and told me almost as much as I knew, which he had then seen in letters from Bruxelles; so that you may say what rare fellows those are, and why anybody should be bound to keep their secrets.[21]

In a second letter a week later Hyde wrote of the Talbot brothers that ' hardly anything can be more evident that they are all naught ', and that ' the Jesuit should be sent to a remote convent, and kept close from further activity '.[22]

At this point in the extremely complicated story Richard found that he was himself coming under suspicion on account of his extraordinary escape from the Protector's clutches which, it was said, could only have been the result of treachery on his part. These rumours were spread on the Continent by no less a person than his own nephew, Dongan, who had crossed the Channel as soon as he could get away from England, and on 30 January 1656 he reached Dunkirk, where he found Stephens, who, as has been shown, had been lying ill and destitute there ever since his departure from London in the previous September. At Dunkirk he had received a visit from Masten whose treachery was still unsuspected. It is only natural to suppose that Dongan and Stephens had discussed the failure of the plot in which they had been engaged, and doubtless commented on Richard Talbot's escape, concerning which Dongan had heard rumours before he crossed the Channel.

However this may be, he wrote a note to Ormonde announcing his safe arrival at Dunkirk, and in the course of it he said, ' I make no questions you have herd of them reports that were of Dicke Talbot, but I could not gett any ground for them. But every body must answer for himself as I hope all them that knows annything of that business will answer for mee, for I can answer for nobody but my selfe.'[23] Not content with this, Dongan wrote again: ' I am very much out of countenance to lett your Lordshipe understand a thing which my duty commands mee to, which is more to me than all the friends in the world. The thing I mean is that there was strange reports of my oncol concerning his betraying of Halsy and myself for this bisiness. I could fine noe ground at al but reports, which I thought it my duty to let your Lordship understand, and as for my part, I will neither accuse him nor justify him because I cannot doe it by profes either ways, which if I could I would not trubel your Lordshipe with giving you this relation, but would take a cours with him myself. My Lady Issabela bids mee tell you that shee thought him innocent now since Manning was put to death; but tim will bring out all.'[24]

The facts of Dongan's disloyalty to his uncle are clear, but the reason for it is more difficult to fathom: possibly it was to distract attention from himself, since he was already under suspicion for having wrecked the plot by his indiscretion. Indeed, as far back as the beginning of the previous December Stephens had written to Ormonde to the effect that the three conspirators had been ' betrayed by the too lavish discourse of Dongan '.[25] When Dongan reached Brussels he was left in no doubt concerning what was being said about him. 'I here,' he wrote to Ormonde on 26 February, 'Mr. O'Neil reports and tels everybody that I tould everybody my bisnes into England before I went, which is the greatest untruth that ever was.'[26]

The Talbots could hardly be described as a united family, and they appear to have been ready to believe anything about one another, so when Dongan moved on to Antwerp, still peddling his story about his uncle, he had no shame in repeating it to Peter Talbot, whom we then find writing to Ormonde as follows:

> Robin Dongan . . . tells me of a strange report of Dick amongst some people in London. He thinks it had noe ground and sayes it is now (?) to Halsey's man or some other. Tyme will discover the truth. In the interim I will neyther flatter my inclination with judging him innocent nor bee rash in condemning him; but truly I will bee wary of all persons which lye under a cloud and such a base aspersion as this is. Whosoever betrays his King will betray his brother. I am apt to believe that Gilbert's businesse hath given some occasion to this blemish of his brother, who came this night to me from Brussels and is mad, swears and damns himselfe, wondring how people can as

F

much as admit any such thoughts against him. Truly I thinke Gilb. would have more credit with his correspondent than hee hath if Dick were a knave.[27]

This was hardly the attitude which one brother might have been expected to adopt towards another, but Peter would appear before long to have become less suspicious, for in another letter to Ormonde he says, ' Dick hath received the Blessed Sacrament in confirmation of his innocency. Truly, all circumstances and obligations both of honour and conscience considered, it is not only improbable but morally impossible that he should not only betray his King, but, in His Majesty, all his own kindred, friends, and country for a little sum which he must never enjoy or show, unless he be resolved to be deemed of all the most perfidious and infamous rogue.'

The one person who comes well out of the affair is Richard Talbot himself. He knew of the charges against him before his nephew arrived in Antwerp, and as early as 1 February he wrote to Ormonde vindicating himself in a letter of which the most important passages are as follows:

I always thought that the testimoneys all those of our family gave of thyr fidelity to the King's servis and in particular to Yr. Ex.cey and the many hazard that myself hath lately run in order thearunto ought merit a better opinion of mee than I find thear is held of mee by some of the King's ministers thear, to be Cromwells onely intelligence hear, if the loss of as much blood as I have lost in his servis, and the quittering of my fortune hear the last summer to go into England to venter the lives of my friends and my owne, my imprissonment thear for six months (which is a thing publikely knowne to the Kings best friends thear that it stood me in 400 St.), and lastely my leyfe lost (if I had not made my escape) bee not motives sufficient to justfy mee.

My Lord, I am a gentleman, and if I wear so wicked as to be so voyd of all fidellity to my lawfull Prince as to turne rogue for interest, yet I am not of soe despicable a sperrit as to doe an act so much below a Gentleman. . . If I had stayed in England thear maught me som ground for that scandalous reporte. . . I cannot imadgin how this should com to pass, but I hope my innocensy will apear, when som of those that accuse mee wil be blak enow.

I belieeve Robin Dongans coming hether now will confirme them in it, and that his escape was permitted as being of relation to me, for it was that that roysed the first reporte in England of it. I should never have knowne that I was suspected but that the Chancelor thear writ to a certaine gentleman[28] at Dunkirk to send into England to know the certainty from Halsy, but I am of opinion that Halsey is to honest a man to tax mee, if it bee not that he hath heard that I said the attempt had beene made upon the Protectors person, but that hee, eyther through cowardis or some other private end, had obstructed it, and that I sayd to those that I was sure would tell him of it, and that I will justify . . .

Though I bee held now to have a correspondecy with Cromwell I hope before many dayes pass that my actions will declare the contrary. All the favor that I beg of your Lo.p is that you will not prejudicate mee, and soe that his Ma.tie and Yr. Excy. bee satisfied (as you may be very justly) those others that harbour that opinion of mee may make further enquiry of it and if they finde any evident proofes for it all the favor I desire from them is that they will prosecute me. . .[29]

Ormonde's reply is not in existence, but that it was not unsatisfactory may be gathered from a second letter to him from Antwerp on 12 February 1656.

My Lord

I expected with much impatience Yr. Excye's letter, which came to my hands soe very late yesterday that I had not time by the last poast to returne you my humble thanks for the hor you did mee, and to say further, if it wear possible, to bind mee more faythfully to his Ma.ties servis or more firme to yr. interests, soe oblidgeing a letter would infallibly doe it, but that being as impossible as my being the person I was represented thear to bee I do promis myselfe that his Ma'tie. and yr selfe will (at least) suspend yr. ill opinions of mee untill you have some more convincing evidence of my guilt, and that once made aparent I shall very patiently submit myself to the punishment (in the publick view of the world) that the infamy and wickedness of my tongue doth requyer; and on the other syed,

Yr. Excy., I am confident, will allow that my petition is not unreasonable, if I beg that noe inconsiderable persons or little envoyes in England words be taken for it if they give not som other proofes than thyr owne base surmises . . .

Though little, my Lord, I have seene of the world, I have observed that whenever thear was any undertaking by any person never so desserving and never soe really ment without other end then the public good, and that it proved unsuccessful, wear it never so cleare that nothing was lost for want of care or contrivance, because it succeeded not according to expectation. God forbid I should pleade the former and present endeavours of all those of our own familyes (in serving his Ma'tie) for my own justification. I will only say one word, that in my opinion is convincing enow, that if interest were soe prevalent with mee as to make mee quit all honestye it is not by giveing intelligence from hence that I could make my greatest benefit. I could before I came out of England by slipeing but a very few words gaine myself a fortune, and my friends likewise during our lives, and nobody know neyther who hurt him. But I prays God for it, I am not of soe covetous a disposition as to prefer money before my contience, my loyalty and my hon'r. I have lived hitherto without beeing a trouble or discredit to my friends, and I hope will continue it.

I shall not trouble Yr. Ex. further in this matter. I know not what I may suffer at present in yr. opinion, but I hope tyme will give mee opertunity to make the contrary evidently apear. The dayly hazard of my life shall justify mee whear (I fear) my acusers dare not show thyr faces, and since you have always been the Patron of us all I humbly crave yr. assistance in my vindication in this particular that so neerely concerns the reputation of,

My Lord,

Yr. Ex'cyes. most faithfull and obedient servant,

R. Talbot.[30]

Such was the end of the episode which may be said to have brought Richard Talbot on the stage of history for the first time, and it seems clear that there was not a shred of evidence in support of the charges brought against him, while his relatives certainly do not come out of the affair any too well. Ormonde showed himself as the great gentleman he proved to be throughout his whole career, while Hyde was blinded by the prejudice of a narrow, if honest, man.

NOTES

1 *History of the Rebellion*, Book XII. Oxford. 1839.

2 *Ibid.*

3 Hyde was created Earl of Clarendon at the coronation of Charles II in April 1661.

4 *MSS*, Record Office, S.P., Spain 42.

5 *History of the Rebellion*, Bk. XIII. Oxford. 1839. Of course Clarendon was naturally somewhat prejudiced.

6 *Cf.* Hume, Martin: *The Court of Philip IV*, pp. 430-437. London. 1907.

7 *Cf.* Moran, Cardinal P. F.: *Spicilegium Ossoriense*, Vol. II, p. 133. Dublin. 1874-1884.

8 Vol. III, pp. 119-120.

9 Surely a mistake for Cologne.

10 *History of England*, Vol. I, Ch. VI.

11 *C.S.P.* D, 1655. Manning to Thurloe, July 3/13, and July 10/20.

12 *Cf. Thurloe State Papers*, Vol. III, p. 659.

13 Treachery certainly paid, for Masten is said to have received at least £2,000 for betraying Halsall, Richard Talbot, and Robin Dongan, and Manning was paid £120 a month.

14 *History of the Rebellion*, Bk. XIV. Oxford. 1839.

15 *Cal. Clar., St. P.* III, Art. 211.

16 The story of Richard's examination and escape, as told by himself and Peter, is to be found in the *Clarendon Papers*, Vol. 51, ff. 6, 8, 10, 12, and 17. Miss Eva Scott, in her *Travels of the King*, Chap. V gives a very full story, from the original sources, of the plot and its failure.

17 *Cal. Car. St. P.* III, Art. 222.

18 *Cf.* Chapman, Hester: *The Tragedy of Charles II*, p. 294. London. 1964.

19 *Cal. Clar. St. P.* II, pp. 75-77.

20 Fuensaldaña. Luis-Perez de Vivero, Conde de Fuensaldaña, was a soldier and diplomat. He had been the Archduke Leopold's general from 1648, and had been in command of the Spanish cavalry at the battle of Lens. The Baron de Woerden described him as 'un homme d'une extreme probité, froid, pas communicatif, mais dont l'amitié, une fois donnée, ne se démentait pas'. He and Condé disliked one another from the outset, and at the former's request Fuensaldaña was superseded in 1656 as commander in the Netherlands and was sent as Viceroy to Milan.

21 Carte, *Original Letters*, Vol. II, pp. 63-64.

22 *Ibid.*, Vol. II, p. 68.

[23] *Cf.* Moran, Cardinal P. F.: *Spicilegium Ossoriense*, Vol. II, p. 159. Dublin. 1874-1884.
[24] *Cf.* Moran, Cardinal P. F.: *Spicilegium Ossoriense*, Vol. II, p. 160.
[25] Carte Papers, 131 f. 160.
[26] *Cf.* Moran, *op. cit.* Vol. II, p. 167.
[27] *Ibid.* Vol. II, p. 160.
[28] Stephens.
[29] *Spicilegium Ossoriense*, Vol. III, pp. 161, 162.
[30] *Spicilegium Ossoriense*, Vol. III, pp. 163-164.

CHAPTER IV

Last Years of Exile

RICHARD TALBOT was still only in his middle twenties, but he had already served an adventurous apprenticeship to what was to prove a stormy life. Lately he had been in the Royalist limelight, but now for a space he was to retire into the background, and chiefly to be concerned with the exiles' military activities. In the high politics of the period he was not involved, and thus the somewhat tedious negotiations between Charles and the Spanish government are not the affair of his biographer; suffice to say that the alliance between Cromwell and Mazarin had to some extent revived the old attraction of the Spanish service for the Irish, and such of the latter as had joined the French armies were induced to desert the Lilies of France for the Lions and Castles of Castille. Richard, having served under the Spanish flag, was ideally suited to take part in the formation of an Irish Brigade in many way analogous to that which was to cover itself with glory in the following century.

The facts were these: on 12 April 1656 Ormonde and Rochester had signed a secret agreement with Cardenas and Fuensaldaña in Brussels, and an important clause in the document provided for the employment by Spain of English and Irish troops in the war against France. Certain Irish regiments had remained in the Spanish service since their first exile, and among their officers were Walter Dongan, now by the death of his brother a baronet, and his brother William; but their numbers had constantly dwindled through discontent over pay and rations. The rising sun of France was definitely proving a counter-attraction, and there was already a large body of

English, Irish, and Scottish troops in the French army. A necessary consequence of the Brussels agreement was the transfer of all Royalist volunteers from the French to the Spanish flag. The advantages of this from the point of view of Madrid are obvious, but it was equally valuable to Charles, for it meant that he would have a force ready to move across the Channel if and when an armed attempt to overthrow Cromwell became practicable. In the assembling of this force Gilbert and Richard Talbot were given a leading part, so it may safely be assumed that they had been acquitted of all suspicion of disloyalty.

Ghent would appear to have been the scene of most of Richard's recruiting activities,[1] and considerable progress was made there in spite of the shortage of money. By November 1656 the number of men collected was in the neighbourhood of six thousand, but a good many officers were loath to change their coats, though the better conditions in the French service may well have had something to do with their reluctance to transfer their allegiance. Nevertheless in due course four regiments were formed which were assigned respectively to the Duke of Gloucester, Ormonde, Sir Thomas Middleton, and Rochester; to these were later added a fifth under the Duke of York, and a sixth, at first under the Earl of Bristol. Richard, however, was not content to be a mere recruiting officer for Philip IV, for he also saw some active service at this time: a new Governor-General of the Netherlands had arrived in the person of Don John of Austria, an illegitimate son of the King of Spain, and the bearer of a historic name. His mother was a famous actress in Madrid, Maria Calderón, usually known by the name of the Calderona, and he was both brilliant and able. Don John's education had been carefully conducted, his ambition was boundless, and his handsome face and popular manners made him the idol of his father's subjects. Until he died in 1679 the second Don John of Austria was a powerful factor in Spanish politics. With his coming to the Low Countries the war became more active, and Don John and Condé, who was in the Spanish service as a result of his disagreements with Mazarin, severely defeated a French army under Turenne which was besieging Valenciennes where a Spanish garrison was beleagured. At this battle ' Dick, with some English gentlemen placed by him[2] among Condé's troops ' was present; this we learn from a letter from Peter to Ormonde.[3]

This year, 1656, which had begun with Richard Talbot under a cloud, was to end with his fortunes very considerably mended, for it brought him into touch with the Duke of York, with whom he was to be closely associated for the rest of his life. For this reason his biographer must look in greater detail at the character of his patron.

The Duke was three years younger than his elder brother, Charles II, having been born at St James's Palace on 14 October 1633. Few monarchs have been so bitterly attacked as James II. The admirers of his predecessor on the throne can hardly find words strong enough to express their disapproval of the man who destroyed his heritage in less than four years; while those who appreciate the sterling qualities which might well have made James III one of the best British monarchs are equally ready to blacken the character of the father whose folly prevented his succession to the throne. The facts of his career are undisputed, but it is difficult to resist the conclusion that the correct interpretation has never yet been put upon them. In spite of the centuries which have elapsed since the Revolution of 1688, the passions which that event aroused have hitherto prevented a just estimate of the monarch who lost his throne as a result. Perhaps one reason for this is that James had the misfortune to become implicated in Irish politics, and, like many another Englishman, both before and since, he was unable to escape unscathed from the ordeal.

In common with his brothers and sisters, he had a stormy youth. On the outbreak of the Civil War he was placed by his father at Oxford for greater safety, and he was captured there by the Parliamentarians in 1646. His captors imprisoned him, together with the Duke of Gloucester and Princess Elizabeth, in the place of his birth, St James's Palace; but after two years he succeeded in making his escape to Holland, and from there he joined his mother in Paris. During the Commonwealth he served as a soldier on the Continent. First of all, he went through four campaigns in the French army under Turenne, who conceived a high opinion of him,[4] and to whom he was devoted, while Condé said that ' in the matter of courage in a man, he desired to see nothing better than the Duke of York '.[5] After the treaty between Cromwell and Mazarin, which obliged him to leave the French service, he entered that of Spain, and fought bravely for the Spaniards at the Battle of the Dunes in 1658. On the eve of the Restoration two years later James was appointed by Philip IV to be High Admiral of Spain, with a command in the expedition that was being prepared for the re-conquest of Portugal. When the monarchy was restored in England the Duke of York was made Lord High Admiral, and as such he commanded the British fleet in the victory over the Dutch off Lowestoft in 1665. In this action he remained on deck for eighteen hours exposed to such heavy fire that more than one man was killed by his side.

The fact is that until James came to the throne no charge of cowardice or vacillation can be laid to his account. At the time of the Popish Plot and the Exclusion Bill he never lost his head, and his attitude was absolutely correct. It is true that once having joined the Church of Rome he refused to leave it but even those who are not of that communion can hardly blame him for such devotion to principle. On the other hand, his short reign seems completely to have broken his nerve, and his conduct after the landing of William of Orange was pusillanimous in the extreme. The first resolution to advance against the invaders was unquestionably the right one, and would most certainly have given him the victory; but the man who had charged the famous *tercios* of Spain and the redoubtable Ironsides of Cromwell abandoned the campaign when he had already got as far as Salisbury because his nose had begun to bleed. Shortly afterwards, on his return to London after his first attempt at flight, he was entreated by Dundee to stay and fight it out, but he flatly refused, with the remark, ' You know there is but a small distance between the prisons and the graves of Kings '.[6] Finally, he fled with such precipitance from the battlefield of the Boyne as to earn the reproaches of no less devoted a Jacobite than Richard Talbot's wife.

Much of this is to anticipate, but the explanation of these apparent inconsistencies would seem to lie in his training during his most impressionable years. In exile he had little to do with the extremely complicated politics of the period, and he had left the handling of them to his elder brother. Furthermore, like the vast majority of soldiers and sailors in civil life, James proved to be a bad judge of character, and the two men whom he principally trusted, namely Sunderland and Churchill, both turned out traitors. The effort to solve problems with which his upbringing had not fitted him to cope appears to have affected James's nervous system to such an extent that the moment things began to go wrong he fell into a panic. He became increasingly more bewildered as he found himself called upon to deal with questions which were beyond him; thus he got into deeper and deeper water, losing his nerve in the process, so that by 1688 he was completely nonplussed even by the problems that he could have taken in his stride ten or twenty years before. It was his misfortune that at the very crisis of his fate his powers of resistance were at their weakest.

James reached Flanders from Paris at the end of September 1656, but at what date he added Richard Talbot to his household is uncertain. Hyde in recording the fact merely states, ' He was a very handsome young man, wore good clothes, and was without a doubt of a clear, ready courage, which was virtue enough to recommend a man to the Duke's good opinion, which, with more expedition than could be expected, he got to that degree that he was made of the bedchamber.'[7] His next step upwards was to be appointed Lieutenant-Colonel of the Duke of York's Regiment, but he only secured this promotion in the face of a good deal of opposition.

The nucleus of this unit were the men whom Cormac Mac-Carthy had taken with him from Ireland to Spain. Their commander was a notable figure in Royalist circles, for he was the eldest son of Viscount Muskerry,[8] and his mother was Eleanor

Butler, a sister of Ormonde; according to Hyde he was 'a young man of extraordinary courage and expectation . . . and had the general estimation of an excellent officer.'9 His regiment was composed of Munster men, largely his own tenants and other dependents, and they had followed him when he changed from the Spanish to the French service, in which they had fought with distinction. When the Brussels treaty required another change of allegiance they unhesitatingly followed Mac-Carthy back into the armies of Philip IV, and they were then renamed the Duke of York's Regiment, while MacCarthy remained their colonel.

About this time a vacancy occurred for a lieutenant-colonel in this regiment, and it would appear that MacCarthy not unnaturally wished to promote one of his own officers; Richard Talbot also applied, and when his application was rejected a duel took place between him and MacCarthy, but it clearly settled nothing, for Richard then appealed to the Duke of York, who came down on his side. MacCarthy thereupon invoked the support of his uncle, and Ormonde and Hyde took the matter up to the King in person. They stressed the impropriety of putting a Leinsterman into one of the highest positions in a Munster unit over the heads of its senior officers and against the wishes of its colonel. Indeed, the two noblemen seem to have rated the unfortunate Charles in a manner which was to become only too familiar to him in the years which lay ahead. However, he refused to interfere in the matter, and Richard got his lieutenant-colonelcy; nevertheless, in this dispute may have lain the seeds of his later intermittent antipathy to Ormonde whose friendship he had hitherto courted most assiduously.

If such was indeed the case, it is to be regretted, for in happier circumstances the older man might have exercised a restraining influence over the younger. Ormonde stood by Charles II and his father in good weather and in bad, and in the none too scrupulous world of Restoration politics he seemed to incarnate the nobler traditions of the old Cavaliers: Dryden, in *Absalom and Achitophel*, depicted him as Barzillai, ' crowned with honour and with years ', and wrote:

> Large was his wealth, but larger was his heart,
> Which well the noblest objects knew to choose,
> The fighting warrior and recording muse.

These events seem to have given Richard a taste for duelling, a method of settling disputes which was much in favour among the exiles, though the King himself thoroughly disapproved of the practice. More often than not the seconds also participated, and among the Sutherland Papers is preserved a letter to Sir Andrew Newport in England from a correspondent in Amiens under the date of 4 September 1658, which says, ' 'Tis strange to hear of the dissensions among the exiled English, Scotch, and Irish in Flanders. . . I saw a relation of a quarrel, under my Lord Taaffe's hand, between him and a Scotchman of my acquaintance, one Sir William Keith; the dispute was only for three royals[10] and a half at tennis. Sir William Keith was slain upon the place; upon this great occasion also were engaged four persons besides the principals. Upon Taaffe's side Dick Talbot fought and wounded Dick Hopton in two places; and on Taaffe's side, again, one Davis fought with Sir William Fleming, but no harm done.'[11]

In the previous year Richard had met an old acquaintance in John Reynolds, who had saved his life at Drogheda and was now in command of the British forces which were co-operating with Turenne. For some reason Reynolds conceived a desire to be presented to the Duke of York, and he got in touch with Lord Newborough and Richard asking them to arrange the matter for him, which they duly did. According to James ' the conversation lasted nearly a half hour, and they separated well satisfied on both sides ': he goes on to say that ' it is not known what instructions Reynolds may have had ', and the mystery is not now likely to be solved for the Cromwellian general shortly afterwards perished in a shipwreck.[12]

All this while hope deferred was making the hearts of Richard and his fellow-exiles sick, which probably accounted for many of the quarrels between them. Cromwell died on 3

September 1658, and when Evelyn noted in his diary, 'Died that arch-rebel, Oliver Cromwell, called Protector' he was but expressing the views of the majority of the British people; all the same, there was no immediate demand for the return of the King. Oliver was succeeded as Protector by his eldest son, Richard, and so firm a grip had the army obtained over the country that there was not a sign of opposition in any quarter, and congratulatory addresses poured in as if a Prince of Wales was succeeding his father on the throne. In quieter times Richard might have done well enough and he has been some-what unfairly treated by historians; yet even if he was not the 'foolish Ishbosheth' of Macaulay's caustic pen, he was unable to control the soldiers upon whom the regime rested, and before the summer of the following year the House of Cromwell had ceased to reign.

These events naturally raised the hopes of the exiles, and Charles and James hastened to the coast, the later accom-panied by Richard Talbot, but they were doomed to disappoint-ment; it is true that there was a Royalist rising in Cheshire, but treachery had been at work, and had the King landed at Deal, as he was on the point of doing, he would have been seized and murdered. His supporters in Cheshire were routed by Lambert at Winnington, and there was nothing for it but to return to Flanders. A letter of 14 September 1659, says, 'All the Duke of York's people, viz., the Barkleys, Talbot, Bron-kart,[13] Leyton, with my Lord Longdale etc., are returned to Bruxells, and the Duke himself expected to-morrow.'[14]

The dawn might not be far away, but this was the darkest hour preceding it. The autumn witnessed the negotiations which led to the Treaty of the Pyrenees between France and Spain, and although Charles went to Fuenterrabia in the hope that Louis and Philip would do something for him, he was dis-appointed, for all that happened was that the Spanish subsidies came to an end with the peace. Poverty was more acute than at any time during the long exile, and Colonel Richard Grace, who commanded Ormonde's regiment, wrote of the 'unspeak-able sufferings and miseryes' of himself and his men in

Brussels. Grace was not the man to complain lightly, for if ever the Stuart cause had a devoted adherent it was he. A member of an old Kilkenny family, and descended from Raymond le Gros, he was born about 1620, and saw service with the Royalists in England during the Civil War. He returned to Ireland in 1646, and eventually became such a thorn in the side of the Roundheads that a price of £300 was placed on his head. In due course, Grace surrendered on terms, and was allowed to take a regiment of twelve hundred men into the Spanish service; he afterwards fought at their head at the Battle of the Dunes. Much later he was successfully to defend Athlone against the Williamites, but he was killed in the second siege of the town.[15]

In March 1660 the dawn at last broke, and Monk, who held the destiny of the three kingdoms in his hands, declared for the King. On the afternoon of the fifteenth of that month there appeared in London an ordinary workman ' with a ladder upon his shoulder and a pot of paint in his hand, and set the ladder in the place where the last King's statue had stood, and then went up and wiped out that inscription, *Exit Tyrannus*, and as soon as he had done it threw up his cap and cried " God bless King Charles the Second ", in which the whole Exchange joined with the greatest shout.'[16] Next day, by the votes of the excluded members, the Long Parliament brought its existence to an end, and Monk, judging the time now ripe, gave a secret interview to the King's emissary, Sir John Grenville.

Grenville reached Brussels on 30 March, delivered Monk's message to Charles, the main purport of which was to advise him to leave the territory of a state with which England was still at war. The King at once saw the point of this, and next morning he crossed the frontier to Breda, where he signed the famous Declaration. The Dutch were not slow in realizing which was the winning side, and were equally quick in seeking to profit by it, so that the reception accorded to Charles and his followers left nothing to be desired. Shortly afterwards the English fleet arrived, and when all was ready for the journey to England the Duke of York, accompanied no doubt by Richard

Talbot, boarded the *Naseby*, now renamed the *Royal Charles*, and took command of the squadron. On the morning of 25 May 1660 the exiles reached Dover, where they were received with great demonstrations of thankfulness and joy. Evelyn was typical of his contemporaries when he wrote in his diary, 'It was the Lord's doing, for such a restoration was never mentioned in any history, ancient or modern, since the return of the Jews from the Babylonish captivity.'

Richard Talbot was now thirty, a Gentleman of the Bedchamber to the Duke of York, and a ' Lieutenant-Colonel of his regiment ', so that he seemed to have the world at his feet; just at this moment, however, he became involved in what was an extremely discreditable episode – that is to say if it ever took place at all. The case against him has been in modern times most succinctly stated by Macaulay.

> Soon after the Restoration, Talbot attempted to obtain the favour of royal family by a service more infamous still.[17] A plea was wanted which might justify the Duke of York in breaking that promise of marriage by which he had obtained from Anne Hyde the last proof of female affection. Such a plea Talbot, in concert with some of his dissolute companions, undertook to furnish. They agreed to describe the poor young lady as a creature without virtue, shame, or delicacy, and made up long romances about tender interviews and stolen favours. Talbot in particular related how, in one of his secret visits to her, he had unluckily overturned the Chancellor's inkstand upon a pile of papers, and how cleverly she had averted a discovery by laying the blame of the accident on her monkey. These stories, which, if they had been true, would never have passed the lips of any but the basest of mankind, were pure inventions. Talbot was soon forced to own that they were so; and he owned it without a blush. The injured lady became Duchess of York. Had her husband been a man really upright and honourable, he would have driven from his presence with indignation and contempt the wretches who had slandered her. But one of the peculiarities of James's character was that no act, however wicked and shameful, which had been prompted by a desire to gain his favour, ever seemed to him deserving of disapprobation. Talbot con-

tinued to frequent the court, appeared daily with brazen front before the princess whose ruin he had plotted, and was installed into the lucrative post of chief pandar to her husband.[18]

It would be difficult to imagine a more damning indictment, and it clearly calls for the closest scrutiny in any examination of Richard Talbot's career. The story is, indeed, a complicated one, and it is not made any easier to follow by the utter lack of credibility attaching to most of those concerned. The basic facts, however, are not in dispute.

Among the English girls in Holland during the period immediately before the Restoration was Anne Hyde, daughter of the Chancellor, and between her and the Duke of York there had existed an acquaintanceship since the days when both were little more than children. The Duke's sister, Mary, Princess of Orange, early offered to make Anne one of her Maids of Honour, whether because she was attracted by the girl, or out of a desire to gratify Hyde, her brother's trusted minister. The Chancellor was at first opposed to the idea, but he was overruled by his wife, and the Princess took Anne with her on a visit to Queen Henrietta Maria in Paris, when she met James, who was then serving in the French army: later they saw a good deal of one another in the Low Countries. Anne ' inherited no good looks and was a plain woman ',[19] but she was both vivacious and intelligent, and she soon established an ascendancy over James, who wrote of her, ' Besides her person, she had all the qualities proper to inflame a heart less apt to take fire than his: while she managed so well as to bring his passion to such a height as, between the time he first saw her and the winter before the King's restoration, he resolved to marry none but her; and promised her to do it.' The not unnatural result of such a friendship between a young man of twenty-six and a girl of twenty-two, on whose hands time hung heavily, soon ensued, and in February 1660 Anne Hyde found herself pregnant. This put Charles in the delicate position of a monarch whose chief minister's daughter was with child by his brother, the heir presumptive to the throne.

What then ensued is subject to several interpretations. Hyde

G

clearly lost his head: he was overwhelmed simultaneously by anxiety for his daughter and by ambition for her advancement, and he roundly declared that he would rather she were James's mistress than his wife, though why he should have made such a statement is not easy to follow. Of course, the position of James was drastically changed at the Restoration which occurred in the middle of Anne's pregnancy, for from being a penniless exile he became from the matrimonial angle an extremely eligible match. At this point the evidence of the *Mémoires du Chevalier de Grammont*, upon which Macaulay based his attack on Richard Talbot, must be cited. Of this book, it may be recalled, Sir Winston Churchill has written, ' Anthony Hamilton, who is famous for the authorship of Grammont's memoirs, has penned some mischievous pages from which historians diligently fail to avert their eyes.'[20] What he has to say about Anne Hyde fills some of the most mischievous of them.

Anthony Hamilton was born at Roscrea, Co. Tipperary, in 1646, but as his family were Royalists he spent the years of the Commonwealth and Protectorate in exile in France. He had a sister called Elizabeth who married the Chevalier de Grammont. It would appear to have been something in the nature of a shot-gun wedding, for the story goes that Grammont, on leaving England after a visit, was stopped at Dover by the lady's brothers with the words, ' Chevalier, have you not forgotten something?' To which the answer came, ' Of course; I forgot to marry your sister: let us return.' Anthony Hamilton in due course wrote his brother-in-law's memoirs, and published them anonymously in 1713, seven years before his own death. They are characterized by wit, malice, and gaiety, and it is to be noted that the author himself admits that he wrote for those who only read for amusement, and he had nothing but contempt for the exact narrative: such being the case it is surely permissible to question his credibility as a historian, especially when writing of Ricard Talbot, since he was a mere fourteen years of age at the time of the events which he purports to describe; his testimony can therefore only have been based on gossip which he heard in later life or upon his recollections of what Grammont had told him.

However this may be he asserts that at first James was so far from repenting of his secret marriage with Anne Hyde that he seemed only to wish for the King's restoration that he might have an opportunity of declaring it with splendour. Nevertheless, when he saw himself enjoying a rank which placed him so near the throne, and reflected on the indignation which the announcement would create at Court, and indeed throughout the whole kingdom, the matter took on a different complexion; he also feared that his brother would refuse his consent. On the other hand, his conscience bound him to adhere to his marriage contract,[21] even if, after his earlier enthusiasm for Anne had subsided, he had eyes for the many beauties of Whitehall.[22]

In his perplexity James ' opened his heart to Lord Falmouth ', that is to say to Sir Charles Berkeley, for he was not raised to the peerage as the Earl of Falmouth until four years later – so much for Hamilton's attention to detail. The Duke could not have turned to a better man in his own interests, or to a worse one in those of Anne Hyde. Berkeley assured James that not only was he not married, but that it was impossible he could ever have had any such idea: in any case his marriage would be invalid without the King's consent even if the lady in question were a suitable match, but that it was a mere jest when she was only the daughter of ' an insignificant lawyer, whom the Royal favour had made a peer of the realm without any noble blood, and Chancellor without any capacity '. This was a little hard in view of the fact that Hyde had for fifteen years been Chancellor of the Exchequer to Charles I and his son, and on Sir Edward Herbert's death in 1658 had been made Lord Chancellor of England. Finally, Berkeley told James that if he would listen to four gentlemen whom he could introduce, he would hear enough about Anne's previous life to make up his mind about the proposed marriage.

According to Hamilton, or Grammont, the Duke agreed to meet the four, who turned out to be the Earl of Arran, Jermyn,

Richard Talbot, and Killigrew, 'all men of honour, but who infinitely preferred the interest of the Duke of York to Miss Hyde's reputation, and who, in addition, were greatly dissatisfied, like the whole of the Court, at the insolent authority of the Prime Minister'. Of Richard's three companions in this quartet, Arran was the younger son of Ormonde; Henry Jermyn the Younger was a famous knight of dames who was later to fall into disfavour with the King for ogling Barbara Villiers; while Killigrew may have been any one of the contemporary bearers of that name. All four were briefed by Berkeley before being presented to James, who then exhorted them to tell him all they knew. At first they were somewhat reticent, but after further entreaties by the Duke they each told their story.

Arran testified that one day in Holland when he and Jermyn were playing skittles Anne pretended to faint, whereupon the two men saw her to her room and cut the laces of her stays. Richard told the story of the monkey upon which Macaulay fastened with such eagerness, and stated that the ink had been spilt while he was pleasuring the Chancellor's daughter. Killigrew went even further, and described how Anne accorded him the last favours in a summer-house by the water's edge, so well hidden from observation that while he was possessing her 'the only witnesses of his happiness were three or four swans'. When James had heard what the four had to say he thanked them for their frankness, told them to keep the meeting to themselves, and went to the King's apartments. While Charles and his brother were discussing what had happened Berkeley was in the ante-chamber, where he met Ossory, Arran's elder brother, to whom he told the whole story.

In due course James reappeared, and told them to meet him in about an hour's time at the Chancellor's house. This they accordingly did, and when they got there they found Anne drying her tears, and her father leaning against the wall in a state of emotion. Only the Duke of York was completely at ease, and as Ossory and Berkeley entered the room he said to them, 'As you are the two men of the Court whom I most esteem, I desire that you should first have the honour of paying your respects to the Duchess of York. There she is.' On this the two men went down on their knees, and kissed Anne's hand ' which she held out with as much stateliness and majesty as if she had never done anything else all her life '.

Having told this disreputable, though highly entertaining, story which reflects no credit upon anybody mentioned in it with the possible exception of Anne Hyde, Hamilton clearly felt that his readers would expect some reason to be given for the friendly relations which subsequently existed between Anne and her four traducers, so he goes on to say that out of the goodness of her heart she treated them with studied kindness, and told them that nothing was a greater proof of the attachment of a man of honour than to put the interest of his friend or his master above his own reputation. Hamilton concludes this extremely improbable tale with the remark that Anne's behaviour constituted ' a memorable example of prudence and moderation not only for her own sex but for those who value most their knowledge of ours'. Now since Anthony Hamilton was only fourteen when this incident is alleged to have taken place, he can hardly be described as a contemporary witness to the events he describes; whether he got the story from Grammont, from some other source, or merely invented it himself is another matter.

Macaulay's credibility as a historian has never been more in question than in his attitude to Talbot, and what he has to say on this occasion is typical. The *Mémoires* do not say that Richard undertook to furnish the necessary plea for the Duke of York to break off his marriage, but that Berkeley did so; they do not make Talbot's, but Killigrew's, the chief evidence; and they do not state that Richard was forced to own that his story was a pure invention, and that he did so without a blush.

The *Mémoires* themselves can be dismissed as mere gossip, and quite unworthy of the notice of a serious historian: if there had been anything in the charges against Richard one would have expected to find it in Hyde's own account of his daughter's marriage to James, but in the *Continuation* there is no mention of him at all, which is the more surprising in

view of Hyde's dislike of the Talbot family. In all these circumstances it would seem safe to acquit Richard of the charges
which Macaulay brings against him where the affairs of James
and Anne are concerned.

The historian's further accusation that Richard was ' installed into the lucrative post of chief pandar to her husband '
is also based on Grammont's *Mémoires* as well as upon a statement by Gilbert Burnet, Bishop of Salisbury, who in one place
speaks of ' Richard Talbot, one of the Duke's bedchamber men,
who had much cunning, and had the secret of his master's
pleasures for some years '; in another he says, ' the Duke had
always one private amour after another, in the managing of
which he seemed to stand more in awe of the Duchess than,
considering the inequality of their rank, could have been
imagined. Talbot was looked on as the manager of these
intrigues '.[23] The credibility of the *Mémoires* has already been
discussed, so there is no need to consider them any further as
a reliable source, while so far as Burnet is concerned the final
judgment upon him was surely passed by Sir Arthur Bryant
when he wrote that most of the Bishop's statements, where he
is not speaking from his own personal experience, may be disregarded.[24]

In all these circumstances it would seem fair to claim that
in 1660 Richard Talbot was neither better nor worse than
those with whom he came into contact at Whitehall. The men
of the Restoration were not, as a whole, equal to their opportunities. It is one of the great misfortunes of revolution that it
is generally followed by a period in which the statesmen at the
top are not of the first rank. Whether it is that times of disturbance favour the second-rate, or whether the effort of making a revolution so exhausts the common stock as temporarily
to lower the standard, is difficult to decide, but the fact remains
that, when the revolutionary era comes to an end, it is followed
by an age, possibly of great events, but usually of little men. So
it was with the Restoration: after the storms of the Civil War
a good deal of scum rose to the surface, and it was some years
before things began to settle down again.

NOTES

[1] *Cf. Cal. Clar. St. P.* III, Art. 364.
[2] Don John of Austria.
[3] *Cf. Clar. St. P.,* III, Arts 416, 433, and 445.
[4] *Cf.* Turner, F. C.: *James II,* pp. 40-42. London. 1948.
[5] *Cf.* Hay, M. V.: *The Enigma of James II,* p. 132. London. 1938.
  also Belloc, H.: *James the Second,* p. 74. London. 1928.
[6] *Cf.* Tayler, A. and H.: *John Graham of Claverhouse,* pp. 207-208. London. 1939.
[7] *Continuation,* Vol. III, p. 120.
[8] Created Earl of Clancarty in 1658.
[9] *Ormonde,* Vol. IV, p. 67 *et seq.*
[10] The Spanish *real.*
[11] Quoted by Sergeant, P. W.: *Little Jennings and Fighting Dick Talbot.* Vol. I, p. 87. London. 1913.
[12] *Cf. The Memoirs of James II,* pp. 244-246. London. 1962.
[13] William Brounker.
[14] *H.M.C., Bath MSS,* Vol. II.
[15] *Cf. The Irish Sword,* Vol. I, p. 173. Dublin. 1949.
[16] *Cf.* Bryant, Sir Arthur: *King Charles II,* p. 74. London. 1931.
[17] That is to say than ' the infamous service of assassinating the Protector '.
[18] *History of England,* Chapter VI.
[19] Connell, N.: *Anne,* p. 21. London. 1937.
[20] *Marlborough, His Life and Times,* Vol. I, p. 45. London. 1933.
[21] This had been made in the autumn of 1659.
[22] This summary is based on the edition of the *Mémoires du Chevalier de Grammont* edited by Claire-Eliane Engel. Monaco. 1958.
[23] *History of My Own Time,* Chs. V. and IX. Oxford. 1833.
[24] *King Charles II,* p. 47n. London. 1931.

CHAPTER V

The Irish Champion

WHILE RICHARD TALBOT was plotting in England and campaigning on the continent much had been happening in his own country, and with the resultant situation he was now to be intimately concerned. The two outstanding problems, as so often in Ireland, were religion and the land, but the settlement of Church questions, the most contentious issue in the other two kingdoms, gave rise to comparatively little difficulty in the third, for the established church there had never been legally abolished, though it had fallen into chaotic impotence during the years of civil strife. Ormonde, as loyal an Anglican as Clarendon, had no trouble in persuading Charles II, busy with what must have seemed to him to be much more important matters, to assume that the old Church organization was to be revived as a matter of course, so the surviving bishops were restored to their sees, and the vacancies were all filled within a year of the King's return, while in every act dealing with the land the restoration of ecclesiastical estates was insisted upon. The only real point at issue was the fact that many churches in the North and elsewhere had passed into the hands of the Presbyterians, who were supported by the Ulster Scots as well as by the Cromwellian settlers.

The Irish Parliament,[1] however, had no more sympathy with Presbyterians than it had with Catholics: it had itself been suppressed during the Protectorate, and so was in favour of restoring the old order alike in Church and State. In 1666 it passed an act of uniformity on the model of that which had been enforced in England in 1662, and the English Prayer Book, having been approved by the convocation of Irish clergy, was ordered to be used in every cathedral, parish church, and chapel. Furthermore, every holder of a benefice was to declare his acceptance of its doctrines before the feast of the Annunciation, 1667, and every person appointed in the future must make a similar declaration within two months. After 29 September 1667 no benefice might be held by a man who had not received episcopal ordination. All clergy, professors, schoolmasters, and private tutors must accept the doctrine of non-resistance, conform to the liturgy, and repudiate the Solemn League and Covenant; and schoolmasters and private tutors must also take the oaths of allegiance and supremacy, and receive a licence from the bishop of the diocese. English supremacy in Ireland rested upon Protestant ascendancy, and no stone was to be left unturned to ensure that this was maintained.

Richard Talbot took no particular interest in the affairs of the Church of Ireland, nor was there any reason why he should, but it was otherwise where the land was concerned. In a non-industrial economy the possession of land confers power on its owner, and in such a society the balance of power rests with the class that has the balance of land. In seventeenth century Irish history there were, apart from the plantations, three main settlements of the land problem, but in actual fact they amounted to nothing more nor less than the settlement of the balance of land according to the will of the strongest. The first of these was the Cromwellian Settlement by which is to be understood the dealings of the Commonwealth of England with the lands and habitations of the people of Ireland after the conquest of the country in 1652. As the object of the English was genocide they seized the lands of the Irish, and transferred them (and with them all the power in the State) to a flood of new English settlers who were filled with a consuming national and religious hatred of those whom they had displaced.[2]

Two other so-called settlements followed, which may be called the Restoration and the Revolution Settlements. The first was in reality a counter-revolution by which some of the Old English, who had espoused the Royalist cause, and a few of the native Irish, were restored to their estates under the Acts of Settlement and Explanation – with this Talbot was to be intimately concerned – and the second followed the victory of the Williamites after Talbot was dead: by it the lands recently restored to the supporters of the Stuarts and the few native Irish were again seized by the Parliament of England, and distributed among the conquering nation.[3] Evidence of what was intended is shown by the fact that at the court for the sale of estates forfeited on account of the war of 1689-91 the land in question could only be purchased by Englishmen; no Irishman, high or low, could buy an acre of them or occupy more than the site for a cabin. It was clearly intended that the relics of the nation should be reduced to the condition of labourers.[4]

To give the statesmen of the Restoration their due they were under no illusions as to the problems that confronted them. They realized only too well that the claims with which they had to deal were of baffling intricacy, so much so that Clarendon, no friend of Ireland or Irishmen anyway, begged that ' no part might be referred to him ', while Ormonde, who knew more of the problem than any other minister, was extremely loath to quit the easy life of the English court to settle the disputes of his fellow-countrymen.

Evidence of this attitude on the part of the royal advisers is to be found in some Council Notes which passed between the King and Clarendon:

King. When will it be fit to call in the Irish as they desired last night?

Clar. Whenever you have a mind to spoil the business; really all will come to nothing if you call them in.

King. I cannot imagine, with any justice, how I can refuse to hear them since they desire it.

Clar. Have you not heard them? If you do call them, the other side must be called too, and then we are in till morning. If you are tenderhearted on their behalf I pray leave them to the House of Commons, and their work is done. They are mad, and do not understand their own interest.

> Sir Nicholas Plunkett is desperate, and would make all others so too.
>
> *King.* For my part, rebel for rebel, I had rather trust a Papist rebel than a Presbyterian one.

On another occasion we find Charles remarking, ' But methinks 'tis an ugly thing for me to make a party judge.'[5]

As we have seen, English policy under the Commonwealth had been avowedly genocidal, and there had been a wholesale eviction from their holdings of the native Irish, who had incurred the bitter hatred of the English on account of the atrocities which they were alleged to have committed in 1641-43. All of them, save such as were needed to serve as labourers, were compelled to choose between exile and migration to the province of Connacht or the county of Clare, where land was to be allotted to them. A very considerable number, amounting to some 35,000, chose expatriation, and like Richard Talbot entered the service of the exiled Charles or one of the Continental Powers, while the rest accepted the offered lands in Connacht and Clare: there was thus a very large area of Irish land at the disposal of the English government.

By the Cromwellian Settlement most of this land went to two classes of recipients: the first category was composed of what were known as adventurers, that is to say men who had advanced money in 1642 for the suppression of the Irish rising, and to whom Irish land had been pledged as security by Act of Parliament; the second class consisted of the Roundhead soldiers who had conquered Ireland, and whose arrears of pay were to be liquidated in land at what were known as adventurers' rates. The primary question in 1660 was whether, or how far, this settlement should be maintained.

There were strong arguments on both sides. On the one hand the Act which pledged Irish land to the adventurers had actually, if not very willingly, been signed by Charles I; both they and the soldiers had in a greater or lesser degree contributed to the final defeat of the Irish; and their displacement would be a serious blow to ' the English interest ' in Ireland, while it would certainly rouse grave discontent among just that section of the population whose hostility could be most dangerous to the government of the Restoration. On the other hand, the money actually contributed by the original adventurers had not been spent in Ireland at all but equipping the Parliamentary forces in England against the King, while a large proportion of the soldiers who were settled on the land had been in the service of the Commonwealth rather than in that of the Crown. Thus the mass of the settlers had no claim whatsoever on Charles's gratitude except that they had made no resistance to his restoration to the throne. Above all, the Cromwellian Settlement could clearly not be maintained in its entirety without the grossest injustice to the native Irish, many of whom had not been guilty of any disloyalty.

There can be no question but that the King sincerely desired to see justice done, not least to the native Irish, but he had not been back in England long before he realized that where Irish questions were concerned truth was a very relative term, while investigation soon proved that there was not enough land to go round. All through 1660 Ireland was very much in his thoughts, and by the end of the year he hoped that a real settlement was in sight. Originally Monk had been made Lord-Lieutenant, but it never seems to have occurred to him to visit Dublin, so Lord Robartes was appointed as deputy; he was a sullen and morose man according to his contemporaries, and his repellent manner alienated most of the Irish who came into contact with him. He also showed no desire to go over to Ireland. It was thus found expedient to buy him off with the office of Privy Seal, and the government of Ireland, after a rather serious delay, was entrusted to three Lords Justices, one of whom was Richard Talbot's old jailer, Sir Charles Coote, now raised to the peerage as Earl of Mountrath.

As the year 1660 drew to a close the time seemed to have arrived for Charles to take action; having been furnished with an optimistic estimate of the amount of land available for restoration to what were described as the loyal Irish after the settlers had been confirmed in their possessions he expressed his delight that it would be in his power to satisfy the interests of all his subjects. 'His inclinations,' as Carte says, 'led him to make them all happy; and he eagerly embraced a scheme which flattered those inclinations.'[6] On 30 November 1660 he accordingly issued a Declaration which was to frustrate his good intentions, and which it is reasonable to believe he would never have signed had his information concerning conditions in Ireland been more accurate, or had he paid the briefest of visits to the country.

The general principle laid down in the Declaration was that the adventurers and the soldiers who had received land in payment of arrears of pay should be confirmed in the estates held by them on 7 May 1659. There were, however, a number of exceptions: the Church of Ireland and certain loyalists such as Ormonde were to recover the whole of their lost property, while all Protestants and what were termed 'innocent Papists'[7] were to be restored to their land, even though this had been given to adventurers and soldiers. In all these latter cases the displaced holders were to receive compensation elsewhere. Those Irish who had served the King faithfully abroad, such as Richard Talbot and the Dongans, were also marked out for favourable treatment. Papists who were not innocent, and who had accepted land in Connacht and Clare, were to be bound by their own act, and were to have no claim on their previous holdings. The great importance attached by the 'English interest' to the corporate towns in Ireland is proved by the clause which provided that no Papist, however innocent, was to recover lands or houses in any town, but was to have the equivalent in the neighbourhood.

The next step was to appoint Commissioners to carry out the terms of the Declaration, and as soon as they got to work it became clear that the scales were heavily weighted against the Irish, for in their instructions the qualifications of an 'innocent Papist' were made exceedingly strict. There were numbers who had never drawn sword against the King, and though living in rebellious districts had held themselves aloof from their neighbours' treasonable activities, while others had actually been driven out of Dublin by the Lords Justices of the day into the rebels' country on pain of death, but still had not opposed the King; yet all these were, by the instructions to the Commissioners, not classified as 'innocent'. By contrast, Cromwellian soldiers who had actually fought against the King were confirmed in the possession of the land assigned to them, unless they were regicides or notoriously disloyal. In these circumstances the Protestants were naturally exultant that from so wide a definition of guilt few of the native Irish could escape.

From London the discussion of the land question passed to Dublin, where Parliament was convened in May 1661. Election for the Commons was in the hands of the existing holders of land and offices, and from these Catholics had been so diligently excluded during the Commonwealth that they had no chance of being returned, especially for the boroughs which elected about two-thirds of the Lower House. The representatives of the adventurers and soldiers, who were in a great majority, proposed a bill to confirm the royal Declaration as it stood. On the other hand the House of Lords, containing the bishops and the heads of the old-established families in Ireland, was by no means enamoured of the new settlers whose ascendancy, established so recently under a republican administration seemed likely to be made permanent. The Lords held that the Declaration had been based on inadequate and partial information, and proceeded to propose considerable modifications; this disagreement between the two Houses necessitated another appeal to London.

The adventurers and soldiers lost no time in preparing their case. They decided to send commissioners to England to press for the immediate passage of their bill into law, and they raised a sum of between twenty and thirty thousand pounds to back the commissioners' efforts. The Lords also sent agents to London to present their views, and on the prorogation of the Irish Parliament at the end of July 1661, the scene of the struggle shifted to England. As for the Irish Catholics, both of the Pale and elsewhere, if they were at a disadvantage in their own country through the control exercised by their enemies over Parliament they were still worse placed when the fight was transferred to London. They had no funds at their disposal as was the case with the adventurers and soldiers; they had few friends at Court, where Catholics in high places were still extremely rare; and English public opinion was prejudiced against them, not merely on account of their religion but also because they were Irish. In these circumstances it behoved them to secure as powerful a patron as possible.

Generations of historians have censured them for not invoking the aid of Ormonde, though it is difficult to see why they should have done so. The Butlers had always been strong supporters of the English connection, and, as we have seen, ' the Black Earl ' in the reign of Elizabeth I had done more than most men to help the Queen in her struggle with his fellow countrymen. The present head of the family, recently made a duke, was admittedly one of the most honourable men of his age, and unbiased in matters where others felt strongly, but he was a Protestant with an English mother, and circumstances had earlier brought him into conflict with Rinuccini, whose memory was still dear to many Irish Catholics. Had a judge been required, Ormonde would have filled the bill admirably, but what the Irish wanted was an advocate, so it is easy to see why their choice should have fallen on Richard Talbot instead: they may have made a mistake but they surely had every reason for making it. Ormonde was clearly none too pleased that he was passed over, and ' seeing that his advice would not be followed and that his character was every day torn in pieces by some or other of their country ',[8] he refused to take any prominent part in the adjustment of the Bill of Settlement, and until his appointment as Lord-Lieutenant in November 1661, confined his activity in Irish affairs to helping his personal friends and giving certificates of good behaviour on behalf of those Irish whose loyalty was unjustly called in question.

Richard Talbot was a singularly bad choice; at this stage of his career he was not the man to take charge of a negotiation for which the prerequisite was tact, quite apart from the fact that those on whose behalf he was acting were extremely wild themselves. Admittedly, Ormonde was prejudiced, but he was not far out when he wrote to his friend, Sir Maurice Eustace:

> I fear the liberty allowed the Irish to speak for themselves will turn to their prejudice, by the unskilful use they make of it, in justifying themselves, instructing the King and his council in what is good for them, and recriminating of others. Whereas a modest extenuation of their crimes, a humble submission to and imploring His Majesty's grace, and a declaration of their hearty desire to live quietly and brotherly with their fellow-subjects for the future, would better have befitted the disadvantage they are under, and have prevailed more than all their eloquence. But it is long since I have given over any hope that they would do, or be advised to do, what was best for them.

Any influence that Richard possessed was quite unavailing to help his clients who were their own worst enemies, for while loudly protesting their own loyalty to the Crown, they attacked with injudicious violence those who had formerly espoused the Parliamentary cause; they spoke of them as if they had all been regicides, thereby provoking the obvious retort that they had themselves been guilty of the 1641 massacres, and had attempted to put Ireland under foreign domination – an accusation that would not have done them any harm in Dublin but was enough to damn them in London. Above all, their handling of the King himself was remarkedly maladroit, for they were continually harping upon their rights and his duties, while the representatives of the adventurers and soldiers were profuse in their protestations of loyalty and submission. The limit of the royal patience was reached when Sir Nicholas Plunkett was suddenly confronted before the Privy Council with his signature on a document authorizing the offer of Ireland in 1647, first to the Pope, and, if he refused it, to any Catholic prince willing to protect her. Plunkett was banished from Court, all further addresses from Irish Catholics to the Council were forbidden, and the Bill of Settlement, including the clauses to which so much objection had been taken, received the royal assent.[9]

This incensed the Irish, who placed the responsibility on Ormonde for not using his influence at the Privy Council to further their case, and they called upon their champion to do something for them. Richard did as he was asked, and, according to Carte, 'came in so huffing a manner, and used such impertinent and insolent language in his discourse, that it looked like a challenge'; so Ormonde went to the King, and asked if it was his pleasure, 'that at this time of day he should put off his doublet to fight duels with Dick Talbot'. This time Richard had gone too far, for Charles was notoriously opposed to duelling at Court, so the offender was sent to cool his heels in the Tower. This was in October 1661, but he was not destined to remain there for long, for he was sent, probably through the influence of the Duke of York, on a minor diplomatic mission to Portugal; this ensured that he should be out of the way until the storm he had aroused had died down. The exact date of Richard's return is fixed by Pepys, for in the only entry in the *Diary* which mentions him, under the date of 10 April 1662, occurs the entry, 'Yesterday came Col. Talbot with letters from Portugal that the Queen is resolved to embarque for England this week.'

The dissatisfaction of the Irish Catholics at the treatment they were receiving was only equalled by that of their more extreme opponents at the alleged sympathy shown by the Commissioners administrating the Act of Settlement to innocent Papists, and before long there was a getting-together of disgruntled and embittered Republicans, Anabaptists, Fifth Monarchy Men, and other 'fanaticks', which in Ireland in 1663 blossomed into a plot to seize Dublin Castle. In this conspiracy a prominent part was played by Lieutenant Thomas Blood, who was later to obtain infamy by his attempt to steal the Crown Jewels in the Tower of London.

His immediate family history is obscure, but his grandfather is believed to have come from Derbyshire to Ireland, and may have been connected in some capacity with Lord Inchiquin; at any rate, he sat for Ennis in the Irish Parliament of James I. The grandson, Thomas, is believed to have been born in 1618,

H

and twenty-two years later for services which are unknown the family received a grant of land in Meath and Wicklow. Thomas would seem to have played an equivocal part in the ensuing wars, for although Prince Rupert said he had known him ' as a very stout, bold fellow in the royal service ', he was given a commission in the Parliamentary forces, and was further rewarded by Henry Cromwell with some confiscated Irish property. When the Restoration took place he was a little slow in once more changing sides, so the Commissioners relieved him of his doubtfully-gotten estates. This soured his mind, and made him only too ready to co-operate in any conspiracy to overturn the existing regime.

The plot in which Blood now became involved had as its principles, besides himself, his brother-in-law, Lackie, a Fellow of Trinity College; one Philip Alden; and several lawyers and former Cromwellian officers. In spite of his comparative youth and minor rank, Blood was regarded by his colleagues as their leader owing to his courage and initiative. It was he who was credited with having written the declaration which was to have been published should the conspiracy have proved successful, and it was he who worked out the details of the plot to surprise the Castle.

The plan was simple. Several conspirators were to obtain entrance to the building on the plea that they wished to present petitions to the Lord-Lieutenant, while outside, waiting for a signal, was to be a body of about eighty disbanded soldiers disguised as artisans and tradesmen. As soon as Ormonde made his appearance a man in the guise of a baker was to upset a basket of white loaves. While the guards were scrambling for the bread the pseudo-petitioners were to seize and disarm them, admit their accomplices, capture the Castle, and arrest or kill Ormonde. Unfortunately for Blood and his friends Philip Alden turned traitor, and so the Lord-Lieutenant had plenty of time to make his preparations. The date fixed for the attempt was 21 May 1663, and early that morning several of the plotters, including Lackie, were arrested and flung into jail. Blood escaped and went into hiding, but was promptly declared an outlaw with a price on his head, and what remained of his property was confiscated.

To what might have been tragedy succeeded farce. Lackie in prison feigned madness, and his wife and the Fellows of Trinity vainly petitioned for his release, so he made an effort to escape, which was also unsuccessful. With commendable courage he refused to betray his associates by turning King's Evidence, and was duly sentenced to be executed. A crowd of about two thousand people turned out to enjoy the spectacle when a rumour suddenly went round to the effect that Blood was going to attempt a rescue with a band of desperadoes, and so great was his reputation as a gangster even at this early date that the audience immediately panicked and ran away, including the executioner, 'leaving the person that was to suffer in the dreadful posture of a person preparing for his untimely Death, the Rope about his Neck, and nobody to do the Office'. However, Blood failed to put in an appearance, so it was not necessary to hand his task over to any enthusiastic amateur, for the professional hangman regained his courage, and duly returned to the gallows to turn the luckless Lackie off. Four other persons were also executed for this failure, one among many down the centuries, to take Dublin Castle by a *coup de main*.[10]

After his lack of success in this conspiracy Blood appears to have roamed about the more remote parts of Ireland, posing as an Anabaptist, a Quaker, or sometimes even as a priest, suiting his disguises and professions to those among whom he moved, but always striving to rally a party together. On one occasion Ormonde, when he went to his castle at Kilkenny, was warned to be on his guard because Blood was alleged to be in the neighbourhood, and to have declared that his object was to seize or kill the Lord-Lieutenant. Blood was, it may be added, on the run for some time, but finally escaped to Holland.[11]

Such was the Ireland, and such were at any rate some of the people in it, with whom Richard Talbot resumed dealings after his sojourn in the Tower and his mission to Portugal. The Irish House of Commons had drawn up and transmitted to England[12] a Bill of Explanation, designed to make clear the mean-

ing of the King's Declaration of November 1660, and among
other things it endeavoured ' to make provision for eminent
and deserving persons who were cut off from all manner of
relief by the power of the Court of Claims being determined '.
Now this Court of Claims was the body which had been set up
to investigate the pretensions of the innocent Papists who
wished to come under the Declaration, but its competence only
extended down to 22 August 1662, by which time out of four
thousand claims not more than four hundred had been heard.

In these troubled waters there was obviously some profitable
fishing to be had, for, however conscious of their own rectitude
large numbers of the Irish Catholics might be, they were also
fully aware of the difficulty of being restored to their estates
if they relied upon virtue alone, so they were willing to give
bonds, in some instances running into four figures, to influential patrons to be redeemed as soon as their names were duly
recorded in the Bill of Explanation. Such patrons were by no
means slow in coming forward, and prominent among them
was Richard Talbot; others who acted in the same capacity
were such prominent figures of the day as the Earl of St
Albans,[13] Sir Charles Berkeley, Sir Gilbert Gerard, Lord Carlingford, and the Speaker of the Irish House of Commons, Sir
Audley Mervyn.

In addition to this work for the dispossessed Irish, there
was an opportunity of making money through commissions
from Englishmen wanting estates in Ireland at the smallest
possible cost to themselves, so it is hardly surprising that, by
the summer of 1663 when Talbot returned to London from
Dublin, he was in possession of £18,000 in lands and other
securities from those interested in acquiring, or being restored
to, property in Ireland. Things, however, did not go as smoothly
as Richard wished, for the King and the Privy Council, on
examining the Bill of Explanation, entirely disapproved of it,
and orders were sent to Ormonde to draw up a new measure.
This upset Talbot's calculations, but he seems to have turned
the situation to his advantage all the same, for Grammont says
of him at this time, ' There was no man at Court who had a

better appearance. He was, indeed, but a younger brother, of a family which, though very ancient, was not very considerable, either for its renown or its riches. Yet, though he was naturally of a very careless disposition, being bent, however, on making his fortune, and much in favour with the Duke of York, and fortune likewise being propitious to him at play, he had improved both so much that he was in possession of about 40,000 livres a year in land.'[14]

NOTES

[1] For the first time an Irish Parliament was composed almost wholly of Protestants.

[2] *Cf.* Prendergast, J. P.: *The Cromwellian Settlement of Ireland, passim.* London. 1865.

[3] *Cf.* Simms, J. G.: *The Williamite Confiscation in Ireland, 1690-1703, passim.* London. 1956.

[4] The Penal Laws, which lasted nearly in full force until the outbreak of the War of American Independence, were merely the complement of the Forfeited Estates Act, and the Cromwellian Settlement formed the basis of the government of Ireland until the days of George Wyndham.

[5] *Cf.* Bryant, Sir Arthur: *The Letters of King Charles II,* pp. 108-109. London. 1935.

[6] *Ormonde,* Vol. IV, p. 32.

[7] Those who had not acted against the Crown since 22 October 1642.

[8] Carte, T.: *Ormonde,* Vol. IV, p. 66.

[9] The commission appointed to administer the Act, which included Sir Winston Churchill, however, tempered its provisions to a number of innocent Papists.

[10] *C.S.P. Dom.* 1663.

[11] Petherick, M.: *Restoration Rogues,* pp. 13-39. London. 1951.

[12] By Poynings' Law of 1494 the Irish legislature was subordinate to, and completely dependent on, the English Parliament. It was not repealed until 1782.

[13] Among his clients is said to have been Patrick Sarsfield.

[14] *Mémoires,* p. 235-236. Monaco. 1958. Berwick wrote of him at the end of his life that 'although he had acquired great property, it could not be said that it was by ill means; for he never seemed greedy for money' (*Memoirs,* Vol. I, p. 95. London. 1779.)

CHAPTER VI

The Court of Charles II

IT IS only too easy to exaggerate the degradation of public and private life during the reigns of Charles II and his brother. The evidence is too often taken merely from books and plays, and however attractive these may prove to the salacious, the historian is bound to regard them with a certain amount of suspicion. The private letters of the period lend no support to the charge of widespread debauchery, and, after all, if modern London, Dublin, and Edinburgh were to be judged by similar evidence they would go down to posterity as veritable Babylons. Honesty among politicians and chastity among women are as rare in the books and plays of today as they were in those of the latter half of the seventeenth century, but to frame an indictment against the morals of a whole generation on such grounds is a risky proceeding. What has given the Restoration a bad name, and here the comparison with modern England is very striking, was not its immorality but its lack of reticence. Once the shackles imposed by the Puritan regime were struck off, both sexes began to take a delight in outraging the conventions to which they had previously been subject.

It is impossible to acquit Charles personally of all blame for this state of affairs, though his responsibility has been grossly exaggerated. The excesses of a section of London society at the present time are not being prevented by the obvious disapproval of Buckingham Palace, but they do not receive the encouragement which would be the case were the Queen openly tolerant of them. As a statesman, Charles I cannot be mentioned in the same breath as his son; but as a man he was immeasurably superior, and his Court elevated the standards of English social life just as that of the others lowered them. It is impossible not to detect a general deterioration. Whatever view one may take of Puritanism, there were men associated with it, if not in Ireland, who were actuated by the highest motives: it is difficult to name a single one, with the possible exception of Algernon Sidney, fit to be compared with them among the self-seeking adventurers who clustered round Shaftesbury and Titus Oates. Charles was too much of a cynic to bother about appearances, and the story of his father rapping him over the shoulders for inattention during a tedious sermon is typical of the two men and their respective generations.

It was in his letters to his beloved sister, Minette, Duchesse d'Orléans, that Charles most fully revealed himself. On one occasion he wrote to her, 'We had a design to have a masquerade here, and had made no ill design in the general for it, but we were not able to go through with it, not having one man here that could make a tolerable entry.' At another time he sympathized with Minette for the sermons to which she was compelled to listen: 'We have the disease of sermons that you complain of there, but I hope have the same convenience that the rest of the family has, of sleeping out most of the time, which is a great ease to those who are bound to hear them.'

Sometimes he was more than a little indelicate, as when he wrote, 'The Queen showed me your letter about the operation done upon Mdlle. Montosier, and by her smile I believe she had no more guess at the meaning than you had at the writing of the letter. I am confident that this will be the only operation of that kind that will be done in our age, for, as I have heard, most husbands had rather make use of a needle and thread than of a knife.' When the fourteen-year-old Duke of Monmouth was married to the heiress of the Buccleughs, two years his junior, Charles commented, 'You must not by this post expect a long letter from me, this being James's marriage day. And I am going to sup with them, where we intend to dance, and see them abed together, but the ceremony shall stop there, for they are both too young to lie all night together.'[1]

It may not be out of place to a better understanding of the Restoration outlook to observe that in writing to his sister in this vein the King was not doing so merely for the purpose of being bawdy. Whatever may be the case today there were far too few people in the England of the seventeenth century, and matrimony was regarded, to quote the Anglican Prayer Book, very literally as ' ordained for the procreation of children ', and a newly-married couple were expected to lose no time in taking the necessary steps to this end. ' To begin my letter to a new married lady,' wrote Mary of Orange to her friend, Lady Bathurst, on her wedding, ' it must be with wishing you much joy, and nine months hence two boys, for one is too common a wish.'[2] Charles himself on the day after his wedding to Catherine of Braganza, wrote to Clarendon, ' It was happy for the honour of the nation that I was not put to the consummation of the marriage last night, for I was so sleepy by having slept but two hours in my journey as I was afraid that matters would have gone very sleepily.'[3]

In these circumstances it is hardly surprising that the ceremonies attendant upon a wedding were what until recently at any rate would have been regarded as indecent. After the actual ceremony was over there was a feast in which the consumption of sack poset[4] played a prominent part; when the assembled company had drunk its fill the bride was undressed by her maids and the bridgegroom by his male friends, and at this point the revellers came upstairs to see them to bed, scramble for ribbons and garters, fling the bride's stockings, and draw the curtains of the bed on the married couple.

Naturally anything which impeded the procreation of children was to be deprecated, and in 1674 there appeared a pamphlet entitled *The Women's Petition against Coffee*, a beverage which would seem to have enjoyed a bad reputation on this score.

> The dull lubbers want a spur now, rather than a bridle: being
> so far found doing any works of supererogation that we find
> them not capable of performing those devoirs which their duty,
> and our expectations exact . . . The occasion of which insuffer-

able disaster, after a serious enquiry, and discussion of the point by the learned of the faculty, we can attribute to nothing more than the excessive use of that newfangled, abominable, heathenish liquor called coffee, which rifling nature of her choicest treasures, and drying up the radical moisture, has so eunucht our husbands, and crippled our more kind gallants, that they are become as impotent as age, and as unfruitful as those deserts whence that unhappy berry is said to be brought. . . Wherefore the premises considered, and to the end that our just rights may be restored, and all the ancient privileges of our sex preserved inviolable; that our husbands may give us some other testimonies of their being men, besides their beards and wearing of empty pantaloons. . . But returning to the good old strengthening liquors of our forefathers; that Nature's exchequer may once again be replenisht, and a race of lusty heroes begot, able by their achievements to equal the glories of our ancestors.

Charles was a wit in an age of wits. When William Penn was received in audience the Quaker kept his hat on his head, whereupon the King promptly removed his own. ' Friend Charles,' said Penn, ' Why doest thou not keep on thy hat?' ' 'Tis the custom in this place,' Charles replied, ' that only one man should remain uncovered at a time.' When Rochester produced his famous epitaph,

> Here lies our Sovereign Lord the King
> Whose word no man relied on:
> He never said a foolish thing,
> And never did a wise one.

Charles neatly parried the thrust with the observation, ' My words are my own, but my acts are my ministers'.'

He was, indeed, excellent at avoiding an inconvenient question. Once when the Duke of Buckingham had been sent to Paris on a special mission, the President of the Royal Society, who was the King's guest at Windsor, endeavoured to find out what was afoot: meeting Charles in one of the corridors of the Castle he ventured to ask, ' And when does Your Majesty expect to see the Duke of Buckingham again?' With a twinkle in his eye, his host replied, ' On the Day of Judgement in the Valley of Jehoshaphat ', and disappeared into his private apartments.[5] On another occasion a clergyman preaching before the King had read his sermon, and had been duly rebuked for so doing at dinner afterwards; however, before the meal was over, Charles unbent, and the cleric was emboldened to ask why he objected to a read sermon when he always read his speech to Parliament: to which the King replied, ' Because I like to have something to hold in front of me. I've asked those damn fellows for money so often that I am ashamed to look them in the face.' Sometimes Charles was himself the object of a quick retort, as, for example, when he remarked to a lady-in-waiting, ' I am very pleased to see you here again, for a rumour reached me that you had been laid up with twins.' The instant reply was, ' But, Sir, you must never believe more than half what you are told.'

It was in these exalted circles that Richard Talbot, as an intimate of the Duke of York, now moved. To say that he was a paragon of virtue would manifestly be absurd, but he was nothing like so promiscuous in his amours as were most of his contemporaries, female as well as male. There seems little doubt that he had an *affaire* with the Countess of Shrewsbury, whom Grammont described as ' this beauty less famous for her conquests than for the misfortunes which she occasioned ' The lady, who had been born Anna Maria Brudenell, was certainly a reigning toast, and we are told that three or four of her lovers wore an ounce of her hair made into bracelets. She attained a notoriety remarkable even for that age when the story went round how the Duke of Buckingham fought a duel with, and mortally wounded, her husband, while she, dressed as a page, stood by holding the Duke's horse.

Talbot would appear to have had an illegitimate son, possibly sired about this time, who was later to take part in the defence of Limerick, but the identity of his mother has never been established. This young man, also called Richard, served with Mountcashel's brigade in France, and by 1694 had attained the rank of brigadier, but there his promotion came to an end, for, reminiscent of his father at the same age, he made some indiscreet remarks concerning the failure of Louis to give further assistance to James to regain his throne. They were duly repeated to the French King who by no means relished criticism of this nature, so Talbot was called to Paris, deprived of his command, and sent to the Bastille, where he remained a prisoner for about a year; after his release he was not restored to his rank, but, as a volunteer in his old regiment, he was killed in 1702 at the battle of Luzzara.

More serious than any intrigue with the Countess of Shrewsbury was Talbot's siege of the heart of Frances Jennings, who was subsequently to become his wife, but not before both he and she had already been married elsewhere. The exact date at which she appeared at Court as a lady-in-waiting to the Duchess of York has never been established, but there can be no doubt as to the sensation she created when she arrived there, and Sir Winston Churchill has written of her, 'Fair and impregnable, she shone upon that merry, easy-going, pleasure-loving society.' She had beautiful flaxen hair and a dazzlingly fair complexion, together with an animated expression which redeemed her face from the insipidity that too often accompanies such fairness. Her weakest points were her nose and, as is the case with so many English girls, her hands; nor was her mouth very small, but it was beautifully shaped. Grammont was almost lyrical where Frances Jennings was concerned, and he compared her with 'Aurora, or the goddess of spring'. 'With this amiable person,' he continues, 'she was full of wit and sprightliness, and all her movements were unaffected and easy. Her conversation was charming when she had a mind to please, subtle and delicate when she was disposed to raillery; but as she was subject to flights of the imagination, and frequently began to speak before she had finished thinking, her utterances did not always convey what she wished.' Considering that she was probably not more than fifteen at the time this is not very remarkable.

Her father, Richard Jennings, came of a Somerset family which, though long entitled to bear arms, had no crest before

the reign of Henry VIII: for some time they had been settled
in Hertfordshire, at Holywell House near St Albans on the
banks of the Var. Locally the Jennings were of some note, for
the grandfather of Frances was High Sheriff of the county in
1625, and like his son, Richard, was repeatedly returned to the
House of Commons for St Albans. At one time the family were
by no means badly off, for they had property in Somerset and
Kent as well as in Hertfordshire, and their income may well
have reached the neighbourhood of £4,000 a year. By the time
that Frances met Richard Talbot her father was dead, and
concerning her widowed mother various views were held by
contemporaries: Mrs Manley, in *The New Atlantis*, referred
to her as ' the famous Mother Shipton, who by the power and
influence of her major art had placed her daughter in the
Court '. In our own time Sir Winston Churchill has said that
' she certainly bore a questionable reputation, suffered from a
violent temper, and found in St James's Palace, where she had
apartments, a refuge from hungry creditors who, armed with
the law, bayed outside '.[6]

At first Talbot's suit prospered: he was a good-looking
man; he was clearly a favourite of the Duke of York; and he
had a substantial income, which particularly appealed to
Frances, who shared that respect for money which was so
prominent a characteristic of her sister, Sarah, the formidable
Duchess of Marlborough. The course of true love was not,
however, destined to run smooth, for Richard began to over-
play his hand. One of the closest friends of Frances was a girl
called Goditha Price, who had recently been dismissed from
the service of the Duchess of York, whereupon she had entered
the household of Lady Castlemaine, which was hardly a school
of morals. Talbot objected to this friendship, and made no
bones about letting Frances know what he thought. ' In the
tone of a guardian rather than a lover ', says Grammont, ' he
took upon himself to chide her for the disreputable company
she kept. Mdlle Jennings was haughty beyond conception when
once she took it into her head; and as she liked Mdlle Price's
conversation much better than his, she ventured to ask him to

attend to his own affairs, and told him, if he only came over from Ireland to read her lectures, he might take the trouble to go back again as soon as he pleased.'

If Talbot was somewhat tactless in his handling of the matter it would seem that he had some justification for the belief that Goditha Price was far from being an ideal companion for one who valued her chastity as highly as did Frances Jennings, as one of their joint escapades serves to show. The two girls conceived a desire to consult a soothsayer in the City, who was in actual fact none other than the notorious John Wilmot, Second Earl of Rochester, in disguise, for London was barred to him as he had incurred the displeasure of the King. It was necessary for them to disguise themselves before undertaking the excursion, so they decided to go as orange-girls: now although the selling of oranges may have been a profitable occupation in those days it was hardly a reputable one owing to the liberties which the male purchasers of the fruit were liable to take with the female vendors. Of this particular episode Pepys noted in his *Diary,* ' What mad freaks the Mayds of Honour at Court have: that Mrs Jennings, one of the Duchess's maids, the other day dressed herself like an orange wench, and went up and down and cried oranges; till, falling down, or by some accident, her fine shoes were discerned, and she put to a great deal of shame.' Needless to say the frolic was not long in reaching Grammont who commented that ' the enterprise was certainly very rash, but nothing was too rash for Miss Jennings, who was of the opinion that a woman might despise appearances, provided she was in reality virtuous.' What Frances forgot and Richard realized, is that the world is governed by just these appearances.

In the spring of 1666 she married one of the Hamilton brothers, George, who was knighted in the following year, and thirteen years were to elapse before Frances and Richard came together again as widow and widower.

The marriage of his *inamorata* to another must have been a severe blow to Talbot, and, like many another man in similar circumstances, he turned to an earlier love for consolation: in this case the earlier love was Katherine Baynton, but three years passed before he did turn to her. She was the elder daughter of a Colonel Matthew Baynton, who had lost his life fighting for the King in the Civil War, and for his services pensions had been assigned to her mother, her sister,[7] and herself. Like so many pensions of that period, it was not very regularly paid, and presumably by way of compensation Katherine was appointed to the household of the Queen. There was nothing to be said against her on the score of looks, but otherwise she seems to have been rather insipid – more a Victorian than a Restoration type: she certainly did not appeal to Grammont, who portrays her as swooning when the situation arose in the best nineteenth-century manner. The only reference to her by Pepys is at least consistent with the sneers of Grammont, and it is in a description of the launching of the *Royal Catherine* at Woolwich when both the King and Queen were present: ' Mrs Baynton and the Duchess of Buckingham had been very sick coming by water in the barge, the water being very rough; but what silly sport they made with them in very common terms, methought, was very poor, and below what people think these great people say and do.'

For some unknown reason there seems to have been a good deal of secrecy about the actual marriage of Richard and Katherine. What presumably was a wedding-present from the King was referred to in an order from Charles to Sir George Carteret, Vice-Treasurer of Ireland, on 3 April 1669, to pay £4,000 to Colonel Richard Talbot, without account, out of the first money coming into his hands of any arrears of revenue in Ireland,[8] while a second warrant to the Vice-Treasurer exactly a month later says, ' We have promised to give £4,000 to Katherine Baynton, Maid of Honour to the Queen, in consideration of her services, and the merits of her father, Colonel Matthew Baynton, who was killed in the late King's service, and also to promote her marriage with Colonel Richard Talbot '.[9] The wedding would therefore appear to have taken place at some date in May, but the first public reference to it occurs in a newsletter of 8 June 1669: ' It is now become a less secret that Colonel Talbot, of the Duke of York's Bedchamber is married to Mrs Baynton, one of Her Majesty's Maids of Honour.'[10] As a wife Katherine made no history, so perhaps we may assume that the marriage was a happy one. It lasted nine years, for Katherine died in March 1679 and was buried at Christchurch Cathedral, Dublin. She and Richard had no sons, but apparently two daughters, Katherine and Charlotte.

Richard Talbot was not solely concerned with the affairs of the heart during the early years of the Restoration. If the Court of Charles II earned its reputation as the Court of Cuckolds, it was also a hotbed of personal and political intrigue, and the mutual relations of the various celebrities were both extremely complex and also very liable to sudden changes, which makes them in retrospect by no means easy to follow. One of the constant factors was Buckingham's enmity to James and Clarendon, and this dated from before the Restoration; amongst others temporary alliances were formed from time to time in order to undermine the position of someone disliked by them in common: in this way Buckingham and his cousin Lady Castlemaine, who were on the worst of terms with one another in 1666, are found in the following year to be in league with Arlington and others to destroy Clarendon. This they succeeded in doing, with the result that Ireland lost her greatest enemy in the highest circles. The fall of Clarendon also made the King master in his council as he had never been before, and no subsequent minister ever acquired the same ascendancy as had been held, at any rate for a time, by the late Chancellor. Furthermore in the struggle to free himself from a distasteful control Charles acquired an increased sense of independence and a keener interest in politics: his intimate advisers believed that they were guiding him, whereas in reality they were doing nothing of the sort.

In these intrigues in high places Richard Talbot played no part – not, we may be sure, because he was repelled by them, but because outside Ireland his political position was still too humble to allow him to participate in them; there is also to be taken into consideration the fact that his activities were circumscribed in view of his membership of the Duke of York's Household, for at no point in his career was he ever found acting in opposition to James's interests. In 1664, however, came a further clash with Ormonde, which resulted in a second period of incarceration in the Tower.

The seeds of the trouble were sown earlier that year when on the King's orders the Lord-Lieutenant had come to England to advise on the Settlement of Ireland of which the details were still far from complete, and in August 1664 he was set to work with a committee on the Bill of Explanation. Now Talbot was toiling away on behalf of his clients with the £18,000 in bonds in his pocket, and it was over one of these, a certain James Allen, that the clash came. Although Allen seems to have been a far from innocent Papist yet Talbot had succeeded in obtaining on his behalf a decree from the Court of Claims restoring him to his estate; but he had only managed to secure this, so his enemies maintained, by the corruption of witnesses before the Court in question. Unfortunately for him, the Earl of Mount-Alexander[11] got hold of some letters from Talbot to his brother Peter and Sir Brian O'Neil, which revealed the fraud which had been perpetrated: Ormonde had left his son Ossory as Deputy in Dublin, and it was before him and the Irish Privy Council that Mount-Alexander proceeded to lay these papers with a demand for a reversal of the decree.

The matter was further complicated by the fact that Allen had already sold part of his restored estate to no less a person than Talbot himself, so the latter's embarrassment is not difficult to understand, and this was considerably increased when Ormonde made a suggestion to the Privy Council in London that a clause should be inserted in the Bill of Explanation to annul all decrees of restitution already obtained by bribes, payment, or both. Talbot now lost his head completely, for he believed, or affected to believe, that this proposal was aimed at him personally, so he went about London making threats against Ormonde's life. These soon reached the King, who declared that the offence was unpardonable, and including the whole Talbot family in his condemnation said that all the brothers were

' naughty fellows and had no good meaning': in consequence, Richard was sent to the Tower on 22 December 1664, ' committed for high misdemeanours' as the warrant to the Lieutenant has it, and two of his brothers went to the Fleet. He stayed there for a month, but it is interesting to note that when he came out he still had enough influence to get the decree in favour of Allen confirmed.

The fact is that Ormonde's position was undermined by the fall of Clarendon, for the Cabal ministry was determined to have him out as the only one left of the King's old advisers. Their reasons were mostly the reverse of creditable, and the most eager of the ministers was Buckingham who coveted his two posts as Steward of the Household and Lord-Lieutenant of Ireland; behind him was Lady Castlemaine, who could never forgive Ormonde for having stopped a grant to her of Phoenix Park. The extent to which his enemies were prepared to go in their vendetta against him was shown in December 1670, even after he had ceased to be Lord-Lieutenant.

On the sixth of that month Ormonde was returning from a banquet in the City of London to his house in St James's Street, and he was nearly home when his coach was stopped by a body of masked men, at the head of which was Thomas Blood. For some reason the Duke's footmen had lagged behind, so the moment was particularly opportune for the conspirators. As soon as the coach was at a standstill Ormonde was seized and dragged out of it. He shouted for help, and he struggled hard, but he was sixty years of age, and not in too good a state of health, while he had to deal with five determined ruffians, armed with knives and pistols. The Duke's life would not have been worth a moment's purchase had not Blood conceived the plan of hanging him at Tyburn, so that when London woke up next morning it would see the ex-Lord Lieutenant of Ireland dangling from the gallows. This refinement was destined to bring the whole attempt to naught.

When the Duke's struggles had been overcome, he was tied back-to-back to one of the conspirators, a man of great size, and mounted on a horse with his captor, who then set off

I

towards Tyburn. Meanwhile Blood, once Ormonde's immediate resistance was at an end, rode off down Piccadilly towards Hyde Park to see that all was in readiness for the execution. Five minutes sufficed to tie the end of the rope, and slip the noose, after which Blood retraced his steps to see what had become of his companions. Things had not gone so well as he had hoped, for Ormonde was not so spent as to be powerless. He was not an Irishman for nothing, and he realized in a few moments that he was the victim of an ordinary murder-plot, when safety lay in cunning rather than force. If he wished to save his life he must keep still and be on the alert, while disarming suspicion by appearing to be in a far worse condition than was actually the case. This ruse succeeded, for after Blood had left three of his associates did likewise, and then the Duke began to work for his liberation. He managed to get his foot underneath the stirrup, and by a sudden twist and jerk dismounted his captor. Down into the mud they both tumbled, but the way in which they were bound prevented them from doing anything except roll about struggling on the ground.

As murderers Blood and his companions seem to have been peculiarly incompetent, for they had neglected to silence Ormonde's coachman; it may have been that they thought he was too frightened to foil them, but if that was their assumption it was to cost them dear, for the first thing he did was to drive on to his master's house, and give the alarm. Near Hyde Park two men were seen, in the light of torches, to be struggling on the ground, and when the strap that bound them was severed, the Duke of Ormonde was saved, for his assailant made his escape in the darkness and confusion. No one was ever arrested for this crime, but it was widely attributed to Buckingham and Lady Castlemaine.

Such being the case, it was indeed fortunate for Richard Talbot's reputation that he only left Dublin for London on the day that Blood made his attack on Ormonde, for had he been in England at the time he would unquestionably have been implicated in the crime by his many detractors from that day to this; for in spite of his position in the Duke of York's household he was mixing with some very undesirable company indeed, and company that would stop at nothing, including murder, to gain its ends.

What brought him over to London at this particular juncture was a further effort to secure redress for the wrongs which many of his fellow-countrymen claimed that they had suffered through the Acts of Settlement and Explanation. A just complaint was of little effect, and bribery was beyond the means of most of the aggrieved parties. Those who remained dissatisfied found very considerable obstacles in their path, such as the power of the purse, political influence, and religious and racial prejudice. It was decided to see if anything could be effected by a direct petition to the King, who, it was rightly felt, was more likely to be favourable to the Irish cause now that Clarendon's influence was removed. An impressive number of signatures was obtained to the petition which set forth that the signatories had been dispossessed of their lands by ' the late usurped power' for their loyalty, and that they had faithfully served the King and suffered for him at home and abroad; and that for want of a just presentation of their cases their estates had, contrary to His Majesty's declared intentions, been kept by others, so that they were in extreme misery for want of subsistance.' What was asked for was an impartial tribunal to hear their grievances, and in the meantime it was requested that all further grants of undisposed land in Ireland should be stopped. Richard Talbot was chosen as the representative to take this petition to London.[12]

On 18 January 1671 he appeared before the King in Council and delivered it to him. It was soon clear that a favourable impression had been created, for Charles and the majority of the Privy Councillors considered reasonable the requests for the appointment of an impartial commission to hear the petitioners' grievances, and for the cessation in the interval of all further assignments of Irish land. Accordingly a committee of thirteen was appointed to deal with the matter, and it met three days later when Talbot appeared before it, with a list of those whom he represented and his proposals for their relief.

He stated that he appeared on behalf of a large number of innocent men who had been condemned before their cases had been heard, and he proposed as a remedy an amendment to the Acts of Settlement; he also asked to be heard by his counsel, one Ayloffe.

This proposal at once aroused the opposition of Ormonde, who was a member of the committee: he maintained that it was better to uphold the Settlement, in spite of a few errors, than to waste time and money in doing the work all over again, while bringing the trade of Ireland to a standstill in the meantime, though why this last should have been the case is not quite clear. Of the ministers, Arlington was alarmed at the idea of the amount of work certain to be involved by a new Settlement, and complained that the petitioners were going too far. All the same the majority supported Talbot, who was allowed to introduce Ayloffe into the proceedings. Thereafter the verbal battle raged furiously, with the Confederate War being fought all over again, Ayloffe maintaining that his clients were without exception innocent Papists, while Ormonde related the story of the events of the forties from his point of view. Finally it was decided to submit the papers in the case to the Attorney-General, Sir Heneage Finch, who quickly gave his opinion against the petitioners' claims. Charles and the Council as a whole, however, did not choose to be guided by Finch, and before long the controversy was more or less where it began. A further Commission of Enquiry was sent to Ireland, and Talbot went to Dublin a few days before they arrived in the capital. There he found that tempers were roused by the prospect of upsetting the Acts of Settlements, as a contemporary letter clearly proves: ' The petition lately delivered by Col. Talbot has made no small noise here. Yesterday morning, on occasion of discourse thereof, Sir Henry Ingoldsby and Mr Thomas Cusack, nephew to Col. Talbot, fought a duel, when, it's said, the latter in closing broke his sword, but notwithstanding was too strong for the other. However, both came home unhurt, but 'tis feared the occasion will breed much greater animosities yet.'[18]

While these investigations into the complexity of Irish land tenures were pursuing their weary course Talbot got himself involved at the end of May 1672 in a naval battle, where his experiences were decidedly unpleasant if not unduly prolonged. The Duke of York, in command of an Anglo-French fleet, allowed himself to be surprised by the Dutch in Southwold Bay; although the ensuing combat was tenacious and both sides claimed a victory, the best opinion was that the Dutch had the better of the encounter. James was eager to have his revenge by following the enemy into his own waters, but the King was imperative that he should lie in wait for the enemy's merchant ships from the Indies, whose cargoes were valued at several millions which would have gone a long way to relieve Charles from dependence upon either Louis XIV or the House of Commons. The upshot, however, was that the ships managed to elude James and reached their home-ports in safety.

Talbot reached the fleet just before the battle, and was on board the *Catherine,* which, according to a contemporary writer, ' was taken by the Dutch, and in her Sir John Chicherley and Colonel Richard Talbot, with several others, who were carried prisoners into other ships; and then the Dutch going to fire her, the rest of the souldiers that were in her saved her and brought her off '.[14] Talbot cannot have remained a prisoner in Dutch hands for long since on 16 October he was at Chester, and four days later he reached Dublin, where he ran into some very serious trouble indeed.

The English people in general, and the House of Commons in particular, were showing signs of a restlessness where Roman Catholics were concerned which was later to develop into the Popish Plot agitation, and they were further stirred up by the news which was going round about the tenderness displayed towards Papists, innocent and otherwise, by Dublin Castle since Ormonde had ceased to be Lord-Lieutenant. The long-standing rules against their admission into the corporations had been relaxed all over Ireland,[15] and they had also been accepted as Justices of the Peace, while nine or ten had been elected to the Common Council of Dublin subject to the King's approval, which was soon given. As may be supposed this

development was very pleasing to Talbot, who probably gave
evidence of his satisfaction too loudly. He and his friends made
no secret of their determination to see what they could do to
ameliorate the lot of the English Catholics too, and a considerable sum of money was ' collected at the masses throughout
Ireland by directions of the priests, Jesuits, and friars, to be
disposed of in England for the advantage of the Roman Catholic
cause ', and with this Talbot and two other colonels, Fitzpatrick and Dempsey, crossed to England in March 1673, the
actual disposition of the money being left in the hands of
Talbot and Fitzpatrick.

A close examination of the situation at this time, however,
makes it abundantly clear that the desire to do justice to the
Catholics originated with the King and was viewed with grave
suspicion by the authorities at Dublin Castle, who, nevertheless, had to do as they were told, though fully conscious that
such a policy was by no means in the interest of the English
garrison whom they considered it to be their duty to support.
Genocide of the Elizabethan and Cromwellian type was out of
the question with Charles II on the throne, so in its place the
Castle had recourse to the principle of *divide et impera*: on
14 November 1673 the then Lord-Lieutenant, the Earl of
Essex,[16] wrote to Ormonde:

> Soon after my coming hither Molooney,[17] the titular Bp. of
> Killaloe, whom I look upon as the most dangerous, because the
> wisest, man of all their clergy, made a composure of all their
> differences which were amongst the men of their religion, par-
> ticularly of the disputes which were between their Primate and
> Peter Talbot, as also the dissentions betwixt Collonel Talbot
> and Collonel Fitzpatricke, and had upon the matter well near
> made an union among them all. I soon found if this proceeded
> I should have no intelligence of any of their practices or acting,
> and believing it to be one of the most important things I could
> do, both for his Majestye's service and the security of his
> Protestant subjects here, either to keep these men divided, or
> if they were united to breeke them again, I made use of some
> of their ffriars, who always have their little wrangle with the
> secular clergy, to set up factions against their Bp., and by

encouraging these little annemostyes among themselves at length brought them to that pass that they openly accused one another of exercising ecclesiasticall jurisdiction contrary to the laws of the land.[18]

That these views coincided with those of Ormonde cannot be doubted, for in one of his letters, quoted by Carte, he wrote, ' My aim was to work a division among the Roman clergy, and I believe I had accomplished it, to the great security of the government and the Protestants, and against the opposition of the Pope and his creatures and nuncios, if I had not been removed.'

Unfortunately these sentiments, rather than those of the King, were soon to appeal not only to the Protestant minority in Ireland, but to the Protestant majority in England, and it was not long before Richard Talbot and his master were to feel the backwash of this growing antagonism to the Church of Rome. As the years of the second decade of the Restoration passed the political situation in England, with which that in Ireland was always inextricably entangled, was increasingly less influenced by what had gone before, and new factors, difficult for an Irishman to appreciate, soon began to make themselves felt. In particular, the growing power of France was not long, first in attracting attention, and then in arousing alarm, on the English side of the Channel.

For a good many years English public opinion had been slow to realize either the decline of Spain or the rise of France, and Cromwell was by no means alone in his failure to appreciate the true significance of what was taking place on the mainland of Europe. However, before the Restoration was ten years old not only were the armies of Louis XIV over-running the territory of his neighbours, especially those Low Countries with whose fortunes England had so long been associated, but, worse still from the English point of view, France was building up a navy of the very first rank. In these circumstances it is hardly surprising that the ordinary citizen should have come to regard France in the same light as his grandfather had looked upon Spain. The kingdom of Louis XIV was, too, in his uncritical eyes the sword-arm of the Papacy, for the French monarch's differences with successive Popes had no meaning for him: all he knew was that his co-religionists, the Huguenots, were losing their privileges one by one, and at this he took alarm. Nor was national suspicion in any way allayed by the attitude of France during the English wars with the Dutch, for it was generally believed that Louis was deliberately playing the two Protestant powers off against one another in order to weaken them both, and there was much in French policy to justify the suspicion.

The second decade of the Restoration thus witnessed a revival of the old fear of Rome and a growing mistrust of French intentions, with the result that England had an attack of nerves during which she showed herself capable of running to any extreme. National hysteria is at once a dangerous and an unpleasant phenomenon, and it is one from which England during her history has on the whole been fairly free; even Charles I gave it as his opinion that ' the English are a sober people ',[19] but when an outbreak does occur it takes a particularly violent form.

Such being the case it is in no way surprising that Talbot and his two companions should have found the situation extremely grave when they crossed to England. The discovery on the recent death of the Duchess of York that she was a Catholic had roused suspicions that her husband was probably one too, and so added fuel to the fire of Protestant bigotry. On 8 March the King had been forced to cancel his year-old Declaration of Indulgence, and on the twentieth the Test Act was passed: by this measure all civil and military officer-holders and all members of the household of the King and the Duke of York were to take the oaths of allegiance and supremacy, while by 1 August they were to have received the sacrament according to the service of the Church of England. This was bad enough, but worse was to follow where the Talbots were concerned, for on 26 March the House of Commons petitioned the King that for the establishment of the possessions of his subjects in Ireland he would be pleased to maintain the Acts of

Settlement and Explanation, as well as to recall his Commission of Enquiry as calculated to disturb the peace of the kingdom. The petition further demanded that ' Colonel Richard Talbot, who had notoriously assumed to himself the title of agent-general of the Roman Catholics of Ireland, might be immediately dismissed out of all commands, either civil or military, and forbid all access to Court '.

As if this were not enough, the Commons went on to demand that no Papists should be continued or admitted as judges, justices of the peace, sheriffs, mayors, etc. in Ireland; that the titular Popish ecclesiastical authorities, ' and in particular Peter Talbot, pretended Archbishop of Dublin[20] for his notorious disloyalty and disobedience and contempt of the laws ' should be sent abroad; that the regular priests also should be banished and all Roman Catholic convents, schools, etc. be closed; that the permission to live in corporations should be recalled; that all Papists in Ireland should be disarmed; and that ' His Majesty should give further directions for the encouragement of the English planters and the Protestant interest in Ireland and the suppression of the insolencies and disorders of the Irish Papists, by whose practices, and particularly of the said Richard and Peter Talbot, the peace and safety of Ireland had been so much of late endangered '. That Ireland was an overwhelmingly Catholic country, and that her inhabitants had any right to run their own affairs in their own way, did not occur to the House of Commons, whose members never ceased to claim just that right for themselves. Such being the case it is hardly surprising to find Sir Arthur Forbes writing to Viscount Conway, ' What was the commission of those three colonels from Ireland is not to be learnt here, for at their arrival they found affairs altered from what they expected, and found it convenient to bear a lower sail.'[21]

In face of this onslaught Charles did his best to temporize, so he answered the petition of the Commons with an assurance that no man should have reason to complain. He dissolved the Commission of Enquiry, and declared that he was resolved to preserve the Settlement of Ireland and to disturb nothing which had been confirmed by the Acts. All the same, he appointed another committee from the Privy Council, though with much reduced powers, but it effected little. The injustices which the Irish Catholics suffered through the Settlement remained unredressed for the rest of Charles's reign: prior to 1673 Richard Talbot had been able to do something for them, but for relief on any more extended scale he and they had another twelve years to wait.

During the greater part of this time he was either in prison or on the run. At first he did not realize how great a storm was brewing, and he tried to ride it, confident that he could rely upon the support of the Duke of York; but before long it became evident that James's own position was precarious in the extreme, so in September 1673 Talbot crossed to France,[22] where he remained for some eighteen months before returning to England and going into hiding in Yorkshire; during the whole of his life up to this date he had done all he could to call the maximum amount of attention to himself, but now his object was to draw the minimum, and in this he was remarkably successful. In the summer of 1677 Ormonde became Lord-Lieutenant again, and in view of his forgiving nature Talbot felt it safe to show himself in his own country once more, which he accordingly did in time to be present at his wife's funeral in March 1678.

By this time the conversion of the Duke of York to the Catholic faith had added fuel to the fire of public-house Protestantism, and in the van of the movement had appeared Titus Oates. At this absence of time it is by no means easy to understand why so unattractive a scoundrel exercised so great an influence over the country for so long. There is, indeed, evidence that he was by no means contemptible as a preacher in the style of those days, and he certainly enjoyed the backing of the extremely efficient Whig organization, to which he owed his position of a national hero; furthermore, the country was in a frenzy of anti-Catholic hysteria. Yet, even so, his record was such that it is surprising that so many people were deluded by him. Perhaps the explanation is to be found in the fact that in the seventeenth century it was easier for a man to dissociate himself from his past than it is in the twentieth, though the exposure of more than one financial scandal of late years has left one wondering how men with such shady pasts ever induced the investor or the banks to trust them again.

Oates was of this type, and he had been peculiarly successful in getting out of one scrape after another. A product of Cambridge University, which sent him down without a degree, he was by no means devoid of intelligence, and it was only when the Plot was waning that he began palpably to contradict himself; though at a banquet given in his honour in the City he once seriously embarrassed his Whig supporters by engaging in a public discussion of no little heat with one Tonge as to which of them had the honour of originating the conspiracy. For the rest, his superb health did much to aid him, and he lived to die in his bed.

This evil man's tentacles began to extend to Ireland in October 1678, and the first to be seized by them was Peter Talbot. Some letters written by him while he and Richard were in France had been found among the papers of Father Coleman, one of the earliest victims of Oates, and his enemies in Dublin were not slow in joining in the campaign against him; the fact that he was in the worst of health in no way assuaged the malice of his persecutors, and on 30 September a warrant was issued for his arrest. Ormonde had no choice but to comply with it, and on the eleventh of the following month the Archbishop was carried in a chair from Luttrell's Town to Dublin Castle where he was henceforth confined. Carte, who speaks of ' his miserable, helpless condition, the violence of his distemper being scarce supportable, and threatening his death every moment ', relates that he was allowed to have an attendant to wait upon him in prison.[23] He required this attendant for two weary years, for he survived – he can hardly be said to have lived – for that length of time. Confined in a cell near him was Oliver Plunket, Archbishop of Armagh and an old ecclesiastical rival, and a touching incident in his captivity was that shortly before his death Talbot received absolution from the hands of Plunket, who was himself to die on the scaffold in the following year.

Richard was left at liberty a month longer than his brother, and he was at the Castle on the day that the order from London arrived for his arrest as Ormonde testified in a letter to Lord Conway, ' I received this morning directions from the King for the securing of Colonel Richard Talbot, who was then walking the gallery, and, I believe, expected with every post to be so treated. I immediately gave the Deputy Constable of the Castle order to take him into his custody, where he now is.' The vindictiveness of his enemies at this time is well illustrated by Marvell's ferocious picture of him in *Advice to a Painter*:

> Next Talbot must by his great Master stand,
> Laden with Folly, Flesh, and ill-got Land:
> He's of a size indeed to fill a Porch,
> But Ne'er can make a Pillar of the Church;
> His Sword is all his Arg'ment, not his Book,
> Altho' no Scholar, he can act the Cook;
> And will cut Throats again, if he be paid;
> In th'Irish Shambles he first learn'd the Trade.

From these lines it would appear that Talbot was beginning to put on weight, and an inactive life in prison would be unlikely to help matters.

The fates were kinder to him than to his brother, or his medical adviser was more persuasive, for he obtained his release in eight months. On 21 June Sir Robert Southwell wrote from London to Ormonde in Dublin, ' On a petition yesterday from Colonel Talbot to go to his house upon bail, by reason of his sickness in prison, there was a long debate, and it was finally agreed that he should, upon ten thousand pounds bail, be allowed to come over and live in Yorkshire, where he lived before. Some thought he would rather choose to stay in prison than to come over on this side, and most were against his being free on that, which yet his agent does much struggle for, especially till his health be restored; and how the order will settle at last I know not, but it will not go till Tuesday.'[24] Another three weeks elapsed before the order was settled, when, thanks largely to a certificate from Dr Meara, Talbot was given leave to go to France ' for cure ', which he immediately did, but before long it was going round Whitehall that ' Col. Talbot is as well at Paris as ever in his life ', so it would seem that Dr Meara had more than earned his fee.

From the safe distance of the French capital Richard Talbot was able to watch the panorama of English politics, and the King's masterly handling of them. Behind the popular panic which had caused him and his brother to be imprisoned, and behind Oates and his associates, stood the First Earl of Shaftesbury, whose character has been so well delineated by Dryden:

> Achitophel, grown weary to possess
> A lawful fame, and lazy happiness,
> Disdain'd the golden fruit to gather free
> And lent the crowd his arm to shake the tree.
>   Now, manifest of crimes, contriv'd long since,
> He stood at bold defiance with his Prince:
> Held up the buckler of the people's cause
> Against the Crown; and skulk'd behind the laws.
> The wish'd occasion of the Plot he takes;
> Some circumstances finds, but more he makes.
> By buzzing emissaries, fills the ears
> Of listening crowds, with jealousies and fears
> Of arbitrary counsels brought to light,
> And proves the King himself a Jebusite.
>   Weak arguments! Which yet he knew full well,
> Were strong with people easy to rebel.

The English populace hardly knew what it feared, and its idol was carried away by his own verbosity, but ' the great little Lord ' was under no illusions as to the end which he had in view. Shaftesbury's outlook on the world was undoubtedly embittered by physical suffering, and for the last twenty-four years of his life he was in constant pain from a suppurating internal cyst. His model was Pym, and he played upon the passions of the crowd in the same way that Pym had done; the ' brisk boys ' whom he led to demonstrate against all who opposed him were the equivalent of the mobs whom the earlier demagogue had summoned to Whitehall in the early days of the Long Parliament. The easy-going Monmouth as King, with himself as dictator, that was his goal. His fundamental mistake was his assumption that Charles II was Charles I. Old Rowley had his father's example before him, as well as being himself a much more adroit politician. He committed no such blunders as the attempt to arrest the Five Members, but gave Shaftesbury enough rope to hang himself. Few rulers or statesmen have known their people as well as Charles II knew the English, and he realized from the beginning that the more extreme his opponents became, and the more unreasonable he could make them appear, the sooner the reaction against them would develop. Above all, he had a standing army, if only a small one, to protect him, so he could not be overawed by Shaftesbury's thugs as his father had been by those of Pym. Shaftesbury had, it may be observed, the same weakness for women as his proto-type. 'Here comes,' Charles is reputed to have said in the hearing of 'the little limping peer' as he passed before him with the mace and seal, 'the greatest whoremaster in England.' 'Of a subject, Sire,' the Earl replied. Like many another apostle of liberty, Shaftesbury was far from practising what he preached, and in his native Dorset he did not hesitate to enclose commons and ride rough-shod over the rights of his poorer neighbours.[25]

The Popish Plot, properly handled, was to pave the way for the Exclusion Bill, which would rule the Duke of York out of the succession; and at first all went well. The public, in its panic-stricken condition, had no objection to the judicial murder of a number of innocent Catholics, and it welcomed the removal of members of the Church of Rome from official positions; but when the question came to be one of placing Lucy Walter's bastard on the throne of England to satisfy the ambitions of Shaftesbury there was the revulsion of feeling which Charles had foreseen. The King then made his first move, and summoned Parliament to meet at Oxford where it would not be intimidated by the 'brisk boys'. To prove his moderation he went so far as to offer that the Duke of York should be banished for life, and that on his own death there should be a regency for his brother; but Shaftesbury would not hear of any compromise. Charles knew that his hour had come, and when he dissolved Parliament the Whigs found that they had gone too far; but for a combination of circumstances which no one could have foreseen at the time, they might have paid for their leader's mistakes, not with seven, but with seventy years' exclusion from power. Charles won because he had done what his father had never been able to do, that is to say convince the English people that the opponents of the Crown were revolutionaries, and that he stood for the old order; once he had succeeded in this he was allowed to interpret that old order in his own way.

All this Talbot saw from his vantage-point in Paris, but he by no means spent the whole of his time there in the rôle of a political observer, for he met his old love, the former Frances Jennings, and this time she consented to marry him, not, apparently with her brother-in-law's approval, for on 15 January 1680 John Churchill added a postscript to a letter to his wife, ' Pray present my services to the widow and tell her that I am very glad she is not married, and if she stays for my consent she never will be.' All the same the marriage took place in the following year, when Richard was a widower of fifty-one and Frances a widow of thirty-three. That it was a love-match, at any rate on his part, admits of no question, and it goes a long way to disprove the charge that Talbot was of a mercenary nature. By now he was, as we have seen, a man of some substance, but his wife's circumstances were by no means equal to his, for by her first husband Frances had three daughters, of whom the eldest was fourteen. It is true that she and her sister, Sarah, were joint-owners of a small property in Hertfordshire, but this cannot have gone far towards relieving her necessities. She had, it is true some influence at Court, but then so had her husband. In effect, Richard's second marriage was no more brilliant than his first.

Matrimony seems to have turned his thoughts towards home,

and on 17 February 1683 he put his case in a letter to that most forgiving of Lords-Lieutenant, Ormonde:

> I am confident if your Grace had believed me guilty of so much as a thought against His Majesty's service, you had not so generously appealed for my liberty when I was a prisoner in the Castle of Dublin, and I hope that the same reason will now prevail with you to move the King that I may return to put some order to my small affairs, that extremely suffer by my absence for now almost four years from home. My Lord, should I be obliged to live here any longer time, I must certainly be ruined, the expense of this place being excessive for any man that must live as I, and that has so numerous a family. And though His Majesty shall be pleased to approve of my return to my own house, I do assure your Grace I shall need be a good husband to pay the debts I have contracted since I had the misfortune to be named in the Plot, and that your Grace may the more freely move His Majesty to grant this my most humble request, pray be pleased to know that I am none of those persons that are impeached by the House of Commons, and that all that ever was laid to my charge was a story of Mr. Oates that he had seen some commission which was sent me into Ireland, and at the same time he said it was sent me into Ireland I lived in the north of England and did not come thither in six months after, all which is but a bare hearsay and cannot so much as bear any action at common law.[26]

Ormonde would appear to have had no great difficulty in obtaining permission for Talbot to return to Ireland, but, however urgent were his private affairs, it was not long before he was dabbling in politics once more. Plans were afoot for extensive changes in the administration of Ireland, both civil and military, and as it was clear that they must necessarily involve the supersession of the Lord-Lieutenant, purists have held that, after what Ormonde had done for him, it would have behoved Talbot better to stand aside at this particular juncture. It was, however, a cause which he had very much at heart, and the existing situation was one that called loudly for redress, since the Catholic majority in the country only possessed some two and a half millions of the eleven million acres of surveyed land in the kingdom. In addition to calling attention to this scandal, Talbot called for changes in the Privy Council, the magistracy, and the army, which were Protestant monopolies, and as an Irishman and a Catholic he could hardly do less, but there is no evidence that he made any personal attack on Ormonde.

How long it would have been before Talbot's programme was put into operation had Charles lived it is impossible to say, but at the beginning of February 1685 he died, and almost Ormonde's last official act in Dublin was to proclaim James II on the eleventh of that month.

NOTES

1 *Cf.* Hartmann, C. H.: *Charles II and Madame*, pp. 68, 73, 95, 96-97, and 126. London. 1934.
2 *Cf.* Bryant, Sir Arthur: *Postman's Horn*, p. 109. London. 1936.
3 *Lansdowne, MSS* 1236, f. 124.
4 This was a hot drink consisting essentially of sweetened and spiced milk curdled with ale or wine, and sometimes thickened with bread.
5 Dasent, A. I.: *The Private Life of Charles the Second*, p. 249. London. 1927.
6 *Marlborough, His Life and Times*, Vol. I, p. 116. London. 1933.
7 Isabella, who married the Fourth Earl of Roscommon.
8 *Col. St. P. Ireland*, 1669-70.
9 *Cal. St. P. Dom.* 1668-69.
10 *H.M.C. XII. Pt. 7. Le Fleming MSS.*
11 Whom Talbot described as 'the greatest cowhyerd living'. (*C.S.P., Ireland*, 1663-5).
12 *C.S.P. Ireland*, 1669-70.
13 *C.S.P., Dom.*, 1671. Letter of 14 February.
14 *C.S.P. Dom.*, 1672. Letter of 1 June.
15 The Irish mayors were often elected in curious ways. In Cork, for instance the election of the Mayor took place in the open Court of D'Oyer Hundred, and the procedure was somewhat peculiar. The mayor, sheriffs, and commonalty having assembled at the Guildhall on the day of election, the mayor for the time being ordered the names of all the burgesses or persons who had served as sheriffs of the City, and who were resident within the city, to be written on several tickets of equal bigness, and the tickets having been placed in a hat by the mayor five were drawn out by a child nominated by the mayor; these five persons whose names were so drawn out were the candidates put in nomination for the mayoralty for the ensuing year. Thereupon in open court every freeman and member of the whole city or body politic then present were polled; and whichever of

K

the said persons had a majority of the votes of all the freemen then present was duly elected to serve as mayor of the said City for the ensuing year. It was further the custom of the populace assembled outside the Guildhall to pelt the newly-elected Mayor with bran, to which has been attributed the origin of the phrase 'bran-new'.

[16] He was later suspected of complicity in the Rye House Plot, and was incarcerated in the Tower where in due course he was found with his throat cut from ear to ear.

[17] John O'Molony, Bishop of Killaloe, 1672-1689, when he was translated to Limerick.

[18] *Spic. Oss.* II, pp. 222-223.

[19] In a letter to the Prince of Wales, under date of 29 November 1648.

[20] Consecrated 9 May 1669.

[21] *C.S.P. Dom.* Letter of 19 April 1673.

[22] His pass to transport himself beyond the seas with servants etc. was issued on 19 September.

[23] *Ormonde*, IV, p. 550.

[24] *H.M.C., Ormonde MSS*, Vol. IV (New Series).

[25] *Cf.* Bryant, Sir Arthur: *Samuel Pepys, the Years of Peril*, pp. 10-11. Cambridge. 1935.

[26] *H.M.C., Ormonde MSS.* Vol. I (New Series).

CHAPTER VII

A Great Viceroy

WITH THE accession of James II the great days of Richard
Talbot may be said to have begun: previously he had only
played minor parts in the drama of Anglo-Irish politics, but
for the remainder of his life he was to be in the centre of the
stage. The first signs of the quarter from which the wind was
now blowing were not long in becoming visible. Ormonde had
known for some time that he was to be replaced by Laurence
Hyde, Earl of Rochester of the second creation and second son
of Clarendon, and consequently the new King's brother-in-law;
but it was only from a newsheet which he read on the journey
from Dublin to London that he learnt his cavalry regiment on
the Irish establishment had been taken from him and given to
Talbot. This event seems to have been regarded by contemporaries as particularly significant, for at the end of the entry in
his diary for March 1685 Narcissus Luttrell says, ' The Duke of
Ormonde, lord-lieutenant of Ireland, is removed from that
government, and two lords justices appointed for that purpose
at present: his regiment is given to Col. Talbot: the privy
council is dissolved, and a new one appointed, and some talk
as if there were a design for the papists regaining their estates
in that kingdom.'

It was clear that in all parts of the British Isles there would
be changes, for it was hardly to be expected that James would
allow members of his own Church to remain subject to oppres-
sive laws and humiliating disqualifications – to do so would
be equally derogatory to his royal dignity and to his religious
sincerity. For some months it seemed that the King would be

satisfied with very moderate demands which it would be unreasonable to refuse. He was not, as his brother had been in
1660, a young man assuming the government in a country of
which he had little personal knowledge. He was in his fifty-third
year, and for more than two decades he had been an active and
keenly interested politician. He had for his guidance all the
experience of the previous reign, and though he lacked the
cleverness and versatility of his predecessor, he could not be
wholly blind to lessons which were written so large in recent
history. The most distinct of these lessons was that in all three
kingdoms, though for different reasons in each, every step in
the direction of Catholic relief was fraught with difficulty and
danger; another lesson, which had been clearly emphasized
during the previous four years, was that in England a
monarch who had the support of the Established Church
might exercise his prerogative without much fear of national
opposition.

Towards the end of his life Charles II said to Sir Richard
Bulstrode, ' I am weary of travelling, and am resolved to go
abroad no more; but when I am dead and gone, I know not
what my brother will do. I am much afraid that when he comes
to wear the crown he will be obliged to travel again; and yet I
will take care to leave my kingdoms to him in peace, wishing
he may long keep them so; but this hath all of my fears and
less of my reason.'[1] Certainly he had bequeathed to James a
heritage to which few English monarchs had succeeded. The
opposition to the Crown had been broken, and its leaders were
either dead or in exile. The steady increase in revenue from the
Customs had made the poverty of the King in the early days of
the Restoration a mere memory, and there seemed no reason
why this increase should not be maintained. As for the House
of Commons, the line taken with the borough charters had
ensured a majority for the Crown, and the final returns for the
Parliament of 1685 were such that James himself said ' there
were not above forty members, but such as he himself wished
for '.[2] Above all, the Rye House Plot and its ramifications had
convinced the average Englishman that the King alone stood

between him and anarchy of the same type as had followed the fall of the Protectorate. All James had to do was to follow his brother's example, prove that the Catholics did not constitute a menace, and he could certainly have secured a measure of toleration for his co-religionists. Instead, he behaved in such a way that emancipation was postponed for nearly a hundred and fifty years; Ireland was saddled with the Penal Laws, and he himself lost his throne in forty-five months.

In the spring of 1685, all this lay in the future, and in Ireland as elsewhere there was no undue haste to make sweeping changes; the two Lords Justices were the Archbishop of Armagh and the Earl of Granard, and if the Privy Council of Ormonde's time was reduced in numbers, the vacancies were not filled by the nomination of Catholics. Rochester showed no desire to assume his viceregal functions, so he returned to his former office of Treasurer, and was succeeded as Lord-Lieutenant by his elder brother, now the Second Earl of Clarendon. There were, however, signs that the Talbot family was in the ascendant, for in addition to Richard's military appointment, Frances was in attendance upon the Queen at the Coronation in Westminster Abbey on 23 April 1685, appearing in the records as Countess of Bantry; in the earlier lists of Queen Mary's household she figures as Lady of the Bedchamber in company with her sister Isabel, Countess of Roscommon, the Duchess of Norfolk, and Lady Bellasyse, each at a salary of £500 a year. The inclusion of the Duchess was more than a little unfortunate, for her morals were none too good, and a few months later Narcissus Luttrell noted, ' The Dss. of Norfolk . . . hath been lately found in bed with one Jermyn, to her great scandal.'

In June the calm was broken by Monmouth's landing at Lyme Regis on the twenty-first of that month, and although the Protestant Duke's rising was crushed within a few weeks, forces were set in motion which were in due course to overturn James's throne. The upbringing and character of the King, which have already been discussed, explain his attitude on the morrow of Sedgemoor. Once Monmouth had been captured,

James was in the strongest possible position. All he had to do was to keep his nephew in the Tower, and so long as Monmouth was alive there was nothing to fear from William of Orange. It is true that popular discontent might have looked to the imprisoned Duke for a lead, but from the point of view of James it was better to have his only serious rival under lock and key in London than an independent potentate across the sea with an army and navy of his own. While Monmouth lived it is difficult to see how the Whigs could have run William as their candidate. Yet in spite of the manifest advantages to be gained from sparing his nephew's life, James refused to regard him in any other light than as a rebel who had incurred the death penalty. It may well be that Sunderland, who was playing a very deep game, intercepted the letter in which Monmouth told his uncle of the minister's treachery, but this in no way alters the fact that the King committed a blunder of the first magnitude when he sent his nephew to the scaffold.

The fact is that he completely misinterpreted the lesson of Monmouth's rising. He took its failure to mean that henceforth he had a free hand to do what he liked, whereas in reality it should have served as a signal not to go too far or too fast. What the defeat of Monmouth meant was that the country was intensely loyal to the Crown, and was in no mood for adventures; but the support which the invader received was a warning that an appeal to the Protestant sentiments of the English people would always meet with a ready response. The rebellion showed the necessity of proceeding slowly in religious matters, for there were still many Dissenters who were not prepared to accept the gift of toleration if they had to share it with Catholics. Had James received a political rather than a purely military and naval upbringing, he would certainly have regarded the failure of his nephew as a definite vote of confidence in himself, but also as an intimation that his subjects were still prone to be led astray by agitators. History shows that the suppression of a rebellion is so often either the making or the marring of a regime, and Sedgemoor merely encouraged in James that obstinacy and precipitance which are so often the most prominent characteristics of retired naval and military men in political life.

Monmouth's rising had no repercussions in Ireland. His cause, it is true, was unlikely to make any appeal to the native Irish, but in view of the unrest in the previous reign among the more extreme Protestants it would not have been surprising had there been stirrings in that particular quarter; not a dog barked, however, and the bulk of the army, seven thousand strong and intensely Protestant, allowed itself without demur to be moved into Ulster in case it was required to be shipped across to Scotland to deal with Argyll's insurrection in support of Monmouth, but its services were not wanted. All the same James decided that the Irish militia could not be trusted, and Talbot was entrusted with the task of disbanding it. Needless to say, this step caused considerable alarm in Protestant circles where the force was exclusively recruited.

It was at this time that the King gave the first proofs of his gratitude to the man who had served him so faithfully and so long, for on 20 June he elevated Talbot to the peerage of Ireland with the titles of Baron of Talbotstown, Viscount Baltinglas, and Earl of Tyrconnel on account of his 'immaculate allegiance and infinitely great services performed to the King, and to King Charles II, in England, Ireland and foreign parts, both by sea and land, in which he suffered frequent imprisonments and many grievous wounds'. In default of a son born to him by his wife the remainder was, firstly, to his nephew, Sir William Talbot, Bt. and his heirs male; and, secondly, to another nephew, William Talbot of Haggardstown, son of his brother Garrett. Richard was also raised to the rank of Lieutenant-General. All this was both natural and understandable, but what was neither the one nor the other was the appointment of the Second Earl of Clarendon as Lord-Lieutenant. He had all his father's narrowness of outlook without any of his ability, while he disliked Irishmen and Catholics in general, and Tyrconnel, as he must now be called, in particular. His idea was to rule Ireland by and for the English, and with Tyrconnel's nationalist sentiments he had no sympathy whatever. It is little

wonder that contemporaries were perplexed by the appointment, and that many of them assumed that the two men were
meant to neutralize one another. We know now that the elevation of Tyrconnel to the peerage and to the rank of Lieutenant-
General was as far as James felt he could safely go for the
moment, and that it was only the first step in a revolution of
the Irish administration.

For the rest of that year, 1685, Tyrconnel took no overt step
to put his theories into practice, though he was clearly giving
careful consideration to the best method of doing so. On 9
January 1686 the new Lord-Lieutenant reached Dublin, and
at once the clash came between him and Tyrconnel. Clarendon
had expected to meet Tyrconnel, who had been summoned by
the King to London, at Holyhead, but he sailed straight to
Chester, and so the two men did not meet: Clarendon at once
took this as a deliberate insult, and wrote to his brother,
Rochester:

> I wonder Lord Tyrconnel should take so much pains to have
> some people believe he would have put in at Holyhead if he
> could; when everybody here knows the wind was so fair that
> he might more easily have done it than have gone to Chester.
> But Captain Sheldon, who went over with him, hearing him
> speak so much in public, the morning he left this place, of
> stopping at Holyhead to see my Lord-Lieutenant, asked him,
> ' My Lord, why do you say this, when we all who go with you
> know that you do not intend it?' His answer was, ' Prithee let
> me alone: I know what I say.' When several persons here, Irish,
> asked His Lordship of me and concerning me, etc., his answer
> was that he knew nothing of me more than by sight; that he
> had no manner of acquaintance with me. This some of them-
> selves here have told me when they have heard me speak of
> him in discourse as one I was acquainted with. One cannot help
> smiling at this.

All this did not augur very well for the future co-operation
of the two men, and in the same letter Clarendon accuses
Tyrconnel of making trouble in Dublin before his own arrival
there. ' How is it possible to understand such a man?' the

Lord-Lieutenant continues. ' I speak not of him to anyone here but with that respect which is due to his quality and to one I have lived well with: though I cannot help hearing others speak slightly of him, which I discountenance all I can. Some few more of the extravagancies he has committed between Chester and London, in his last journey, will do his business.'[3] To what this last sentence refers is doubtful, but the wish was probably father to the thought.

The reason why Tyrconnel had gone to London at this particular juncture was because James wished to discuss with him a scheme, which had been in contemplation even before his brother's death, for making the Irish army a real safeguard to the dynasty instead of being merely a garrison to protect the settlers against the Irish; this, in the King's view, involved its transformation from a Protestant into a Catholic force in spite of its loyalty to the Crown during Monmouth's rebellion. The first step in this direction was to separate the civil from the military administration, and this had been done with the removal of Ormonde. Tyrconnel now received his instructions for the next move, and they included a definition of Clarendon's position which laid down that he was not to enjoy the same military power as his predecessors at Dublin Castle. Before Tyrconnel returned to Ireland he went for a cure to Bath, for he was a martyr to gout, and it was not until 5 June 1686 that Clarendon is found writing to Rochester, ' To-day about noon, notice was brought to me that the yacht was in the bay: upon which I sent my coach to Dunlary to meet my Lord Tyrconnel. He first set down his lady at his house and then came to the Castle.'

From then until the resignation of Clarendon in February of the following year there was constant friction between the two men, a friction which left no part of the Irish administration unaffected. For information concerning it we are largely dependent upon Clarendon's own letters, and although these necessarily represent one point of view it is possible to arrive, if not at the truth, at any rate at an approximation to it, by reading between the lines.

Tyrconnel's visit to the Castle on the day of his arrival was a brief one, and after making an appointment for the following afternoon to discuss the matter of the commissions which he had brought from England with him, he said that ' he longed to be out of town and to despatch the business of the army, that he might go over again into England to attend his health '. The next day, which was a Sunday, he dined at the Castle, and in Clarendon's private room after dinner he urged the speedy delivery of the commissions to enable him to leave Dublin in the near future, ' for he longed to make haste back into England for his health, which is every foot the burden of his song '. At this point the Lord-Lieutenant thought that his visitor was about to take his leave, but such was not the case, and the following conversation ensued:

My Lord, began Tyrconnel, I am sent hither to view this army, and to give the King an account of it. Here are great alterations to be made; and the poor people who are put out think it my doing; and, God damn me, I have little or nothing to do in the matter. For I told the King I knew not two of the captains nor other inferior officers in the whole army. I know there are some hard cases, which I am sorry for; but, by God, I know not how to help them. You must know, my Lord, the King, who is a Roman Catholic, is resolved to employ his subjects of that religion, as you will find by the letters I have brought you, and therefore some must be put out to make room for such as the King likes. And I can tell you another thing, the King will not keep one man in his service who ever served under the usurpers.

Clarendon replied that this advice was quite unnecessary, for he never enquired into the reasons for which any man was put in or out of the army; it was his duty to obey the King's commands. He then went on to mention a Lieutenant-Colonel Maguire, a ' hard case ' in his opinion among many others, for he was a man of merit. To this Tyrconnel replied:

My Lord, you do not know all: besides all you have said I will tell you what I know to be true. That gentleman, in the late years of persecution, received and sheltered all the poor Catholics who came to him; and, by God, to have him now laid aside is a terrible thing. But my Lord, when that is done, I would not have you represent any of their cases, which will anger the King and perplex him.

At this point the Lord-Lieutenant referred to the resolution not to employ any who had served under the Commonwealth or the Protectorate, and he expressed the hope that it would not be strictly enforced, although he must have known that it was going to be. In the course of his remarks he let slip the fact that some in this category were still serving, whereupon Tyrconnel, who had admitted that he was personally unfamiliar with the officers of the army but was avid for information concerning them, flared out, ' Who are they who are now employed who ever served the usurpers?' Clarendon realized that he had gone too far, so he proceeded to hedge, and in spite of Tyrconnel's pressure he refused to mention any names. ' And so,' he told his brother, ' I left His Lordship to find out whom I meant.'

The conversation then drifted to the Acts of Settlement, provoking from Tyrconnel the statement, ' By God, my Lord, these Acts of Settlement and this New Interest are damned things!' The number of oaths put into Tyrconnel's mouth is impressive, but it may well be that they were never uttered, merely being included in the narrative because they were what Clarendon's correspondents would expect from any Talbot. However this may be, on this particular occasion either Tyrconnel's language or the subject under discussion caused the Lord-Lieutenant to slip, for in deprecating any further discussion along these lines, he said, ' Neither you nor I are well informed of all the motives and inducements which carried on those affairs twenty-six years since.' To say this to Dick Talbot of all people was hardly tactful, and easily deserved the retort, ' Yes, we do know all those arts and damned roguery contrivances which procured those Acts.' To this Clarendon could only somewhat feebly reply, ' My Lord, I do not know what you mean.'

The two men continued talking for an hour and a half, when Tyrconnel put an end to the conversation with the words,

' Well, I will say no more at present: but, by God, my Lord,
there have been foul damned things done here.'

Next morning Tyrconnel was at the Castle by nine o'clock,
and he was in frequent session with Clarendon until 26 August,
when he set sail for England ' to make projects for Bills '. What
he had in mind the Lord-Lieutenant had no difficulty in guess-
ing, for, he wrote to Rochester, ' By the discourses he and his
friends make here, they are such as will turn this kingdom
topsy-turvy.' Already alarm and despondency were spreading
among the colonists, who began to recall the horrors of the
past hundred years, being fully conscious of the fact that the
Irish had to avenge not only the old wrongs of Elizabethan
days, but also the more recent enormities of Drogheda and
Wexford; it may even be that some of them regretted that they
themselves had not been more magnanimous in the hour of
victory as they saw the forces arrayed against them almost
hourly gaining strength. The appointment of a number of
Catholics, including Tyrconnel himself, to the Privy Council;
the orders for the admission of Catholics into the corporations
and various offices; and the steady progress made in the remod-
elling of the army, revealing the projected Romanization of the
force: these would be sufficient to cause consternation in a less
nervous community than that of the guilt-conscious colonists
in seventeenth-century Ireland.

In his letters Clarendon complains that Tyrconnel was unduly peppery during this period of negotiation, and if such was
the case, as it may well have been, ill-health in the shape of
gout was probably the cause, as it was of a good deal of indiscreet talk in public. There was certainly a flare-up between the
two men on the subject of sheriffs, when Tyrconnel burst out,
' By God, my Lord, I must needs tell you the sheriffs you made
are generally rogues and old Cromwellians. But I justified Your
Excellency to the King, and told him you were not to be
blamed; that you could not at that time know people yourself,
and were advised by the late Chancellor.' The Lord-Lieutenant
demurred to the effect that generally speaking these sheriffs
were ' as good a set of men as any that had been chosen these

dozen years'; only, however, to be told, 'By God, I believe it, for there has not been an honest man sheriff in Ireland these twenty years.' Tyrconnel was certainly touchy on the subject of the sheriffs, for on another occasion, when Clarendon denied that he was partial in Irish matters, Tyrconnel exclaimed, 'By God, my Lord, you must not wonder if the Catholics do think you a little partial after your making such a lot of sheriffs, who are four parts of five rogues.'

During the greater part of these summer months Tyrconnel seems to have been residing with Frances at Carton, which he renamed Talbotstown, probably at the time he received his peerage, but his gout was very bad, and whenever possible he tried to combine a cure with his inspection of the troops. He had hoped to get back to England to make his report to James before the end of August, but he was not well enough, though Clarendon refused to believe that he was ill at all, and it was not until the twenty-sixth that he finally went on board a boat for Chester. At the same time the Lord-Lieutenant took the precaution of writing a letter both to the King and to the Queen putting his side of the case.

The Tyrconnels spent the autumn of 1686 in England – Frances attending to her duties at Court, and Richard intriguing to obtain Clarendon's post as Lord-Lieutenant. This latter occupation has been strongly condemned by historians of the school of Macaulay, though it is difficult to see why this should be the case. At long last he had the opportunity which he had been seeking all his life, that is to see Ireland administered in accordance with the wishes of the majority, not the minority, of her people. His career, it is true, had been as varied as that of any man in those stormy days, but he had himself always been loyal to his country, his faith, and his King, and in spite of numerous temptations he remained loyal to them to the end. His tragedy was that his opportunity came too late from the point of view of his health. He was in his fifty-seventh year – a much greater age then than it is now – and he had lived a hard life. Activity and energy were specially needed in the task that lay before him, but owing to his physical condition they were the qualities with which he was least well provided. On the other hand he knew exactly what he wanted to do, and if any man could transfer the ruling power from the hands of the Protestant minority to those of the Catholic majority, he had the knowledge of Irish affairs and the courage of his opinions to do so.

Neither in London nor in Dublin was there any doubt as to the direction in which events were moving, and men's suspicions were confirmed when on 8 October Tyrconnel was made a member of the English Privy Council. With the beginning of the new year events moved rapidly, and on 11 January Tyrconnel left London for Ireland; at Chester he stayed with that great loyalist the Bishop, Thomas Cartwright, who later landed with James at Kinsale. Thereafter the weather turned against him, and at Holyhead he was detained so long by contrary winds that it was not until 6 February that he reached Dublin. Tyrconnel then sent his secretary, Thomas Sheridan,[4] to Clarendon with a letter from the King instructing him to deliver the sword of office to Tyrconnel within a week after his arrival; this order was not, however, as unexpected as might be supposed, for in addition to the rumours which had been going round Clarendon had already had an official intimation from the Secretary of State, Lord Sunderland, as to what he was required to do.

After all the wrangling between the two men it is pleasant to be able to record that they parted, at any rate outwardly, on good terms. Clarendon only records two meetings with his successor before he left, and at the first of these, a visit paid by Tyrconnel to Dublin Castle, the conversation was purely informal, but when the Lord-Lieutenant returned it Tyrconnel met him on the stairs, and begged him not to leave the Castle before it was convenient to him to do so. The sword was delivered up to Tyrconnel in the presence of the Privy Council on 12 February 1687,[5] and Clarendon could not have been more pleasant, though one sting might have been detected in his allusion to the troubled politics of Ireland: ' The King hath placed Your Excellency in a very great station; has committed to your care the government of a great and flourishing kingdom, of a dutiful, loyal, and obedient people. It is extremely to be lamented that there are such feuds and animosities among them, which I hope Your Excellency's prudence, with the assistance of so wise a Cabinet, will disperse.'

As may be supposed when Tyrconnel arrived in Dublin it had been with full instructions signed by Sunderland. Dalton[6] quotes them from the original document, and the most important are as follows:

Having, upon serious consideration for the peace, prosperity, and good government of Our Kingdom of Ireland, made choice of you for effecting these ends, as a person of approved loyalty, wisdom, courage, moderation, and integrity, to represent Our Royal person there, and caused Letters patent to be passed therefor, We doubt not but you will pursue all prudent courses for the good government and increase of the profits of the same; and for the better enabling you to do so, We give full power and authority unto you to keep the peace, the laws, and commendable customs of Our said Kingdom, to govern all Our people there, to chastise and correct offenders, and to countenance and encourage such as shall do well; and We do also think fit to prescribe unto you some things which will be necessary for you to observe in your government; and therefor We do direct and enjoin you forthwith to inform yourself of the present state of that Kingdom, in all parts thereof, and what is therein amiss, and by what means the same may be best provided for, and thereof transmit an account . . .

We do well know how much it concerns the happiness of Our subjects, as well as the reputation of Our Government, that there be an equal and impartial administration of justice in Our ordinary Courts, and therefore it must be your particular care to enquire diligently into the same . . .

You shall, as soon as conveniently may be after your arrival, order an exact muster to be taken of all Our forces there, so that it may appear if each regiment, company or troop be effectually of the number it ought to be and which We allow upon the pay-rolls . . . and you shall then and there cause the following oath, and no other, to be administered to all officers and soldiers of the Army, and to all governors of towns, forts, and castles; and such of them as shall refuse the said oath, you are to cashier and dismiss the service . . .[7]

Having directed your predecessor in that government to give orders for disarming all disaffected or suspected persons there, and to require the sheriffs of the several counties to give in an account what arms there were in each and in whose hands, and to give order also that the arms which have been bought up by the several counties, or were in the hands of the militia, should be brought into Our stores: Our pleasure is that you inform yourself what has been done in pursuance of these directions and give such further order as shall be requisite for having the same effectually executed. You are further to give order that the arms which were taken from Our Catholic subjects in the year 1678, upon Oats' pretended discovery of a plot, be forthwith restored to them; and, Our intention being that they should be in the same capacity with Our other subjects of being sheriffs, justices of the peace, etc., as they were heretofore, and that they should be admitted to all the privileges and freedoms which Our other subjects enjoy in all ports and corporations, you are to take care thereof accordingly, and give orders therein from time to time as shall be requisite.

To carry out these instructions Tyrconnel took three measures as soon as he became Lord Deputy — one related to the civic charters, another to the abuse of the pulpits as places for the propagation of political views, and a third to the control and reorganization of the army, with which, as may be imagined, little had been done during Clarendon's term of office at Dublin Castle.

The local councils, as we have seen, were entirely in the hands of the Protestants, and had been since the days of Cromwell. Catholics were ineligible for a seat on them, and whenever a change was adumbrated the charters were invoked in support of the *status quo*. In very moderate language Tyrconnel proposed that members of both religions should be placed upon an equal footing, but this suggestion was met with a defiant rejection; whereupon the Lord Deputy invoked the Royal prerogative, as Charles II had done in similar circumstances towards the end of his reign, and issued an Order in

Council calling in the charters. Some local authorities acquiesced without demur, but others protested; among the latter were Dublin and Derry. The capital even went so far as to send its Recorder to London to protest, but James refused him an audience, and ordered him to return to Dublin; the matter was then referred to the courts, which decided almost without discussion that the King could cancel or suspend whatever charters had been granted by the Crown, so finally all were surrendered. There was, in James's own words, ' no great trouble except at Londonderry (a stubborn people, as they appeared to be afterwards), who stood an obstinate suit, but were forced at last to undergo the same fate with the rest '. It is difficult to disagree with Tyrconnel's attitude in this matter for it was only just that the Corporations should be open to all Irishmen irrespective of their religious convictions.

The second matter to which the Lord Deputy turned his attention was the suppression of political oratory from the pulpit. An Order in Council was duly issued, with a warning as to the penalties that persistence in this course would entail, and with pointed reference to ' a few fiery spirits in the pulpit who seek to discuss matters that do not appertain to them, and who declare that the King intends to rule by a new and arbitrary law '. What James did intend was that the Catholic majority in Ireland, who outnumbered their Protestant fellow-countrymen by at least ten to one, should have equal rights with them.

Thirdly there were the measures relating to the armed forces, and these were the most important part of Tyrconnel's programme: the Protestant militia had already been disarmed, and the next task was to build up a regular army which should be reliable. It was to be used for two purposes: one was to supplement the royal forces in England, and the other was to uphold the new dispensation in Ireland itself. A great deal of ink has been spilt by historians over the alleged iniquity of James in bringing Irish troops into England, but it is difficult to understand why this should have been reprehensible: English troops had been poured into Ireland for centuries without arousing

L

any criticism on moral grounds, and there would not appear
to be any reason why Irish soldiers should not be moved in the
opposite direction. On the other hand if James committed no
crime he certainly perpetrated a monumental blunder.[8] The
Irish were not in sufficient numbers to affect the issue, while
their presence enabled his enemies to suggest that he contem-
plated terrorizing England with them. Had the King himself
put up any effective resistance to William the case might have
been very different, but as it was the Irish were useless for all
practical purposes, and were eventually interned in the Isle of
Wight, whence in due course a number of them gradually
filtered back to their own country.

In August 1687 Tyrconnel crossed to England to meet James
and to report on what he was doing to fulfil the instructions
which he had been given on his appointment as Lord Deputy.
The King was on a progress through the West of England,
and Tyrconnel met him at Shrewsbury, thereafter accompanying
him to Chester, where they spent two days together. The dis-
cussions which ensued were naturally held in complete privacy,
but even in these early days James seems to have shown that
there were limits beyond which he would not go in meeting
Irish demands, and one of them was to agree to the repeal of
the Acts of Settlement. For the rest, some extracts from a letter
which Tyrconnel wrote to his master eighteen months later, on
29 January 1689, may afford a clue to the programme which
was discussed at Shrewsbury and Chester.

> Your Ma'tys Kingdome of Ireland is divided into four Pro-
> vinces, vis. Leinster, Munster, Connaught, and Ulster. The
> Catholiques of the Citty of Dublin in Leinster may be guessed
> to equall all other Religions there (not including the soldiers,
> who are all Catholiques). The Catholiques in the rest of that
> Province are forty to one of the people of all other Persuasions.
> The Catholique inhabitants of the Province of Munster are
> thought to be forty to one of all other Persuasions. In the Pro-
> vince of Connaught the Catholiques are two hundred to one
> of all other Persuasions. The Catholiques of Ulster are not soe
> considerable, by reason of the greater number of Scotch Pres-

byterians there, yett may be thought to be as many as all the rest. The said four Provinces contain thirty-two Counties or Shires well planted and inhabited by a numerous people not easily reckon'd; all the Catholiques are unanimous and most zalously affected to your Ma'tys service, but amongst the Protestants, generally tainted with the Principles of England, there are not in the whole Kingdome one hundred that may be relyed on to serve your Ma'ty. . .

There are four Regiments of Old Troopes, and one Battalion of the Regiment of Guards and three Regiments of Horse with one Troop of Grenadiers on Horseback. I have given out Commissions for neare forty Regiments of Foot, four Regiments of Dragoons and two of Horse, all which amount to neare 40,000 men, who are all uncloathed and the greatest part unarmed, and are to be subsisted by their severall officers untill the last of Feb'y next out of their owne purses, to the ruin of most of them; but after that day I see noe possibility for arming them, clothing them or subsisting them for the future but abandoning the Country to them: but after all if I may be supplied by the last of March with those succours that are necessary which I press in my letters, I doubt not but that I shall preserve this Kingdome entirely for yr. Ma'ty.

This, however, is to anticipate, but it shows what was in Tyrconnel's mind when he discussed the Irish situation with James eighteen months earlier.

He had at this time no domestic ties to distract his attention from his duties as Lord Deputy, for from the date of her departure from Dublin with her husband at the end of August 1686 until the same month in 1688 Frances would not appear to have visited Ireland. Her duties in attendance upon the Queen kept her fully occupied, and even when Tyrconnel and his master were communing on the Welsh border she got no nearer to them than Bath, where Mary of Modena was taking the waters. In London she had rooms assigned to her at St James's Palace, and there she lived with her daughters by her two marriages. However, not long after the birth of the Prince of Wales on 10 June she was released from her Court duties, and rejoined her husband in Ireland.

By this time Irish politics were much under the influence of the progress of events in England, where the atmosphere was very heavily charged with suspicion even before James began to show his hand; it was obvious that to carry his plans through would require no inconsiderable amount of that quality in which he was so conspicuously lacking, namely tact. Had he proceeded slowly all might still have been well, but he acted in a most precipitate manner, and what was worse he made some extremely bad appointments. Edward Sclater, Curate of Putney, for example was a pluralist and a time-server, yet he was allowed to keep his emoluments after conversion to Rome on condition of paying a substitute. This was a definite allocation of Church money away from the Establishment for the benefit of an arrant rogue. Still worse was the appointment of a convert to be Dean of Christ Church, for the Dean is not only head of an Oxford College but also a high ecclesiastical dignitary of the Church of England. The interference with the universities of Oxford and Cambridge was in due course followed by the trial of the Seven Bishops for refusing to read the Edict of Toleration, and this had the effect of making the Anglican episcopate really popular for the first and last time in its existence.

The chief reason for the failure of James was not, however, his lack of tact, but his haste, though the two were closely connected. Nevertheless, his motives are intelligible. He was fifty-one years of age when he ascended the throne, and as he was already the only surviving son of Charles I he had no reason to suppose that he had long to live. His heirs were his daughters, Mary and Anne, and as both were strong Protestants, married to Protestant husbands, there was little chance of them doing anything for his co-religionists, though he had as yet no suspicion that they were cast for the parts of Goneril and Regan. It thus seemed to him that what he had to do must be done quickly. Had James known in 1685 that he had another sixteen years of life before him, and that he would be succeeded by his son, he might have proceeded more gradually, and so have achieved his aim. It must be confessed that this assumption is problematical for with all his faults he was too straightforward to be a successful politician.

If time was needed for the Royal plans to mature in England, it was in equal demand in Ireland, where Tyrconnel had to build up a new regime from scratch. An extract from one of the last letters he wrote, on 3 October, to James as *de facto* King of England, testifies to this very clearly:

> I have writ at large by Sarsfield to yr. Ma'ty yesterday, and will not give yr. Ma'ty any other trouble in this but to beg of you to read my letter of this day's date to my lord president, and to consider well the necessetye thear is for yr. service, of dispatcheing with all speed what I desired in it, as well as what I writ to yr. Ma'ty yesterday, being much the same thing. I beg, sir, I may have a quick dispatch to my letters, for noe time is to be lost in raysing new forces: I shall make them subsist as well as I can, tho the Revenue do fale, w'ch it will certainly doe out of hand, for all trade is now given over hear, because of this invasion, but wee have plenty of meat and drink here, tho wee have noe money. The Lord Jesus bless you and preserve you from the power of your enemys. Wold to God your sonn were hear in safety; remember, sir, that Portsmouth is the worst ayre in the world.

One month after this letter was written William of Orange disembarked at Torbay, and the Revolution of 1688 had begun. The contrast between his landing and that of Monmouth is not uninteresting, for which the ' Protestant Duke ' had arrived at Lyme Regis with a mere handful of conspirators he was soon joined by numbers of the peasants and artisans of the district, if not by the magnates. Since then the West had experienced the rigours of the law as administered by the Lord Chief Justice, and William met with the most frigid of receptions, in spite of the fact that, unlike Monmouth, he had a considerable body of seasoned troops with him. Above all, the navy was in a position to cut the Dutch line of communication, and the army had been very considerably increased both in numbers and efficiency since its victory at Sedgemoor.

The vacillation of the King ruined everything. He had already shown signs of panic in things political, and he now displayed the same characteristics in things military. He advanced to Salisbury with every apparent intention of fighting for his crown, and although a few men of note had already joined his rival, the situation was far from unfavourable. There was some disaffection in the higher command, it is true, but Dundee and Sarsfield could be trusted implicitly, and Churchill would have remained with the King had his cause prospered. All the evidence points to the loyalty of the rank and file, so it is obvious that the right policy for James was to engage the enemy at once before any widespread demoralization set in among his own forces. Had he done that, and appealed to the national dislike of foreigners to rouse his subjects against the Dutch, the issue would hardly have been in doubt. Instead, James seems to have had no other end in view than to play for time while the Queen and the Prince of Wales made good their escape from the country.[9] Although he was at Salisbury within a fortnight of William's landing he allowed the fact that his nose was bleeding to reduce him to complete inaction. This decided Churchill that he was on the losing side, so he went over to William.

This proved to be the beginning of the end. James returned to London without making any sort or resistance and tamely allowed the Dutch troops to take possession of the capital; then he made two attempts to escape, the first of which he bungled, and finally he arrived at Ambleteuse on Christmas Day, and from there he went on to join his wife and son, who had proceeded him under the escort of the Duc de Lauzun, at Saint Germain-en-Laye. Among those of his followers who fell into William's hands was Richard Hamilton, who by pretending that he favoured the new regime got himself sent to Dublin in the hope that he might seduce Tyrconnel from his allegiance, which he had no intention of doing even if the Lord Deputy was willing to be seduced.

It only remains to add that immediately upon his arrival at Saint Germain the fallen monarch began to make active preparations to recover the crowns which he had lost, and so persistent were his applications to Louis for help that it is difficult to resist the conclusion that had James displayed as much energy in defending his throne as he did in attempting to regain it the events of the preceding autumn might have ended very differently. The situation, too, in the opening months of 1689 was far from discouraging in view of the fact that in Scotland the Highlands were in arms under Dundee, while Tyrconnel had seen to it that the greater part of Ireland refused to recognize the Revolution. Such being the case, the French Government felt justified in giving some assistance to the Jacobites, though strictly on the principle of limited liability, and with the ultimate purpose, not of restoring James to the three kingdoms he had lost, but rather of weakening William and his allies in Flanders. A bargain was therefore made, by which Louis agreed to lend his cousin a contingent of French troops for a campaign in Ireland, but only on condition that an equal number of Irish recruits was enlisted for the service of France.

NOTES

[1] Bulstrode, Sir Richard: *Memoirs,* pp. 424-425. London. 1721.

[2] *Cf.* George, R. H.: *Parliamentary Elections and Electioneering in 1685, Transactions of the Royal Historical Society,* Fourth Series, Vol. XIX, pp. 167-195. London. 1936.

[3] *State Letters of Henry, Earl of Clarendon.* Letter of 23 January 1686. London. 1765.

[4] Clarendon called him a 'wicked cheating man', and after his dismissal by Tyrconnel for dishonesty he became his bitterest and most unscrupulous enemy.

[5] Tyrconnel was Lord Deputy whereas Clarendon was Lord-Lieutenant.

[6] *King James's Army List,* Vol. I, pp. 53-55.

[7] Then follows a simple form of oath to be true and faithful to the King etc., with no religious implications.

[8] As he did in bringing Dundee and the Scottish army south.

[9] Even so, it is not easy to see why he did not send them to Ireland, as Tyrconnel suggested, rather than to France.

CHAPTER VIII

King James in Ireland

ONCE THE agreement between James and Louis had been made no time was lost by the French in preparing the Royal exile for his Irish expedition, and by the end of February 1689 everything was ready. A number of senior French officers were chosen to accompany James. They were von Rosen, Lieutenant-General, an Alsatian, as Berwick has recorded, ' to command the army under Tyrconnel; M. de Maumont, Major-General, to serve as Lieutenant-General; and MM. de Pusignan and Léry, Brigadiers to be Major-Generals; Boisseleau, a captain in the Guards, was sent to be Adjutant-General; and L'Estrade Guidon in the Life Guards, to be Quartermaster-General of Cavalry.'[1] Above all, as the personal envoy of Louis was the Comte d'Avaux, perhaps the ablest diplomat in the French service. Among the English were, in addition to Berwick himself, his brother the Grand Prior, and Anthony Hamilton. James went to Versailles to take leave of the French King, and as he left Louis said to him, ' I hope never to see you again, but if fate wills that we should meet once more, you will find me as you have always found me.' The expedition was due to sail from Brest, but before it actually got off the ship which was carrying James was fouled by another, and her bowsprit was carried away. This necessitated a return to port for repairs, and the fleet did not finally put to sea until 22 March; on the fifth day after leaving Brest the squadron dropped anchor in Kinsale Bay.

The evidence regarding the King's movements during the next few days is scanty and conflicting, for the civic records of Cork for this period are missing, and whether or not it is true that history repeats itself there can be no doubt that the historians of Cork repeat one another.[2] What is established is that Tyrconnel was not at Kinsale when James arrived, but that the King was greeted there by Justin MacCarthy, shortly to be created Viscount Mountcashel and Baron of Castleinch; Chief Justice Nugent; and the Earl of Clancarty; and was conducted to the Mansion House in Fisher Street.[3] With them he discussed the existing state of Ireland, and present at this conference was d'Avaux. As soon as Tyrconnel heard of his master's arrival he left Dublin, where he had been detained on official business, for the South, but James had reached Cork by the time the two men met. Where this meeting took place is in some doubt, for the statement that James stayed in the Bishop's palace is capable of two interpretations, for it may refer to the palace by the Protestant cathedral,[4] or to one at Bishopstown, a few miles outside the city of which the ruins are extensive, and partly inhabited at the present time. It was not Tyrconnel's first visit to Cork, for he had been there in 1686 when he was given a civic reception by the then Mayor, Christopher Crofts.

Of the warmth of the Royal greeting there can, however, be no doubt, and this is attested by an anonymous contemporary manuscript discovered in Vienna earlier in the present century.[5]

The King of England having arrived at Kinsale the Earl of Tyrconnel came to Cork to receive His Majesty. Could he have gratified the impatience which he had to see him, he would have come to the very spot where he had disembarked, or even further, had it been possible, but his presence was necessary in the heart of the kingdom to maintain all things in their place. He came to see His Majesty followed by the guards allowed him by his quality of viceroy, who he brought to accompany the King. There were besides these a hundred gentlemen on horseback, brought by their anxiety to see and pay their respects to His Majesty. The King did him an honour which sovereigns rarely pay to their subjects, for having perceived him, he advanced to meet him at the door of the chamber and embraced him. He gave him the praises due to the unshakeable firmness which he had shown in his service, and did him the honour not only to make him dine at his table, but sat him at his right and the Duke of Berwick at his left.

In a word, the King gave him all the marks and signs of satisfaction which were due to such a subject, and testified his esteem by creating him duke. After he had received an exact account of all the affairs of Ireland, His Majesty held a council, in which the new duke had the honour to take part. The whole Court of the King congratulated him on his noble firmness and the fidelity to his legitimate sovereign of which he had given proof, so that he tasted now all the pleasure that a true gentleman can experience when he has done what his honour and duty demand of him. The King of France so valued the merits of this Earl of Tyrconnel as to send him the Cordon Bleu and a casket containing twelve thousand louis.

There can be no doubt as to the views of the vast majority of the inhabitants of County Cork, but there were one or two pockets of resistance, such as Bandon and Drimoleague. Bandon had been founded by the ' Great ' Earl of Cork in 1608 and was part of the Protestant plantation of Munster. One of its gates is said to have borne the legend, ' Turk, Jew, or Atheist may enter here, but not a Papist ', which was capped by a Catholic wit who added, ' Who wrote this wrote it well, for the same is written on the gates of Hell '.

If there is some doubt as to the exact spot in Cork where Tyrconnel met the King there can be none as to the encouraging report which he made to him. The whole of Leinster, Munster, and Connacht was in Jacobite hands, and even in Ulster only Derry and Enniskillen, among the towns of any importance, acknowledged William. The plan of campaign, too, was clear enough, for it was to subdue the entire kingdom before the Dutchman could set foot in it, and then to send such a force to Scotland as would enable Dundee to obtain complete control of that country. Actually, the meeting between the monarch and the Lord Deputy was one between two ageing men, neither of whom had worn well, for both were only in their late fifties. Berwick, a shrewd observer of men if ever there was one, wrote of Tyrconnel at this time, ' He was a man of very good sense, very obliging, but immoderately vain, and full of cunning. He had not a military genius, but much courage. After the Prince of Orange's invasion, his firmness preserved Ireland, and he nobly refused all the offers that were made to induce him to submit.' On the other hand, Berwick was of the opinion that as the campaign progressed Tyrconnel deteriorated rapidly, for he continued, ' From the battle of the Boyne he sank prodigiously, being become as irresolute in his mind as unwieldly in his body.'[6]

James and Tyrconnel were old friends, and they thoroughly understood one another, but it was otherwise with their followers, who fell into four main groups. First of all were the English who had come with the King from France. They regarded Ireland as a mere stepping-stone to Whitehall, and they hoped to return there without having in the process surrendered too much authority to the native Irish. Then there were the Anglo-Irish, comprising such families as the Dillons, Nugents, Plunketts, and Talbots, who had long been resident in Ireland; they were, in fact, Irishmen, but owing to historical associations they had a definite allegiance to the British Crown. Many of them belonged to, or were connected with, the old Pale families, and their point of view was that of their fathers in the Confederate was as described on an earlier page. They were Catholics who were ready to fight to regain their lands, and to re-establish the open practice of their religion, but they had no desire to sever the connection with England. Originally, as we have seen, they had regarded their Celtic fellow-countrymen with more than a little suspicion – an attitude which was fully reciprocated, but adversity during the Cromwellian persecution had done a great deal to modify these feelings. They were, in effect, what a later generation would have described as Home Rulers, but they were not hostile to England.

Next came the Old Irish, who were to form by far the largest part of the Jacobite army and who were the most ardent supporters of the Stuarts. In so far as they were politically conscious at all, their aim was to set up an independent Ireland,

and they welcomed James as a means of achieving that end; in any scheme for the reconquest of England they were not interested at all. Lastly, there were the French, of whom the most important was the Comte d'Avaux, the ambassador of Louis XIV. According to Berwick he was ' a man of sense, and had acquired reputation in the different embassies he had been employed in ', but James grew ' dissatisfied with his haughty and disrespectful manner of conducting himself'[7] and d'Avaux was recalled before the end of the year.[8] He and his compatriots were chiefly animated by the desire to attract William from the Low Countries to Ireland, and that with as little loss of life as possible among the subjects of *Le Grand Monarque*. It was, in short, a situation that might have daunted a statesman of the very first order, and as it had to be faced by men of no outstanding ability it is hardly surprising that Jacobite hopes were more apparent than real.

From Cork to Dublin the King's journey was a triumphal procession; indeed, so much was this the case that we are told that in Carlow he ' was slobbered with the kisses of the rude country Irishwomen, so that he was forced to beg to have them kept from him '. Very wisely, Tyrconnel drove in d'Avaux's carriage as far as Lismore, and he seems to have taken full advantage of the opportunity to make a favourable impression on the French ambassador.

On 24 March James made his formal entry into Dublin. Tyrconnel, bearing the sword of state, preceded him, while surrounding him were the Comte d'Avaux, the Dukes of Berwick and Powis, and the Earls of Melfort and Granard. Behind were the Irish, Scottish, and English gentlemen of his household, while to meet him there came out from the capital the old Anglo-Irish nobility in their coaches-and-six. The Catholic clergy were there too, with the Host aloft, as well as the aldermen of Dublin in their robes. It was a gay scene, at once symbolic of Irish traditions and of Irish hopes. ' Forty beautiful damsels scattered flowers upon the royal path, tapestry waved across the streets, every window glowed with loveliness, and a countless multitude vociferated *Céad Míle Fáilte*.'[9] James was the first English monarch to visit Ireland since Richard II, and it is worthy of note that in these early days of the war the line of division of opinion was by no means wholly religious as some authorities would have us believe. The King, it may be noted in this connection, was accompanied to Ireland by Thomas Cartwright, Bishop of Chester, and he was welcomed to Cork by the Protestant Bishop, Edward Wetenhall; furthermore, contrary to what might have been expected, Christ Church Cathedral was the only Protestant place of worship in Dublin that was handed over to the Roman Catholics for their use.

It must have been with a considerable feeling of accomplishment that Tyrconnel participated in the formal entry of James into Dublin, but he is unlikely to have been under any illusions regarding the difficulty of the task that lay ahead. The King was himself a definite embarrassment, and it is doubtful whether Tyrconnel realized how much he had degenerated during his three and a half years on the throne. D'Avaux, in his very first letter to Louis from Kinsale, warned his master that ' our chief difficulty will be the irresolution of King James, who often changes his mind, and then decides not always for the best '.[10] The real cause of the inability of the French ambassador, as later of Tyrconnel, to see eye-to-eye with the King was the latter's determination to abandon Ireland at the very first opportunity he could of crossing over to England or Scotland. This was in the main sound strategy, but it broke down for a variety of reasons, not the least of which was the failure of the French to use their superiority at sea to prevent William from sending troops to assist his supporters in Ireland. To the credit of James he did urge upon his French allies the advisability of establishing a naval base in Dublin Bay, but he was politely told to mind his own business; it is, however, interesting to note that his sense of sound strategy had not entirely deserted him.

Although temporarily dependent upon them, James did not like the Irish, and in this attitude he was encouraged by his English and Scottish advisers. Though himself a Catholic he

shared the traditional dislike which was then felt by English
Catholics for their Irish co-religionists and which is by no
means extinct even today. He also realized that Protestant
England would never allow him to be restored to his throne by
Catholic Ireland, towards whom it had for so long pursued a
policy of genocide. In these circumstances, it would be no
exaggeration to say that the King's mind was set on returning
to London at the earliest possible moment, getting as much
as he could out of the Irish in the meantime, and doing as
little as he could for them – certainly not doing anything that
might alienate the English.

At first Tyrconnel was not opposed to an eventual link-up
with the Scots, and on the King's arrival at Kinsale he wrote to
the Duke of Hamilton:

> If I were not very persuaded that you are the self-same Duke
> of Hamilton in all things that you were when I had the honour
> to be known to Your Grace, I should not venture to assure you
> of my most humble service and respects at this time, nor inform
> you that upon Tuesday last, the 12th, of this month, our King
> arrived at Kinsale, in the West of this kingdom, with a fleet of
> thirty-seven sail of ships, with arms for 24,000 foot, 4,000
> dragoons, and 4,000 horse, and, which is better, 800,000 French
> crowns in ready money. This news, I am confident, will be wel-
> come to Your Grace, as also that I have 50,000 horse, foot, and
> dragoons raised for him here, well armed and disciplined. The
> King brought over with him 200 French and Irish officers, some
> of which were wanted. This good posture of His Majesty's affairs
> will, I hope, encourage Your Grace to stick by him and your-
> selves. I hope before the end of July to have the honour to
> embrace you in Scotland.[11]

Tyrconnel's real views must to some extent be a matter of
conjecture, and his letter to the Duke of Hamilton, with its
optimism concerning the Jacobite strength in Ireland, was
clearly written for propaganda purposes. He was reluctant to
have the King out of Dublin at that particular moment because,
as Parliament was about to meet, he wanted James there to
ensure the passage of certain nationalist legislation which was

very near to his own heart but to which he knew that his master, together with the English and Scottish Jacobites, were opposed; their idea was to get the King out of Ireland before he had time to give way to Irish pressure. The Old Irish of course agreed with Tyrconnel, and so did d'Avaux, for Louis desired above all things to see James firmly established in Ireland, and uncommitted to dangerous enterprises in other directions in which he was not prepared to assist.

French policy was at once consistent and realistic, and it merits close examination if the differences in the Jacobite ranks in the summer of 1689 are to be appreciated. Ireland had only recently entered into the calculations of French statesmen. France and England had been enemies for centuries, but it had hitherto been to Edinburgh rather than to Dublin that Paris had turned for support against their common foe; ever since Edward I had endeavoured to subjugate the northern kingdom at the end of the thirteenth, and beginning of the fourteenth century it had been Scottish policy to work in alliance with France, and for England a war with one Power nearly always led to hostilities with the other. From the French point of view this Edinburgh-Paris axis had everything to recommend it, for it meant that England was perpetually threatened with a war on two fronts: in effect the rôle played by the Turks, the Poles, and the Swedes in relation to the Empire was enacted by the Scots where England was concerned, that is to say they were allies of France, who could be relied upon to attack their common enemy from the rear.

With the union of the English and Scottish crowns in 1603 this policy became more difficult to pursue, but Charles I proved to be no friend to France in spite of the fact that he had married a French wife, and the Scottish opposition to his religious policy gave new life to the Edinburgh-Paris axis. The extent to which Richelieu deliberately fomented trouble between the Scots and their King is a matter of some dispute, but it is clear that French agents and French money had no small part in stirring up that Scottish rebellion which was to prove the undoing of the House of Stuart. With Scottish help available in this way, those who were responsible for French policy were under no temptation to turn towards Ireland, a country with whose potentialities they were as yet very little acquainted.

As the seventeenth century progressed the situation began to change. When Charles II in exile approached Mazarin with the suggestion that he should marry his niece, Hortense Mancini, the Cardinal would have none of it; engrossed in the negotiations preparatory to the Treaty of the Pyrenees, he had not studied the course of events in England, and he was convinced that the monarchy would never be restored there. It must be admitted that there was something to be said for this point of view, for Charles himself was by no means optimistic, though he went to Fuenterrabia while the Franco-Spanish treaty negotiations were in progress in what proved to be the vain hope of persuading one or both of the Powers to do something for him. Within six months he was back in Whitehall without the assistance of either.[12]

Subsequent events were to prove that the sudden collapse of a regime which appeared so stable as the English republic left an ineradicable impression upon Louis XIV. When, in 1688, the Stuarts were forced to take the road of exile once more, he felt that in due course history would repeat itself, and that after an interval there would be another restoration. This explains, in part at any rate, his attitude towards James II and his son. The first restoration had taken France by surprise, and she had got nothing out of it; Louis was determined that this should not happen again. At the same time, it would be a mistake to leave out of account altogether his natural magnanimity, which was fully exhibited in his dealings with the unfortunate Royal Family in England.

Restored to his throne Charles II began to show his hand: Louis might intrigue with his domestic opponents, but in the end his cousin was too clever for him. France was never able to take the attitude of England for granted, and it was dangerous to provoke Charles too far by intriguing with the Scots for fear he should decide to throw in his lot with his Dutch nephew, William of Orange. Louis never trusted Charles, and when he died the French King probably thought that the change to James II was decidedly for the better. Events were soon to prove the opposite.

When opposition to James grew William saw in it an opportunity to bring Great Britain into his war against France, and Louis was under no illusions as to what was in his rival's mind. James, on the other hand, having suppressed Monmouth's rising with comparative ease, was supremely self-confident; he rejected the suggestion of Louis that a junction of the French and English fleets should be effected in order to stop the Dutch expedition, and he resented what he considered to be the patronizing attitude of the French monarch. Louis and his ministers were better acquainted than James with the storm that was brewing in England, but they considered that a long civil war was what was likely to ensue, and, to quote Marshal Villars, ' this suited us better than a settled government under King James '. This miscalculation, natural as it was, proved serious, for the easy victory of the Prince of Orange added England to the enemies of France. Such was the situation when it became clear during the opening weeks of 1689 that Tyrconnel had held Ireland loyal to the exiled James: this gave Louis an opportunity of which he was not slow to take advantage, and henceforth Ireland took the part previously played by Scotland in French strategy.

There was, however, a marked difference between the magnanimity of Louis towards James personally, and the reaction of the French Government to the fallen monarch's desire to regain his throne: Jacobitism was far too valuable a weapon in the hands of French strategy and diplomacy for sentiment to be allowed to blunt its edge. In effect, as a man Louis was prepared to do everything he could for James and his family, and he did treat them most generously, but as King of France he regarded the question of a Stuart restoration solely from the point of view of French national interests. It is in consequence highly arguable if at any time the French Government really desired to see a Stuart back on all three of the thrones which

M

James II had lost: they preferred that the component parts of the British Isles should be divided against themselves, and so the whole kept weak. With this end in view French statesmen were generally ready to give a hand to restore a Stuart in Dublin or Edinburgh, but that was as far as they would go, and in taking this view they were undoubtedly right. During his short reign James II had not proved a special friend of France, and there was only too much reason to suppose that if he were back in London the same policy would be followed again.

In these circumstances the course for France to adopt was clear, and it was to encourage the Jacobites to such an extent as to keep the British Isles in a state of permanent unrest, but without going so far as to effect a Stuart restoration. Naturally this attitude by no means coincided with the views of the exiled dynasty. To any promise of French support which would merely restore them to Dublin or Edinburgh, James II and his successors steadfastly refused their consent, and Prince Charles Edward was but echoing the views of his father and grandfather when, in answer to an offer of Cardinal de Tencin of aid to recover England and Scotland on condition of ceding Ireland to France, he replied, ' All or nothing '. This policy on the part of the French Government explains the scanty resources with which more than one Jacobite attempt was made, and one may be pardoned for supposing that the occasion when Paris really thought the Stuarts a nuisance, was not when they were unfortunate, but when they came so near to success in the Forty-Five.

It was not long before the differences between the King's advisers began to make itself felt at the very highest level. James, on his arrival in Dublin, had formed a small council which met at seven o'clock every evening, and consisted of d'Avaux, Tyrconnel, and Melfort, the Principal Secretary of State. The last-named was one of those unhappy adherents of the Stuart cause who failed to make a single friend except his master. His ' handsome looks and enjoyment of royal favour did not discount his indiscretion and incompetence ',[13] yet James, when dying, bestowed on him a dukedom, promised ten

years before, in reparation for suspicions of his fidelity which
he had been induced to entertain. Melfort declared that it was
against his will that he went with the King to Ireland at all,
and that he dreaded Tyrconnel's 'temper and pride',[14] so he
set to work to intrigue against him. He was, it may be added,
under no illusions as to his own unpopularity, and later in the
year, when he was back in Paris after his dismissal, he said
'all who come from England rail against me as a traitor and
a Sunderland, or worse, if that can be'. He certainly did not
exaggerate, for when he left Dublin he was forced to do so
secretly by night for fear of being assassinated. The immediate
effect of Melfort's hostility to Tyrconnel was to bring the latter
and d'Avaux more closely together.

The first bone of contention was the King's proposed journey
to the North for the purpose of reducing Derry, after which he
hoped to pass on to Scotland. On 6 April he told d'Avaux
that he had been giving considerable thought to the question
of Derry, and that he intended going in that direction in order
to encourage his troops. The ambassador on the contrary
advised him that it would be undignified to take part in the
attack on these 'miserable places', and he was by no means
reassured when the King replied that he had no intention of
proceeding any further than Armagh; the royal presence in
the opinion of d'Avaux was necessary in Dublin, and his
generals could easily deal with the few rebels who were still
in the field. Tyrconnel took the same view in what concerned
the King personally, but even earlier he had told d'Avaux that
a siege of Derry might prove more difficult than was generally
imagined.

What ensued soon justified Tyrconnel's worst apprehensions.
In spite of what he had told d'Avaux, the King did decide to
proceed to Derry in person, for in spite of all that has been
alleged against him he was a merciful man, and he seems to
have imagined that his presence would be sufficient to secure
the surrender of the place without bloodshed. By this time
Richard Hamilton had already summoned the city, and the
governor, Colonel Lundy, was disposed to hand it over, a course

in which the Corporation was not unwilling to concur. In effect, the position was that Lundy and the municipal authorities had announced their readiness to treat, but had stipulated that while negotiations were in progress the Jacobite forces were not to advance beyond St Johnstown. At this point there took place one of those unfortunate mishaps which characterize the history of the later Stuarts. James appears to have been imperfectly acquainted with what was afoot, and without considering what was likely to be the effect of soldiers advancing beyond the agreed point, he appeared on Windmill Hill with an escort of dragoons. At once the cry of ' Treachery ' went up in Derry, and it was believed that the King was leading an army of murderous Catholics to cut every Protestant throat. The mob[15] rose; Lundy was removed from his post; and the defence was organized by the Rev. George Walker, Rector of Donoughmore in County Tyrone, and Henry Baker. When, therefore, the royal trumpets rang out to give the summons they were answered by the fire of a cannon which killed an officer by the King's side. Having thus undergone the same unfortunate experience as his father in front of Hull nearly half a century before, James returned to Dublin with von Rosen and no inconsiderable loss of prestige, leaving the war in the North to be carried on by Hamilton, Berwick, and the two Frenchmen, Maumont and Pusignan.

Louis XIV was by no means pleased when he heard of what had occurred, and on 24 May he wrote to d'Avaux from Versailles a letter in which he stated at length his views on the existing situation in Ireland. ' It seems to me,' he observed, ' that the determination of this Prince to go to Londonderry with so few precautions, and of uselessly summoning the place to surrender when he lacked sufficient troops to reduce it to his obedience, can only produce the very worst effects by depriving the rebels of any fear they might have of his arms, and by discrediting him generally.' What must be done now, the French King continued, is to make sure that James has learnt his lesson, and that he does not embark on any similar adventures either in Scotland or in England unless and until he is assured of widespread support, and has enough troops for his purpose. Louis goes on to say that he is delighted with what d'Avaux tells him of the sentiments of Tyrconnel, 'who seems to me to be devoted to his master's interests' and the ambassador is instructed to work as closely with him as possible. He is also told to bring Melfort along with him so far as possible, but Louis was clearly already becoming suspicious of the Scot. 'Observe Lord Melfort's conduct very closely, and if he continues to neglect my interests, which are only those of the King his master, do not omit to tell me, so that I can take what steps seem suitable to me to persuade the King of England to provide himself with another minister.'

D'Avaux had not accompanied James to Derry. The King had gone by way of Armagh, Charlemont, Omagh, and Strabane, but the ambassador had only followed him as far as Omagh, for he liked neither the purpose of the journey nor the discomfort involved. Tyrconnel did not go at all, for in addition to sharing d'Avaux's views with regard to his master's policy, he felt that an inspection of the Jacobite forces would not come amiss.

Neither in quantity nor in quality did they come up to the standard described in his letter to the Duke of Hamilton. As has been shown on an earlier page the exigencies of politics had done much to diminish the value of the troops as they existed at the death of Charles II. Tyrconnel had purged the army of Protestants, and the Catholics who replaced them were in many instances little, if anything, more than raw recruits when they were put to the test of battle. As if this were not enough, the same mistake had been made in the preceding year as in Scotland, for, as has clearly been shown, some of the best regiments had been sent to England where they effected nothing, while their own country was deprived of their services when these were most needed. When Tyrconnel started his tour of inspection early in April the parade strength of the Jacobite army would appear to have been eight regiments of horse, the same number of dragoons, and forty-four regiments of foot, in all about 35,000 men.

The French observers were appalled at the condition in which they found their allies. Being accustomed to the best military machine in the world they were all the more exasperated by the widespread indiscipline of the men and by the indifferent quality of the officers. Von Rosen summed the Jacobite army up in the disparaging words, ' Nearly all without arms and quite naked: the greater part of the officers are miserable fellows without courage or honour; a single cannon-shot passing at the elevation of a clock-tower throws a whole battalion to the ground, and the only way to get them to their feet is to send horses over their bellies.'[16] This is pretty damning, but, as Professor Murphy of Cork rightly says, von Rosen ' strikes one as being particularly supercilious and arrogant ', and Berwick is not wholly complimentary to him. ' He was,' he wrote, ' an excellent officer, of great bravery and application, very fit to be at the head of a wing; but not capable of commanding an army, because he was always in fear of accidents; in society, he was of a very obliging carriage, and magnificent in his style of living; but subject to passion, even to a degree of madness, and at those times he was incapable of listening to any representations.'[17]

Nearer home, John Stevens, who held a commission in the Grand Prior's Regiment, was also far from flattering. ' What our army either was or might be made,' he says, ' is very hard to give an account of. The common computation was incredible, for most men reckned the whole nation, every poore country fellow having armed himself with a skeine, as they call it, or dagger, or a ropery like a halfe pike, weapons fit only to please themselves, or else to put them into a posture for robbing and plundering the whole country, under pretence of suppressing the rebellious Protestants.'[18] To those accustomed to the troops of Louis XIV they must have looked more like rapparees than soldiers. D'Avaux was equally uncomplimentary about the Irish he saw, but he was able to look a little further, and he formed a high opinion of their inherent military value. All that was needed to convert the raw peasant levies from Ireland into soldiers second to none amongst continental armies was proper training and equipment, and these the French military machine supplied as a matter of course.

In his task of reorganizing the army Tyrconnel had had the invaluable assistance of Mountcashel, as Justin MacCarthy had now become, and, what is more, the two men agreed in the main where politics were concerned: their views coincided with each other's, and consequently with those of d'Avaux. Justin MacCarthy had certainly not allowed the grass to grow under his feet since the Revolution, and but for him Bandon might well have become another Derry, for in February 1689 the townspeople disarmed the small Irish garrison, killed some of the soldiers, and declared for the Prince of Orange. The Earl of Clancarty summoned the town to surrender, but was refused admittance; shortly afterwards, however, MacCarthy himself obtained possession of the place, which he proposed to burn after he had hung the Williamite ringleaders. He desisted owing to the entreaties of a young clergyman of the name of Nicholas Brady, a somewhat unexpected product of Westminster School and Christ Church, Oxford, whose chief claim to fame is his versification of the Psalms and a blank verse translation of the *Aeneid*. Brady persuaded MacCarthy to hold his hand, and the citizens of Bandon were pardoned on payment of a £1,500 indemnity and a promise to make restitution to the soldiers whom they had attacked and robbed. In the circumstances these terms were ridiculously light, and Tyrconnel strongly disapproved of them: so in spite of the identity of their views on general matters, d'Avaux early noted that the two men were not on the best of terms.[19]

To what extent Tyrconnel's tour of inspection was also due to a desire to avoid participation in the King's expedition to the North it is impossible to say, but however this may be he soon came to the conclusion that all was not well with the troops, for we find him writing from Kilkenny on 17 April to say that he was 'wooryed and hurryed about'. As a result of what he saw he suggested that some companies in all the infantry regiments should be disbanded, and that the army should be reduced to thirty thousand men, including two thousand cavalry and three thousand dragoons. These proposals were duly adopted by James. In this connection it may be noted that John Stevens tells us that his regiment originally consisted of twenty-two companies, none of them full, but that it was now reduced to thirteen. The way of the army reformer, however, is always hard, and the author of *The Jacobite Narrative of the War in Ireland*, although a fervent admirer of Tyrconnel, says, ' Whether this was a prudent action it hath long since been argued pro and con. However, we must here acquaint the reader that the disbanded captains and subaltern officers were struck to the very heart by this breach; because their uncommon zeal for the cause, and their treasure spent on the subsistence of their respective bands, and their expectation from thence of lasting honour, were now brought all to nothing in their opinion, though the said officers were dismissed with the King's thanks and promise of preferring them upon the first occasion.'

Tyrconnel complained of illness when he was at Kilkenny, and after his tour of inspection was over it seems to have incapacitated him altogether: indeed a contemporary English newspaper reported that he was ' just expiring of the black jaundice ', the wish being doubtless father to the thought. Whatever may have been wrong with him, his health was sufficiently bad to keep him from taking an active part in public affairs for some months; a portion at least of the time he spent either at Talbotstown or at the Viceregal summer residence at Chapel Izod, where James visited him on several occasions, and he does not appear to have fully recovered much before the end of August, though there is plenty of evidence that he was by no means inactive behind the scenes[20] and none that his illness was a pretext, the result of ' disappointment at his relegation to comparative obscurity ' as one authority would have us believe.[21]

It was not only in the military field that Tyrconnel had been busy since the arrival of the King, for he had inspired several proclamations which James had issued. The first commanded Protestants who had recently left the kingdom to return and accept the royal protection, under penalties for refusal. The second, directed against marauding, ordered all Catholics not belonging to the army to lay up their arms in their houses. A third called on the peasantry to bring in provisions for the troops. A fourth somewhat optimistically raised the value of money. A fifth summoned Parliament to meet in Dublin on 7 May.

No Parliament had met in Ireland since 1666, and Tyrconnel was not leaving anything to chance in the composition of this one. A hostile witness may not have been very far from the truth when he alleged that ' the common way of election was thus: the Earl of Tyrconnel, together with the writ for election, commonly sent a letter recommending the persons he designed should be chosen; the sheriff or mayor being his creature, on receipt of this, call'd so many of the freeholders of a county, or burgesses of a corporation, together as he thought fit, and without any noise, made the return.[22] Owing to his illness Tyrconnel did not take his seat in the House of Lords during the session, but he must have exercised considerable influence behind the scenes in view of the part which he had played in the election of the Lower Chamber: all the same, it is worthy of note that not a single Catholic prelate was summoned to this Parliament, while among those supporting James were the Protestant Primate of All Ireland, the Archbishop of Armagh, as well as the Protestant Bishops of Meath, Derry, Ossory, Limerick, Cork, Raphoe, and Killala.[23]

As soon as the Parliament met the basic differences between James and his followers, and between those followers themselves, were forced out into the open, and its proceedings soon afforded further evidence of the difficulty and weakness of the King's position, for the policy which he must pursue if he was to retain his hold over Ireland was precisely that which would do him immeasurable harm in the other two kingdoms. The Parliament naturally had a large majority of members who were determined to take advantage of the opportunity to right many an ancient wrong, and although it only sat until 18 July, when it was prorogued, it passed no less than thirty-five measures. Most of these were not particularly contentious,[24] but there were three problems of which this certainly could not be said, and they were the repeal of the Acts of Settlement, the Act of Attainder, and the suggested reversal of Poynings' Law, dating from the reign of Henry VII, whereby the supremacy of the King and Council in England over the Irish Parliament was guaranteed.

The first of these was very near Tyrconnel's heart, and represented a course to which he had devoted much of his adult life. D'Avaux, who realized how much the land meant to the Irish people, strongly supported him, for Charles O'Kelly, in his *Macariae Excidium,* says, 'It is much doubted to this day if Count d'Avaux, Ambassador of France, had not warmly interposed, minding him often of his engagement to Louis XIV to redress the injustice done to his subjects, whether any other consideration would prevail with the King to restore to the loyal Irish the inheritance of their ancestors, which they lost in the service of the kings his father and brother – though the late English proprietors were at that time in open hostility against him.' Tyrconnel and the ambassador exerted the utmost pressure upon James from the moment of his arrival in Ireland, and so well informed was Louis about the wishes of the Irish people that in his first letter to d'Avaux he gave a simplified version of the Restoration settlement, urging that James should be persuaded, firstly to return to Catholics the regicides' estates given to him, and secondly to forfeit the property of disloyal Protestants and grant it to Catholics. At the same time Louis recognized that it might not suit James to resume the property of all Protestants as this would alienate Protestant feeling in all three kingdoms.[25]

The Act of Repeal was closely connected with that of Attainder which in the event of a Jacobite victory would have meant that a great deal of land would have been available for distribution to Catholics. By the former measure the heirs of the 1641 proprietors were to recover their ancestors' estates in full, but *bona fide* purchasers were to be recompensed by the forfeiture of property held by William's adherents. The Act of

Repeal also provided for the appointment of commissioners of claims, but this seems to have been a dead letter, for almost immediately a proclamation was issued to the effect that there would be no court of claims for the present, ' lest some should neglect the public safety upon pretence of attending their private concerns '. The only instance of a court of enquiry adjudicating that Dr Simms has been able to find was in Ballyshannon, County Kildare, where it was ordered that as Luke Fitzgerald had proved that in 1641 his ancestors were possessed of the mansion house of Ballyshannon the new holder, one Francis Annesley, was to hand it over to him.[26] Still, Tyrconnel had got his legislation on the statute-book, and had the Jacobite cause prospered he would have changed the course of Irish history.

If the Act of Repeal is defensible on the ground that it meted out justice to those who had been wronged by their political and religious enemies, the Act of Attainder was too comprehensive altogether. In any event, procedure by attainder is open to strong objection in that legislative bodies are not courts of law, that they have no experience in hearing evidence, and that they are apt to be swayed by party passion. In effect, Bills of Attainder ' are nothing more, when passed, than Acts of Parliament for killing or otherwise punishing a man without trial '.[27] Such an act had been used to kill Strafford when James was a boy, and one was to be used in his last years to dispose of Sir John Fenwick. The Irish Attainder Bill contained upwards of two thousand names; no definite charge was preferred against any of the condemned persons, and there was no pretence of a trial. Those condemned were roughly divided into four classes, namely, those actually in arms against James, absentee landlords, Protestants who had fled the country, and – it is to be feared – personal enemies of members of Parliament. There was everything to be said for proceeding against those in the first category, but nothing for taking such strong measures against those in the other three, while the Act definitely encroached on the King's prerogative by removing his right to pardon the attainted persons.

Tyrconnel was himself a beneficiary of this legislation, for out of the attainted estates a sum of twenty thousand pounds a year was voted to him. As any other politician, Whig or Jacobite, would have done precisely the same, this did not cause any comment, though the Williamites were not slow to spread rumours regarding his wife's alleged speculations in the new currency which was the result of the efforts to raise the value of money. Rightly or wrongly, Frances had the same reputation as her sister Sarah where parsimony was concerned, so it was easy for her detractors, notably William King, to make insinuations against her on this score, but what truth there was in them is another matter. Actually, little is known of her activities during 1689, for the condition of Ireland was hardly such as to allow a woman to play a prominent part. During the summer months there was practically no Court, in the social sense of the word, nor had James brought materials for one with him from France. Furthermore, Tyrconnel's temporary retirement through ill-health naturally kept his wife in the background.

The King's determined opposition defeated the efforts of those who desired to repeal Poynings' Law, natural as their wishes in this respect were, and it is by no means impossible that Tyrconnel felt that for the time being at any rate enough Nationalist pressure had been put upon the unhappy James. Even Macaulay pays him a grudging tribute on this score, for he says that ' it was not without difficulty that Avaux and Tyrconnel, whose influence in the Lower House far exceeded the King's, could restrain the zeal of the majority '.[28] Of one thing there was no doubt, and it was that by this time James was as heartily tired of the Irish as the Irish were becoming tired of him. There are contemporary accounts of varying credibility of his resentment at being forced by the Parliament to do what he had no mind to do at all. It was said that the Duke of Powis told the Earl of Granard that ' the King durst not let them know that he had a mind to have them stopped ', and that, when Granard was going to the House of Lords to record his protest against the repeal of the Acts of Settlement,

James said that ' he was fallen into the hands of a people who rammed that and many other things down his throat '. Another story is to the effect that James was so moved by the opposition to him that his nose bled, as it was wont to do in moments of crisis,[29] and that he summed up his experience of Parliaments in the phrase, ' All Commons are alike.' To a Scot who came to ask for assistance for his country James observed, ' What can I do? You see I am left alone. I have none to do anything for me.' Writing many years later, so fervent a supporter as the Earl of Ailesbury confessed that ' King James, to speak naturally as affairs stood between him and his (Irish) Parliaments was a cipher rather than a King.'[30]

Certainly he considered that any promises which he made in Dublin were rendered null and void by the results of the Battle of the Boyne, for in a Declaration which he issued on 17 April 1693, speaking of his intention of summoning an English Parliament if he should be recalled to the throne, he said, ' And in that Parliament we will also consent to everything they shall think necessary to re-establish the late Act of Settlement in Ireland, made in the reign of our dearest brother; and will advise with them how to recompense such of that nation as have followed us to the last, and who may suffer by the said re-establishment, according to the degree of their sufferings, thereby; yet so as the said Act of Settlement may always remain entire.' This Declaration was hardly calculated to recommend James to the Irish.

When Tyrconnel resumed his full activities at the end of August he found a different situation from that which had confronted him earlier in the summer. The Derry commitment had been liquidated by failure, for on 28 July the Williamite vessels sailed up the Foyle, burst through the boom built by the besiegers, and reached the city. There was nothing more to be done, and on the thirty-first, von Rosen withdrew his forces. On the following day came the news that the Williamites of Enniskillen had won a notable success at Newtown Butler. Most important of all, on 27 July Dundee was killed in the hour of victory at Killiecrankie, and his death marked the end of any scheme for a joint invasion of England from Scotland and Ireland. Disasters as these events undoubtedly were, they did at any rate afford an opportunity of concentrating the Jacobite forces in the Dublin area, and of making an effort to organize them properly, which had long been Tyrconnel's wish.

The position then was that the civil and military authority of James was still firmly established in Leinster, Munster, and Connacht but that the failure to take Derry and Enniskillen had provided the enemy with Ulster as a bridgehead into Ireland. On the other hand, Jacobite military inactivity was most marked after the failure in the North, possibly because, to quote Berwick, the army ' which was brought from Derry was reduced almost to nothing ';[31] although it was obvious that the death of Dundee had left William free to concentrate all his strength against Ireland, for he could not much longer ignore the threat to his flank, any more than Elizabeth I had been able to ignore it a century before in her struggle with Spain. As has been shown, some of the blame for this state of affairs must rest with Versailles, for the French never made any serious attempt to use their superiority at sea to prevent Williamite forces from reaching Ireland; for example, they did not follow up Châteaurenard's victory over Admiral Herbert in Bantry Bay in the previous May. So old Marshal Schomberg was not only allowed to land unopposed at Bangor, County Down, on 13 August, but owing to von Rosen's precipitate retreat from Ulster he was not prevented from occupying Belfast and Carrickfergus. At the same time his arrival had the effect of bringing home to the Jacobites the seriousness of their position, and to this extent it facilitated the efforts of Tyrconnel to put the armed forces on a more satisfactory footing.

If ever there was a professional soldier it was Schomberg. By birth he was a great noble of the Rhineland, and in his early years he had fought by the side of von Rosen. He was a soldier and nothing else, for he appeared in this field and that, under this master and that, quite indifferently, though more often than not in the service of France. Indeed, upon the approach of his fiftieth year he naturalized himself and his sons as subjects of Louis, and in 1675 he became a Marshal of France. Then came the Revocation of the Edict of Nantes which lost to France so many an able commander because he was a Protestant. It was not that Schomberg was exiled: he was given an embassy; but he felt that the taking away of privileges from men of his rank on the grounds of their religion rendered it incumbent upon him to leave the service of the French King, so he passed into that of William of Orange.

How far South he intended to press after his landing at Bangor is a matter of opinion, but Berwick very skilfully, by slowly falling back on Drogheda, barred the road to Dublin until it was too late for Schomberg to take it. At Drogheda lay James himself with twenty-two thousand men who had been raised largely by the efforts of Tyrconnel, but they were poorly armed. The King made a determined effort to force a battle on the enemy, and he advanced to within three miles of Dundalk, where Schomberg had taken up his quarters; the attempt, however, was in vain, for the Williamite forces were suffering severely from disease, and their commander was determined not to run any risks. The two armies thus faced each other until the end of October, when Schomberg evacuated Dundalk, which the Jacobites at once occupied. Both sides then went into winter quarters.

That the campaign should have ended so favourably for the Jacobites considering the earlier disasters of the summer was due to two men, namely Berwick and Tyrconnel. Berwick held Schomberg in the field, and Tyrconnel provided James with the forces that enabled him to take full advantage of his son's masterly strategy. Berwick in his *Memoirs* frankly admits that it was 'by the efforts of the Duke of Tyrconnel' that the twenty-two thousand men were collected at Drogheda,[32] while d'Avaux wrote to Colbert de Croissy on 20 September that 'fifteen days ago we scarcely hoped to put affairs upon so good a footing, but since the departure of Lord Melfort, Lord Tyrconnel and all the Irish have laboured with so much zeal that all is in a state of defence'.[33] Throughout his career Tyrconnel had never been much of a devotee of the middle course,

but he seems to have become one on this occasion, for the Rev.
G. W. Story in his *Impartial History*[34] says that von Rosen
' with some others were for deserting Drogheda and Dublin,
and retreating toward Athlone and Limerick . . . This my Lord
Tyrconnel heard of when he was sick at Chapel-Izzard, and
went immediately to Drogheda, where he told them that he
would have an army there by next night of 20,000 men, which
accordingly proved true, for they came in from Munster on
all hands.'[35] On the other hand he and d'Avaux were opposed
to risking a battle with Schomberg if it could be avoided.[36]

Another important event which occurred at this time was
Melfort's departure to France, and it is difficult to believe that
it was a mere coincidence that this should have taken place
at the same time as Tyrconnel's return to duty. The comment
of d'Avaux on the news, when it reached him, was ' If it had
only taken place three months ago it might have done some
good, but now it is too late.' As always in the case of unpopu-
lar politicians, every kind of accusation against him was flying
round Dublin. He diverted the Jacobite funds to his own use;
he mismanaged the stores; he held back horses urgently needed
by Sarsfield as remounts for the cavalry; he took bribes; and
he quarrelled with the King's other advisers. So he took his
departure, and almost immediately began a correspondence
with James in which he neglected no opportunity of portraying
both the Tyrconnels in the worst possible light. As Secretary of
State he was succeeded by Tyrconnel's friend, Sir Richard
Nagle, against whose competence there could be no objection.
This change enhanced, if such were possible, Tyrconnel's prestige, and Charles O'Kelly speaks of James acting ' by the advice
of Tyrconnel, or rather by his orders, for he was in effect the
King of Ireland '.

High Jacobite circles were in considerable disarray at this
time, and Tyrconnel's temporary retirement had done nothing
to bring together the warring elements in James's following.
One member of his family, in particular, seems to have been
more of a liability than an asset, and that was Berwick's brother,
the Grand Prior. D'Avaux had no high opinion of him, as may

be gathered from an extract from a letter which he wrote on 11 February 1690 to Louis:

> One day the Duke of Berwick and his brother entered a room where Lord Dungan,[37] and four or five sparks of the army were cracking a bottle of claret. Presently an officer blamed the Grand Prior for having broken a certain captain of his regiment. Henry FitzJames replying offensively, Berwick good-humouredly suggested that instead of wrangling they should drink to the health of all true Irishmen, and confusion to Lord Melfort, who had well-nigh lost them the kingdom. Whereupon the Grand Prior angrily protested that Melfort was a right good fellow, and a friend of his, and if anyone dared drink such a toast, he would pitch a glass of wine in his face. Some of the gentlemen retorted in terms more or less disrespectful to Melfort, but Dungan carelessly remarked that FitzJames had no business to fall into a passion if they chose to drink the toast; and then, raising an empty goblet, made the usual reverence. Instantly the ill-conditioned Prior flung his wine into Dungan's face, the glass cutting his lordship's nose in two places. The bystanders rushed between the parties. However, Dungan, though a high spirited young man, treated the insult with contempt. 'Never mind,' he said, ' the Prior is not only a child, but the son of my King.'[38]

The upshot of the affair was that James gave his son a sound rating, but d'Avaux was of the opinion that this would do little good, for, according to him, the Grand Prior was a profligate boy who got fuddled every day, and whose debauched habits had prevented him from mounting a horse all the summer.

An army in winter quarters with nothing to do is liable to get out of hand, and the Jacobite forces in Dublin in the winter of 1689-90 were no expection. Although, as Dr MacLysaght has said, ' The generally accepted picture of the hospitable, feckless, fearless, fox-hunting, fire-eating Irish landlord, which is probably no caricature, belongs properly to the eighteenth century,[39] the type was by no means uncommon in its predecessor, and it must have contributed a number of officers to King James's army. In consequence duelling seems to have become almost as common as it had been in not wholly dissimilar cir-

N

cumstances at Cologne and Brussels in the days of Tyrconnel's youth, and it is in no way surprising to be told that the French officers were far from unaddicted to the practice; there were also a number of cold-blooded murders in military circles. One notable instance was the case of a non-attached French officer of the name of Coverent who was killed by one John Wall, an Irish dragoon; Wall was, however, acquitted on the ground that Coverent was not attached to his regiment, and that there was nothing to show that he was an officer. The French, it may be added, were more surprised than pleased to discover that one of their officers might be killed by a private soldier, who could then escape scot-free by the verdict of an Irish court-martial.

It must not, however, be thought that because the King was by no means enamoured of his Irish subjects he was indifferent to the welfare of the Irish troops. In December 1689 he restored to the infantryman his full two shillings a week, to the dragoon his six shillings, and to the cavalryman his eight shillings; of course this was largely paid in base money, but James could hardly be blamed for that, and if his promises could have raised the value of the currency it would not long have remained base. What he could do in other ways to secure value for money he did, and he caused sutling-houses to be opened throughout Ireland where good ale had to be sold by measure at two pence a pint, notices to this effect in French and English[40] being placed in their windows. Again, when meat became so dear in Dublin, although plentiful in the country, that the price was prohibitive, he gave instructions to the Lord Mayor that he was neither to tax it nor hinder its admission to the capital – an order which must have driven many a black-marketeer into the Williamite camp.[41]

Indeed James in Ireland was at his worst as a leader and at his best as a man. While the siege of Derry was still in progress von Rosen determined to try the effect of a little terrorism: to quote Belloc he ' proposed to make war in our modern fashion, and to sacrifice the civilian population at large '.[42] Accordingly he told those within the town that if they did not surrender the place by 1 July he would gather the rebels from all over the countryside, and drive them under the walls to starve. He was as good as his word, and on the second a great crowd of both sexes and all ages, including little children, were driven into the space between the Jacobite lines and the city. The not unnatural reply of Derry was to put up gallows on the walls, on which were to be hanged such prisoners as had been taken. James was horrified as soon as he heard what was taking place; he gave immediate instructions that it was to be stopped; and a circular letter was sent to all senior officers telling them to ' refuse obedience to any order of this nature from our Field-Marshal-General '. He said that ' his honour as a King, and the keeping of his word, was to be preferred to the preservation of his throne ', and he added that if von Rosen had been his own subject he would have hanged him.

He could not bring himself to be severe with Protestants as individuals. His official printer was a Protestant, and a notice calling upon the Protestants to surrender arms and horses under severe penalties was sent to him to print, but somehow he forgot to set it up, and his omission was not discovered for several weeks. The King was urged to make an example of him, but he contented himself with accepting the man's excuses. On another occasion he allowed a Dublin resident, detected in correspondence with William, to escape so that he would not have to give the order for his execution. His son-in-law's methods were very different, for when some months later Mark Bagot was caught in Dublin disguised in woman's clothes he was hanged without mercy. From the point of view of humanity there was nothing to be said against James.

During the winter months in the Irish capital the most stir was made by the escape of Mountcashel from captivity in December, an event which was not much to Tyrconnel's liking. Mountcashel had been taken prisoner by the Williamites at Newtown Butler after his horse had been shot under him, and he had himself been seriously wounded. According to tradition one of the bullets which struck him would certainly have proved fatal if it had not been deflected by his watch which it shattered. An Enniskillener, unaware of his identity, was on the point of clubbing him with a musket when a Jacobite officer called out that the wounded man was his general. At that point the commander of the Enniskillen contingent came up, and formally took Mountcashel and his comrades prisoner. According to a Williamite account the Enniskillen men were glad of the opportunity of saving Mountcashel's life since he had earlier persuaded Lord Galmoy to spare that of Colonel Crichton, the governor of Crom Castle.[43]

Mountcashel was taken to Enniskillen where he remained out of action for five months. He was well-treated by his captors, and James certainly did not forget the man who had suffered so greatly in his cause, for he kept him supplied with both wine and money, as well as arranging for a physician and two surgeons to attend him. Berwick made one attempt to effect his rescue, but without success. When Mountcashel was convalescent he soon became bored with Enniskillen as a place of residence, so he asked Schomberg if he could go to Dublin on parole until his health was restored, but this was refused. Negotiations were then set on foot for his exchange with Mountjoy, still safely immured in the Bastille, but this proposal did not apparently meet with the approval of James – at any rate nothing definite looked like coming of it.

In these circumstances Mountcashel came to the conclusion that he had better effect his own escape, but to do this and still preserve the image – as a later generation would have put it – of an honourable gentleman, since his guard had been removed and he was on parole, was not easy. However, he put about a rumour that he intended to escape, and this had the desired effect, for the guard was restored, and orders came from Whitehall that he was to be more closely confined, ' taking care however to treat him civilly and like a gentleman'. Mountcashel now decided that he was no longer bound by his parole, and with the help of a sergeant whom he had bribed, but who was afterwards summarily shot for his part in the affair, he left Enniskillen by boat under cover of night. This behaviour was naturally interpreted differently in different quarters. The Williamites bluntly declared that Mountcashel had broken his parole, and Schomberg said that he had taken him ' to be a man of honour, but that he would not expect that in an Irishman any more '. On the other hand, Mountcashel's action was afterwards vindicated by a French court, but as Professor Murphy has pointed out 'this was hardly an impartial tribunal '. The whole business leaves rather a nasty taste in the mouth.

When Mountcashel arrived in Dublin his wife[44] was waiting for him and he received a hero's welcome; bonfires burned in the streets of the capital as well as in those of Cork, and James gave him a warm reception at the Castle, which cannot have pleased Tyrconnel, though why the two men should have drifted apart is not easy to say. They appear to have been in almost complete agreement upon matters of civil and miltary policy, so one can only conclude that it was a case of personal dislike, though their background – the one from the Pale and the other of Old Irish ancestry – also the memory of their difference over the terms of the surrender of Bandon, may have had something to do with it. That Tyrconnel should have rejoiced at the departure of Mountcashel to France with the first units of the Irish Brigade may be taken for granted, but what part he played in the appointment is open to doubt; what is often forgotten is that Mountcashel's position in Ireland was precarious after his escape from Enniskillen, for had he become a prisoner of William again he would unquestionably have been shot out of hand. This may have been a further inducement to opt for a posting abroad.

NOTES

[1] *Memoirs,* Vol. I, p. 43. London. 1779.
[2] *Cf.* Tuckey, Francis H.: *County and City of Cork – Remembrancer,* pp. 110-112. Cork. 1837. Also Smith, Charles: *The County and City of Cork,* pp. 112-114. Cork. 1893.
[3] The Council Book of the Corporation contains the following entry:

Kinsale, the fourteenth Day of March, 1688-9. Memorandum, that on the twelfth day of March, inst., his Sacred Majtie, James the Second, by the Grace of God, of England, Scotland, France and Ireland, King, Defender of the faith, etc. arrived in this harbour of Kinsale, with a fleete of twenty-two sayle of shipps belonging to his most Christian Majtie., Lodowick the Fourteenth, King of France, and kept his court at Charles-Forte, in the libertyes of this Towne, till the day of the date hereof, and this day about 3 o'clock, afternoon, removed the Court to Corke.

4 The present building is admittedly of a later date, but there was an earlier one on the site.

5 Quoted by Sergeant, Philip W.: *Little Jennings and Fighting Dick Talbot*, Vol. II, pp. 426-427. London. 1913.

6 *Memoirs*, Vol. I, p. 95. London. 1779.

7 *Memoirs*, Vol. I, p. 59. London. 1779.

8 Jean-Antoine, Comte d'Avaux, Marquis de Givry, was the younger son of Jean Antoine de Mesmes, Comte d'Avaux, and himself nephew of another distinguished diplomatist, Claude de Mesmes (1595-1650). He was born in 1640, and served between 1672 and 1701 on diplomatic missions, usually with ambassadorial status, in Venice, Holland, Ireland, Sweden, and again in Holland. Early in his career he participated as a plenipotentiary in the joint mission appointed in connection with the Peace of Nymegen. He died unmarried in 1709.

9 Wilson, C. T.: *James the Second and the Duke of Berwick*, p. 157. London. 1876.

10 *Negociations de M. le Comte d'Avaux en Irlande, 1689-90*, p. 23. Dublin. 1934.

11 *H.M.C., Buccleugh MSS*. Vol. II, Pt. 1, p. 36. Tyrconnel was clearly unaware when he wrote this letter that Hamilton had declared for William three months earlier, so little was known in Ireland about the situation in Scotland.

12 *Vide supra*, p. 87

13 Middleton, Dorothy: *The Life of Charles, 2nd Earl of Middleton*, p. 144. London. 1957.

14 *Mémoire Justificatif du Comte de Melfort*, Macpherson, Vol. II, p. 674.

15 In those days Derry was mainly Protestant. The modern city has a large Roman Catholic population.

16 *Cf.* Rousset, C. F. M.: *Historie de Louvois*, Vol. IV, p. 198. Paris. 1872.

17 *Memoirs*, Vol. I, p. 59. London. 1779.

18 *Journal of John Stevens*, ed. R. H. Murray, pp. 63-66, and 68. London. 1912.

19 *Negociations de M. le Comte d'Avaux en Irlande*, pp. 23-24, 26 and 29. Dublin. 1934.

20 On 6 August d'Avaux wrote to Louis, 'Lord Tyrconnel has had a relapse, but by taking the local waters, although they are not very good, he is beginning to get better.'

21 Turner, F. C.: *James II*, p. 466. London. 1948.

22 King, William: *State of the Protestants of Ireland*, p. 171. Cork. 1768.

23 *The Complete Peerage*, Vol. III, pp. 631 *et seq.* London.

24 Including one instituting Liberty of Conscience, which would have been unthinkable in England for another century.

[25] *Cf. Negociations de M. le Comte d'Avaux en Irlande*, pp. 31-32. Dublin. 1934.

[26] Simms, J. G.: *The Williamite Confiscation in Ireland, 1690-1703.* London. 1956.

[27] Carter, A. T.: *A History of English Legal Institutions*, p. 109. London. 1902.

[28] *History of England*, Chap. XII.

[29] Notably at Salisbury in 1688, and at Shelton Abbey in 1690 after the Battle of the Boyne.

[30] *Cf.* Turner, F. C.: *James II*, pp. 483-484. London. 1948.

[31] *Memoirs*, Vol. I, p. 56. London. 1779.

[32] Vol. I, p. 63. London. 1779.

[33] *Negociations de M. le Comte d'Avaux en Irlande, 1689-90*, p. 466. Dublin. 1934.

[34] As the reverend gentleman was an extreme Protestant and Whig, and made no secret of his feelings, the title of his work is rather a misnomer, nor, incidentally, is it much of a history.

[35] Pp. 16-17.

[36] *Negociations de M. le Comte d'Avaux en Irlande, 1689-90*, p. 468. Dublin. Dublin. 1934.

[37] Son of the Earl of Limerick.

[38] *Negociations de M. le Comte d'Avaux en Irlande, 1689-90*, pp. 644-45. 1934.

[39] *Irish Life in the Seventeenth Century*, p. 90. Cork. 1950.

[40] Though apparently not in Irish.

[41] *Cf.* Boulger, D. C.: *The Battle of the Boyne*, pp. 130-131. London. 1911.

[42] *James the Second*, p. 248. London. 1928.

[43] *Cf.* Murphy, J. A.: *Justin MacCarthy, Lord Mountcashel*, pp. 22-23. Cork. 1958.

[44] A daughter of Thomas Wentworth, Earl of Strafford.

CHAPTER IX

The Arrival of Lauzun

HARDLY HAD Mountcashel arrived in Dublin than he became immersed in the task of forming the first Irish Brigade.[1] The recent wars in Western Europe had taken a heavy toll of French manpower, and if Louis was to send any substantial body of troops, apart from officers and technicians, to the assistance of James, they would have to be made good by the despatch of an equivalent number of Irish soldiers to France. The idea of an exchange of this nature had been suggested even before James landed in Ireland, and as early as January 1689 Mountcashel was in correspondence with Louvois on the subject. D'Avaux was in complete agreement with the scheme from the moment he realized what excellent material was available. James was at first opposed to it, but he was induced to change his mind when Schomberg landed, and it became clear first that he could not make any effective resistance to the invader without the assistance of a French force, and secondly that this would only be sent by Louis in return for an Irish brigade. From the beginning Mountcashel had been favoured as its commander, but the King was opposed to the appointment, partly because he was reluctant to lose the services of one of his few outstanding generals, and partly because Berwick had been mentioned for the post; finally, however, he gave way.

The French had a decided preference for Mountcashel. He had made a very favourable impression on all the members of that nation with whom he came in contact, while d'Avaux pointed out that he was very popular with his men as well as being highly respected all over Ireland; that he was devoted to France; that he had seen service there; and that he was well acquainted with the French military machine. In addition, there were the indisputable facts of his great personal courage and his qualities of leadership, while he had the reputation of being a good judge of officers. For all these reasons the ambassador considered Mountcashel to be the ideal man to keep the Irish troops faithful and disciplined in the French service. It is also interesting to note that his aristocratic background weighed considerably with d'Avaux who commented that Patrick Sarsfield was ' not a man of the birth of Lord Galway or McCarthy, but he is a gentleman distinguished by his merit, and has more credit in the country than anyone else . . . He is a man upon whom the King can count, and who will never leave his service '.[2] Finally d'Avaux commended Mountcashel to Louvois on the curious ground that ' his short sight will prevent his ever becoming a great general '. In the view of Dr Murphy, ' This was not so much a statement of a defect as a note of assurance: the French[3] were extremely jealous of allowing foreigners to attain the highest military rank.'

It is in no way surprising that the selection of the senior officers of the Brigade should have been a cause of disagreement, and d'Avaux declared that the colonels whom James offered were beneath contempt, being not even fit to be ensigns. The King refused to part with Patrick Sarsfield or Lord Dungan, but he was quite ready to get rid of the Earl of Clancarty, whom the ambassador regarded as ' a young madcap and rather a roué '. Above all, Louis refused to accept any of the Hamiltons as officers in the Irish Brigade.

The French authorities wished that each regiment should be composed of sixteen companies of a hundred men each, and as this condition could not be complied with it explains why the five regiments sent from Ireland were reformed into three on their arrival in France. A start was made with the raising of four, which were originally intended to be those of Galway, Daniel O'Brien, Niall O'Neill, and Feilding. The procedure which was adopted was for James to appeal to the heads of a certain number of Irish families to raise a regiment, the command to

be given to a junior member of the house. Letters of this nature
were on consequence written to the Earl of Clanricard, Viscount Clare, Viscount Dillon, and probably Viscount Mount-
garret. Niall O'Neill proved unable to do what was requested
of him so his name was deleted from the original list; so was
that of Lord Clandicard, who had indeed raised a regiment,
but who was by no means enamoured of the idea of sending it
to France.

On the other hand Viscount Dillon readily gave his consent,
and his second son, Arthur, who was a keen soldier, took command of his regiment. Meanwhile, Lord Mountcashel had
moved to Cork where he was busy beating up recruits for his
battalion which had suffered severely in the North; so successful was he in this task that in a few weeks he raised it from a
skeleton strength of three hundred to a full complement of
twelve. Colonel Robert Feilding made much slower progress
which is perhaps hardly remarkable in view of the fact that he
was not an Irishman at all, but an Englishman who had sat
in the House of Commons at Westminster during James's
reign: he was, however, Mountcashel's brother-in-law, and
with his assistance he got a number of men together, but his
regiment was the weakest of all. The O'Brien regiment was
formed much more speedily, and the Butler one owed its existence largely to the influence of Viscount Galmoye.

The condition upon which these five regiments – Mountcashel, Richard Butler, Dillon, O'Brien, and Feilding – were
sent overseas was that they were to enter the service of the
King of France and to be entirely at his disposal to serve where
he should direct, that is to say against all his enemies ' except-
ing it were the King of England ' should occasion arise. There
was thus a marked distinction in the status of the Mountcashel
Brigade and that of the Wild Geese who followed it after the
Treaty of Limerick. The former became French troops at once,
while until the Peace of Ryswyck the latter were at any rate
nominally King James's men, subject to his orders and not to
those of the King of France. The schedule of pay was also
drawn up before the regiments left Ireland. Each private was to

receive nine francs a month, and the N.C.O.s more in proportion to their rank: an ensign's emolument was 1f. 80c. a day, a lieutenant's 2fcs. 25c., and a captain 5 francs. One sol in the livre was deducted from a private's pay for the personal benefit of the colonel of the regiment, so that if the unit was at full strength it can be reckoned that this would amount to the equivalent of £400 a year for the commanding officer, who also drew a regular annual salary of 2,700 francs.

In all, the Brigade totalled 5,387 all ranks, but they were for the most part exceedingly ill-found, and if James really did refer to them as ' the best regiments in his service ' he was without justification, quite apart from the fact that they were not in his service at all. The men had mostly been raised in haste, and the great majority of them had never shouldered a musket until they received their equipment at Nantes and Bourges. The Brigade sailed from Cork on 18 April 1690 in the same ships which had just brought Lauzun and his force over from France; it would appear that relatives and friends gathered in considerable numbers to see them off, for a contemporary account tells us that ' they were shipped off with a great deal of howling '.

In actual fact far more troops were being sent than Louvois wanted, for he only stipulated for four thousand in exchange for Lauzun's force, but they were to be ' good troops under good officers '. What he actually received was something rather different, for d'Avaux was so anxious to show what a valuable reserve Ireland was in the matter of man-power that he wished to collect as large a total as possible. The immediate consequence of sending too many men in regiments of unequal strength was that the French War Office, who were insisting on each regiment being composed of sixteen companies of a hundred men each, decided to reduce the five regiments to three, and the Butler and Feilding Regiments were the ones chosen for disbandment, the best of their effectives being distributed among Mountcashel, O'Brien, and Dillon. This left a surplus of some six or seven hundred men, who were incontinently shipped back to Ireland on the first excuse that came to hand: for example, the Butler Regiment was accused of having forty valets on the muster-roll under the guise of sergeants. As for Mountcashel himself, he was certainly no loser by changing his service from Ireland to France, for immediately after his arrival he was summoned to Versailles, where Louis gave him a most gratifying reception, making him a present of four thousand écus for his equipage, and an annual grant of the same sum in addition to his emolument as colonel of his regiment.

The French who were to replace the first of the Wild Geese arrived in Kinsale at the end of March, and they were the regiments of Zurlauben (Swiss), Biron, Bouilly, Tirlon, and Chémerault – not Picardie and Auvergne, but still good, and that at a time when the French were the masters of the battle-fields of Europe; what was at fault was their commander-in-chief, for their head was the Duc de Lauzun, who had recently been pardoned by Louis for aspiring to the hand of La Grande Mademoiselle. Berwick had no very high opinion of him, for he wrote, 'When he came to Ireland at the head of the auxilliary troops he made it appear that if he ever had had any knowledge of the military profession he had by that time totally forgotten it . . . In short, in Ireland he showed neither capacity nor resolution; though on other occasions he was said to be a man of great personal bravery. He had a sort of sense, which consisted only in turning everything to ridicule, insinuating himself into everybody's confidence, worming out their secrets, and playing upon their foibles. He was noble in his carriage, generous, and grand in his mode of living. He loved high play, and played much like a gentleman. His figure was very diminutive, and it is impossible to conceive how he could ever have become a favourite with the ladies.[4]

There can, indeed, be little doubt but that the efficiency of the French contingent was to a large extent nullified by the appointment of Lauzun as its commander. An Irish officer with a considerable experience of warfare said of him, 'We lost considerably by this exchange. Lord Mountcashel was a man of honour and great experience, while M. de Lauzun was more fitted to play at gallantries, more capable of unravelling petty court intrigues than of distinguishing himself at the head of a brigade: in addition, he was quick, proud, and so self-sufficient that he treated us as foreigners in our own country.'[5] All this was bad enough, but the French Government made it clear from the start that the lives of French soldiers were not to be recklessly sacrificed in the Stuart cause, for among the instructions drawn up by Louvois for Lauzun was the following: ' Do not allow your love of fighting to carry you away; your glory will be gained by wearing out the enemy. Above all things observe a strict discipline.'[6] Irish soldiers in France were to be more expendable than French soldiers in Ireland.

The squadron which took the Irish Brigade to France also had d'Avaux on board. His mission to Ireland had lasted a bare twelve months, and it was brought to a premature close through no fault of his but as the result of the intrigues of Lauzun at Versailles. In consequence of his assistance to the British Royal Family in 1688 Lauzun had acquired a good deal of credit in Jacobite circles, and in particular he possessed the confidence of Mary of Modena, who, seeing in him the man who had come to her rescue in the hour of danger, appears to have imagined that if he were sent to Ireland he might prove her husband's saviour too. Melfort's arrival at Saint Germain meant an additional critic of d'Avaux in influential circles there, and one may be sure that the ambassador's outspoken criticisms in Dublin of James himself lost nothing in the telling. A much more formidable enemy was Louvois, and in this connection Saint Simon tells a curious story, which may or may not be true, of an incident which greatly contributed to d'Avaux's recall. According to it the ambassador's secretary put by mistake a letter from his master to Colbert de Croissy into an envelope addressed to Louvois; unfortunately the letter contained a number of harsh criticisms of the War Minister's conduct of affairs, and Louvois was the last man to take this sort of thing lying down, so he was added to the growing band of those who wished to bring about d'Avaux's downfall.

Confronted with these intrigues and pressures, Louis seems to have decided to take the line of least resistance, which was to recall d'Avaux from Dublin. In November 1689, therefore, he wrote to the ambassador informing him that he could return to France as soon as Lauzun arrived in Ireland. The letter was in the most flattering terms, for the King wrote, ' Since I have no doubt that in the present conjuncture you will be well pleased to return to me I have accordingly decided to give you permission . . . assuring you nevertheless that I am fully satisfied with the sagacity you have shown in the conduct of this recent embassy, and with the valuable services that you have rendered me.' A letter from Colbert de Croissy was equally complimentary, but it made no attempt to hide from d'Avaux the fact that he was being recalled to avoid the friction that was likely to arise between two men of such opposite temperaments as Lauzun and himself. The ambassador was naturally chagrined at the course which events had taken, not least because he was convinced that all the good work which he had done must now go to waste. That Louis bore him no grudge, however, is attested by the fact that not long after his return to his own country he was appointed to represent his King in Sweden, at that time one of the key posts in the French diplomatic service. With d'Avaux there also left von Rosen, of whom James was even more pleased to be rid.

The simultaneous departure from Ireland of d'Avaux, von Rosen, and Mountcashel both strengthened the influence of Tyrconnel and, for a time at any rate, led to greater harmony in the Jacobite High Command. Whatever Tyrconnel's personal views about Lauzun, the other's obvious desire to help James could not but impress him, and he is found writing to Mary of Modena, ' I must doe M. de Lauzun justice to say I never saw anyone more zealous or more painful in all things relating to the King's service.' As it behoved him to be in the circumstances in which he was now placed, Tyrconnel was extremely circumspect in his behaviour, and that this attitude was paying is proved by the esteem which the Queen had come to feel for him, as shown by an extract from a letter which he received from her at the end of March.

> This is my third letter since I heard from you, but shall not make it a long one, for the bearer[8] of it knows a great deal of my mind, or rather all the thoughts of my heart, for I was so overjoyed to meet with one I durst speak freely to that I opened my heart to him and sayd more than I am like to do again in haste to anybody. I therfor refer myself to him to tell you all wee spoke off, for I have no secrets from you; one thing only I must beg of you, to have a good care of the King, and not lett him be too much encouraged by the good news he will hear,[9] for I dread nothing at this time but his going too fast into England, and in a manner disadvantageous to those of our per-suasion . . . Pray putt him often in mynd of beeing carefull of his person, if not for his own sake, for mine, my sonnes, and all our friends that are undon if anything amiss happens to him. I dare not lett myself go upon the subject, I am to full of it; I know you love the King. I am sure you are my friend, and therefor I need say the less to you, but cannot end my letter without telling you that I never in my life had a truer nor a more sincere friendship for anybody than I have for you.[10]

On one point at least James, Tyrconnel, and Lauzun were all agreed, and that was on the advisability of sending a French fleet into the Irish Sea either to prevent William from landing or to cut him off from England once he was ashore, but as on a previous occasion the proposal was cold-shouldered at Versailles. All the evidence, too, goes to show that Tyrconnel was not the man he had been, though James certainly went too far when he described him as ' old and infirm '. There was clearly no driving-force behind the Jacobite preparations, which explains why Dublin was short of bread, and why many of the guns brought by Lauzun were still at Cork for want of car-riages. Furthermore, according to the *Jacobite Narrative*, ' Far too many regiments of foot were left in garrisons, and that to no purpose, as it happened afterwards, whereby the King's army which took the field proved much inferior to the host of the rebels.' When Lauzun reached Dublin he was far from impressed with the situation he found there, and in a letter to Louvois he described it as ' a chaos equal to that in Genesis before the creation of the world ', though he paid a tribute to the activities of James himself.

Meanwhile Williamite reinforcements were pouring into Ireland, among them seven thousand Danes who landed at Belfast in March 1690.[11] Dutch, Brandenburghers, and some English quickly followed. In May Schomberg forced Charlemont to capitulate: situated on the Blackwater in County Armagh it was the last strong place in Ulster which still held out for James, and its loss was serious. Schomberg gave the garrison the honours of war, and saw that they were observed, which was not always the normal English practice, as we have seen. On 6 June his son Meinhart disembarked at Belfast with a formidable train of artillery, while eight days later William himself landed at Carrickfergus, which he should never have been allowed to do had the French Navy been intelligently handled.[12] The lists were now set.

NOTES

[1] The best recent account of its formation is Murphy, J. A.: *Justin Mac-Carthy, Lord Mountcashel, Commander of the First Irish Brigade in France.* Cork University Press. 1958.

[2] *Negociations de M. le Comte d'Avaux en Irlande,* p. 519. Dublin. 1934.

[3] Unlike the Spaniards, it may be noted.

[4] *Memoirs,* Vol. I, pp. 75-76. London. 1779.

[5] *Cf. The Irish Sword,* Vol. I, p. 69. Dublin. 1953.

[6] *Cf.* Force, Duc de la: *Lauzun,* p. 174. Paris. 1913.

[8] Lord Dover.

[9] The reference is obscure, for there was no good news.

[10] Quoted by Haile, M.: *Queen Mary of Modena,* p. 263. London. 1905.

[11] *Cf.* Danaher, K. and Simms, J. G.: *The Danish Force in Ireland, 1690-91, passim.* Dublin. 1962.

[12] It won the battle of Beachy Head only two weeks later.

CHAPTER X

The Battle of the Boyne

JAMES AND Tyrconnel left Dublin on 16 June. At that date the main Jacobite force lay round Ardee, but before moving on them William concentrated at Loughbrickland, near where Banbridge now stands. The distance to Dublin, his immediate objective, was approximately eighty miles, having regard to the roads available. When he began his advance to the South no serious effort was made to oppose him, although the line of the southern Ulster hills about Slieve Gullion might, one would have thought, have been considered as a possible delaying position. On the other hand, William might have been expected to be in a hurry to come to grips with his enemy, in view of his commitments elsewhere, but he displayed no such desire. If the Jacobite withdrawal from north Louth was made in comparatively easy stages the Williamite advance was leisurely in the extreme. The Dutchman commenced his match on 24 June, but he did not reach the Boyne until the thirtieth – that is to say that he took seven days to cover fifty miles. When he arrived at the Boyne he found the Jacobite forces drawn up along the southern bank.

They held the line of the river from Oldbridge to a point approximately half a mile to the east, while Drogheda was occupied as a detached post by 1,300 men under the command of Lord Iveagh. Up the river from Drogheda there was no bridge before Slane, though there were several fords, notably one on the Jacobite left at Rosnaree. Behind the Jacobite position the then main road to Dublin – the only available line of retreat – ran through Duleek, but owing to the marshy

o

ground on either side it formed such a bottle-neck that two coaches could not pass. From Oldbridge to Duleek the distance, as the crow flies, is about four and three-quarter miles, but it is nearly three-quarters of a mile shorter from Rosnaree. It was, therefore, clear that if a force which crossed the river at Rosnaree could push on rapidly to Duleek it stood a good chance of being able to cut off the retreat of troops holding the Oldbridge position.

What is not easy to understand is why James decided to fight on the Boyne at all. Berwick says, ' It was proposed to encamp on the heights beyond Dundalk, because that country was difficult of access; but as the enemy, by taking a small circuit, could get into the plain behind us, it was resolved to take post behind the River Boyne, near Drogheda.'[1] Lauzun's instructions from Louvois were, as we have seen, to avoid pitched battles, and to wear the enemy out. Berwick was probably right in asserting that it would have been a mistake to have made a definite stand to the north of Dundalk, but it is difficult to resist the conclusion that if a delaying action only was included it might with greater advantage have been attempted there. What is clear is that there were divided counsels in the Jacobite high command, and James himself had become notorious for indecision in moments of crisis: it was many years since he had been the dashing subordinate of Turenne. In any event, little or nothing was done to render the position defensible once the decision to fight had been taken. The garrison of Drogheda should have been used to protect the Jacobite right flank, but it might never have existed for all the part it played in the battle. No attempt seems to have been made to organize any strong redoubts, although their importance in a defensive position was well appreciated in the French army at the time; nor was anything done to render the fords difficult or impassable, or to place any obstructions in the bed of the river.

Futhermore, the Jacobite left flank was as exposed as the right. Richard Hamilton, at a conference on the evening before the battle, begged James to post a strong force at Rosnaree and Slane, but all that was done was to place a regiment of Irish

dragoons under Sir Niall O'Neill. Tyrconnel's nephew, at Rosnaree, and to leave the bridge at Slane quite unprotected.
Finally, the question of a counter-attack never seems to have
been considered at all. In these circumstances it is impossible
not to agree with Hilaire Belloc that the Jacobite position was
weak. 'The troops,' he wrote, 'occupying it were in full view
of the enemy on the northern bank; it was approachable on
many points at low tide; it contained little opportunity for
cover behind which to gather reserves; it could be turned on
the left by a superior force; and behind it was the narrow defile
of Duleek.'[2]

The forces under the command of James were of very un-
even quality, and only the French could be described as first-
class. The cavalry under Sarsfield were good in spite of their
lack of training, but the infantry and dragoons were little more
than untrained mobs of under-nourished civilians in uniform.
Moreover, after their failures in Ulster, the morale of the
Jacobites was none too high.

When one turns to the relative strength of the forces facing
one another it is to be confronted with a variety of widely
different estimates. The late Colonel O'Connell examined these
for a number of years, and eventually put forward the propo-
sition that the only way in which an approximately accurate
account of the strength of the rival armies could be obtained
was by accepting the figures given by each side for its own
forces. On this basis he put the Williamites at thirty-three
thousand and the Jacobites at twenty-one thousand: Berwick's
figures, it may be noted, were forty-five thousand and twenty-
three thousand repectively at the opening of the campaign.
There are, of course, other factors to be taken into consideration, for the Williamites were much superior in artillery, and
their morale was higher than at any rate a large part of the
opposing army.

William's forces were largely composed of trained professional soldiers from the Continent who had plenty of experience of active service conditions. The *corps d'élite* was the
brigade of Dutch Blue Guards under Solms, while also of excel-

lent quality were a further Dutch force under the Prince of Nassau, two French Huguenot regiments, and a brigade of English under Sir Thomas Hanmer. In addition there were the northern Irish, flushed with their successes at Derry, Enniskillen, and Newtown Butler: that they played no part in the ensuing battle was not their fault, but was due to the fact that no such rôle was cast for them by their commander. Not only was the army of William greatly superior in strength and training to that of his father-in-law but it was better posted, for the northern bank of the Boyne is excellently suited for the preparation of an offensive. It contains deep ravines opposite either end of what was the Jacobite position across the river, and in these depressions it was possible to assemble large numbers of troops without being observed from the other side.

Having brought his enemy to battle, it was clearly to the interest of William, given the general political and military situation, to use his superior strength to envelop and destroy him, but this was exactly what he failed to do. The truth is that William proved as indifferent a general in Ireland as in the Low Countries. Indeed, the generalship on both sides at the Boyne was mediocre, though the French historians have dismissed the action too lightly when they talk of ' a skirmish followed by a retreat '; for if a Dundee had been in command of the Jacobites, or had Berwick been twenty years older, the result might have been very different. As it was, the only general who in any way distinguished himself was old Schomberg, and he was killed during the course of the battle.

After a careful examination of the position, during which he came within an ace of being killed, William decided upon his tactics. They were, after a preliminary bombardment, to make a strong frontal attack across the river at low tide upon the main Jacobite position on the high ground at Donore, at the same time sending a force of about seven thousand cavalry and infantry to cross the river at Rosnaree and Slane, and then to push on to Duleek. The weather, it may be added, was perfect the whole time.

The exact nature of the flank attack has presented the greatest difficulty to historians, and it is not easy to discover what really happened. Daylight was about four on that first day of July, and both armies were early astir. Belloc was of the opinion that the flanking party under Meinhart Schomberg moved off not later than six, and he was probably right; in actual fact at whatever time it started it was too late, for it should have been sent off on the previous evening if it was to prove really effective, and this blunder is the measure of William's competence as a general. Some three hours later James and Lauzun were informed that Meinhart Schomberg's infantry under the command of General James Douglas, a former colleague of Dundee, had crossed the bridge at Slane, and that his cavalry under his own hand had forced the ford at Rosnaree. What had happened in the meantime?

The only certain fact is that Niall O'Neill's dragoons had been routed: to quote the Duc de la Force, ' Artillery had rendered untenable the position held by the dragoons, who had fought bravely for an hour, losing many men as well as their colonel.'³ This is a welcome, if unique, tribute to the valour of the dragoons, but in all else the Duc de la Force is at fault. Meinhart Schomberg could not have been held up for an hour if the news of his crossing reached the Jacobite headquarters as early as nine o'clock, and there were no Williamite cannon in that part of the field: they were all firing on Donore preparatory to covering the crossing at Oldbridge. Nor is this all, for the Duc de la Force confuses Rosnaree with Slane – a mistake which he shares with many other commentators – and he places the dragoons at the latter place, which, as we have seen, was not held by the Jacobites at all. What seems to have happened was that the infantry under Douglas were sent round by Slane, but that they were still too far away to threaten the line of retreat to Duleek; the cavalry were nearer, having forced the ford at Rosnaree, but they were held up, pending the arrival of the foot, by the fact that on the southern side of the ford the ground rises abruptly, thus rendering any purely mounted action impossible.

James and Lauzun must have expected that this flanking movement might be attempted or they would not have posted the dragoons at Rosnaree; but where they made their great mistake was in not attacking across the Boyne in the direction of Tullyallen as soon as Meinhart Schomberg's force had been sufficiently detached from the main Williamite army to be beyond recall. Napoleon would have exacted the maximum penalty from William, and even in the seventeenth century Montrose or Dundee would have made him pay dearly. Even if the Jacobite commanders regarded the whole affair as a delaying action, it was their duty to strike this blow, but either their competence or their intelligence was at fault, and they thought solely in terms of the defensive. At the same time Lauzun at once appreciated the threat to his left flank contained in the news which reached him at nine o'clock, and he moved the whole of the French, and some of the Irish, infantry, together with Sarsfield's cavalry, along the southern bank of the river towards Rosnaree. This left twenty-four thousand Williamites facing fourteen thousand Jacobites on the Boyne and at Donore. By this time James had withdrawn his guns, and it might have been better had he withdrawn the troops along the river-bank as well. As for the defence on Donore, that was now reduced to eight battalions under Richard Hamilton and the cavalry on the right under Berwick; both of them were nominally under the orders of Tyrconnel, but as he was himself heavily engaged they were in reality each responsible for his own actions.

By ten o'clock the state of the tide was such that the river could be crossed, and the brigade of Dutch Blue Guards, with fifty drums beating, entered the water upon a front of ten men. The Irish fired one volley, and then broke, as might have been expected of raw troops brought face-to-face with experienced veterans. To the left of the Dutch were the Huguenots; next came the English contingent under Hanmer; then the Danes and more Dutch. All these successfully made the crossing, and before long there were something like ten thousand Williamites to the south of the Boyne.

From this moment the fighting became not a little confused. On the Jacobite left Meinhart Schomberg was still waiting for his infantry who had crossed the river at Slane, and was himself being closely watched by Lauzun and Sarsfield. In the centre the Williamite troops who had reached the southern bank of the Boyne were reforming for an attack on the Donore position and were being repeatedly charged by the Jacobite horse. At this critical juncture it was Tyrconnel who took upon himself the duty of deciding what should be done for the defence of Oldbridge, where, during the earlier hours of the morning, there were only the two regiments of Clanricard and Antrim. When Tyrconnel saw the preparations for the attack developing he moved down five infantry regiments under Richard Hamilton to support the two in Oldbridge. On the sloping ground behind Oldbridge, leading gradually upwards to the Pass of Duleek, he drew up his cavalry. These consisted of Tyrconnel's own regiment, two troops of the bodyguard commanded by Berwick, and Parker's and Sutherland's regiments – a total of three and a half cavalry regiments. ' These troops were as good cavalry as existed anywhere, but it is putting them at a high figure to say they totalled fifteen hundred sabres.'[4] The seven infantry battalions numbered four thousand, so that Tyrconnel had five thousand, five hundred men to oppose Schomberg, who had at least fifteen thousand men under his immediate orders.

Berwick gives a vivid account of what happened in this part of the field.

> Schomberg, who remained in front of us, attacked, and made himself master of Oldbridge, notwithstanding the resistance of the regiment stationed at the place, which had one hundred and fifty men killed on the spot. Upon this, Hamilton marched down with the other seven battalions to beat them back. Two battalions of the Guards broke through them; but their cavalry having found means to pass at another ford, and advancing to fall upon our foot, I brought up our horse, which gave our battalions an opportunity to retreat; but at the same time we had a very unequal combat to sustain, as well from the number of

squadrons as from the badness of the ground, which was cut through in many places, and into which the enemy had introduced infantry. However we charged and recharged ten times; and at last the enemy amazed at our boldness, halted.[5]

Numbers, however, soon began to tell, and William himself, with the English cavalry, commenced to work round the right flank, which should, of course, have been protected by Drogheda. By noon it was clear that a decision had been reached, and that the time had come for the Jacobites to withdraw.

The retreat was very well managed. Douglas joined up with Meinhart Schomberg at about twelve o'clock, and from that moment the threat to Duleek became very real. Lauzun, however, marched parallel with the Williamites, and it was the defensive who won that critical race. As the Jacobite infantry fell back on Duleek the horse drew up behind them as a rearguard, and checked William's somewhat ineffectual attempts at pursuit. Hamilton turned on his pursuers in the neighbourhood of Platin Hall, and chased them back to their main body, until he was himself forced to withdraw. In consequence the Irish foot were able to pass unmolested through Duleek, and the French battalions followed them without losing any of their cohesion. It was Berwick's opinion that if William had been a more enterprising commander the Jacobite army would not have got away, at any rate not without being severely mauled, but this in no way detracts from the skill and bravery shown by the French infantry and the Irish cavalry in covering the retreat.

On the Jacobite side at any rate the Boyne was a soldier's battle, for the generalship was of a very low standard: whether James or Lauzun was the more guilty is not easy to decide. First of all there was the mistaken decision to make a stand on the Boyne at all; then came the failure to cover the flanks; and lastly the incompetence which left less than six thousand men at Oldbridge to fight about fifteen thousand of the enemy. As for the French veterans, up to the time that the battle was decided they might as well never have been present at all. One man who emerges without stain on this day when the Stuart cause went down to defeat was surely Tyrconnel, who, at the age of sixty, and according to Macaulay a physical wreck several years earlier, had headed cavalry charges in a way which would have reflected the utmost credit on a man half his age. He lost, it may be noted, two relatives, for Sir Niall O'Neill died of wounds at Waterford eight days later and Walter Dongan was killed at the head of his regiment at the ford of Donore. As for the total casualties, it is not easy to arrive at any agreed figure. Berwick put the Jacobite losses at not more than a thousand, and said those of the Williamites were negligible. Macaulay estimated them at one thousand, five hundred for the Jacobites and five hundred (including old Schomberg) for their opponents. In the present century Belloc, while adopting Macaulay's figure for the Jacobites, has put the Williamite casualties as high as two thousand.

How ineffective was William's effort at pursuit can be gauged by the orderly arrival of the Jacobite forces in Dublin. The first few mounted stragglers reached the capital at about four o'clock on the day of the battle, and at about sunset James arrived at the Castle escorted by Sarsfield's cavalry; the bulk of the Jacobite infantry followed him between then and midnight. As for the rearguard, it made its appearance in the early hours of the following morning: the cavalry moved in formation and by units, with trumpets sounding, at the walk, and finally there marched to tuck of drum the regiments of *Le Roi Soleil* in perfect order, though tired. At no time did the retreat to Dublin degenerate into anything like a rout.

What happened after James reached the capital has been the sport of legend – how on his arrival at the Castle he was greeted by Frances Tyrconnel to whom he complained that the Irish had run away, only to be told, 'But your Majesty has run still faster.' Whether he had already decided to leave Ireland is uncertain, but as soon as he reached Dublin he was given letters from the Queen urging him to do so. Luxembourg had won a great victory at Fleurus, and in her opinion now was the time, with William absent in Ireland, for James to return immediately to France, obtain the aid of Louis, which she did not doubt would be forthcoming, land in force on the English coast, and march in triumph to London. This advice fitted in very well with her husband's views, for it never seems to have occurred to either of them that Louis had any other object save to put the Stuarts back on the three thrones they had lost. Berwick would seem to have held the same view.

> The King, seeing from the ill success of the battle of the Boyne that he could not keep possession of Dublin, thought it better to leave the command to Tyrconnel, and return to France, as well to solicit a reinforcement as to see if he could not find an opening to take advantage of the absence of the Prince of Orange for an attempt upon England. The opportunity was favourable, for Marshal Luxembourg had gained the battle of Fleurus in Flanders; and the Comte de Tourville, who had lately beaten the enemy's fleet, was then at anchor in the Downs, so that the passage to England being without difficulty or opposition it was to be presumed that the King might with ease make himself master of that kingdom.

Differences inside the French government seemed to him to have ruined his father's chances, for he continues:

> This would likewise have obliged the Prince of Orange to quit Ireland in order to save the great stake: But M. de Louvois, Minister for the War Department, who, out of opposition to M. de Seignelay, Minister of the Marine Department, thwarted all the projects of the King of England, set himself so strongly to counteract this plan that the Most Christian King, overcome by his arguments, refused to consent to it.[6]

However this may be, Dublin was panic-stricken when the result of the Battle of the Boyne become known, as the arrival of William was expected almost hourly, and there was a general exodus to the South and West. On all sides James was urged to get away before it was too late, or he would become his son-in-law's prisoner, though it was most unlikely that the Dutchman would wish to burden himself with such a captive; on the contrary he probably echoed the remark of Maurice of Saxony when he had Charles V at his mercy, 'I have no cage big enough to hold such a bird.' Soon after his arrival James ' spoke

singly with those of his Privy Council whom he trusted most ',
and they left him in no doubt as to their views, which were
that the sooner he departed the better, probably because they
did not want the responsibility for his safety. Next morning,

> Mr. Taaf, the Duke of Tyrconnel's chaplain (a very honest
> and discreet clergie man) came from him to press the King to
> leave Dublin and get into France as soon as ever he could, and
> to send all the troops in town immediately to meet him and
> Mons'r de Lauzun at Leslip,[7] whither he was marching with all
> what he had left, not designing to come into Dublin at all, for
> fear he should not get his tired troops soon enough out of it
> again. Accordingly the King order'd Simon Lutterel to march to
> Leslip with all the forces in the town except two troops of the
> King's own regiment of hors, which he kept to attend upon
> himself, who in complyance to the advice of all his friends
> resolved to go for France, and try to doe something more
> efectual on that side than he could hope from so shatter'd and
> dishearted a body of men as now remain'd in Ireland.[8]

James's last act in Dublin did him the utmost credit, for it
was to order that the city should not be destroyed to prevent it
falling into the enemy's hands.

He rode out of the capital at sunrise on 2 July with his two
troops of horse, and proceeded somewhat leisurely to Bray,
where he left the cavalry to hold the bridge until noon. In his
own account of his flight he says that ' he went to the house[9]
of a gentleman of the name of Hacket, near Arclough ',[10] where
he rested his horses, and then continued on his way to Duncannon. Just a century later, in 1791, Hugh Howard, brother
of the first Viscount Wicklow, wrote of this visit.

> Formerly the road from Dublin to Wexford was not through
> the town of Arklow, but across the river by a ford. It led by
> the herd's house, on the brow of a hill called Stringers Hill,
> at the end of Shelton Avenue across the river to Polehony,
> Lord Carysfort's seat, and so into the county of Wexford; or
> into the County of Waterford through Carlow and Kilkenny.
> This road to the ford has ever since been called King James's
> Lane; it is now impassable. The avenue was at the foot of

Stringers Hill, about a quarter of a mile from Shelton House, to which it led straight up to the door, through a double row of beech trees, having a hill to the right and the Hall Meadow to the Left. At the door was a porch made of wood, with seats.

An old man, one Richard Johnson, who was son to the gardener at Shelton told me that just after the battle of the Boyne, being then a young boy, as he was standing one evening in company with a labouring man of the name of Coghlan in Shelton avenue (this must have been the evening of July 2nd, 1690) he saw two tall gentlemen, grandly mounted and all covered with dust, ride down Stringers Hill in their way to the ford; but instead of proceding onwards, they turned up the avenue, whither he followed them not knowing then who they were. When they came to the house, which was at that time in the possession of one Mr. Hacket, (he was the sequestrator)[11] they alighted, and sat down in the porch, where they had some cold meat and a jug of strong beer. While they continued there, which was only for a few minutes, one of them was seized with a violent bleeding at the nose, which stained that side of the porch where the gentleman sat. When the bleeding was stopped they mounted their horses again, and rode down the avenue and across the ford (probably the short cut way to Dun-cannon Fort). He afterwards knew for certain in that the person whose nose had bled was King James II and that the other was a person of distinction . . . The porch was afterwards taken down, and the post with the blood on it (which I have seen) long carefully preserved, but has since been burned by the care-lessness of servants.[12]

From Shelton the King pushed on to Duncannon, and so precipitate were his movements that when he arrived there no Williamite troops had as yet reached Dublin. At Passage East there was lying a St Malo privateer of twenty-eight guns, appropriately or inappropriately named the *Lauzun*, and her captain was persuaded to drop down the river, embark James and his party, and take them to Kinsale, where a squadron of ten French frigates was waiting for him. These ships had been sent there by Seignelay at the personal request of the Queen so that her husband might have a means of escape if things went badly for him. From Kinsale he wrote to Tyrconnel, whom he had not seen since they parted on the battlefield of the Boyne, reappointing him as his Lord Deputy, and then sailed for Brest, where he arrived on 20 July, bringing the news of his own defeat.[13]

There can be no doubt about French opinion of his conduct. Louvois roundly accused him of having ' spoiled everything by a mixture of ignorance, over-confidence, and folly ', while Luxembourg neatly summed up the situation in the words, ' Those who love the King of England must be very glad to see him safe and sound; but those who think of his reputation have reason to deplore the figure he has cut.' As for the Irish, to this day they have neither forgiven nor forgotten what they consider to be his desertion of them.

NOTES

[1] *Memoirs*, Vol. I, p. 63. London. 1779.

[2] *James the Second*, p. 257. London. 1928.

[3] *Lauzun*, p. 184. Paris. 1913.

[4] Boulger, D. C.: *The Battle of the Boyne*, p. 159. London. 1911.

[5] *Memoirs*, Vol. I, p. 64. London. 1779.

[6] *Memoirs*, Vol. I, pp. 66-68. London. 1779. *Cf.* Churchill, W. S.: *Marlborough, His Life and Times*, Vol. I, pp. 323-5. London. 1933.

[7] Leixlip.

[8] Clarke, J. S.: *Life of James II*, Vol. II, pp. 401-2. London. 1816.

[9] Shelton Abbey, but not the present building.

[10] Arklow.

[11] The owner was Dr Ralph Howard, a Williamite, who had taken refuge in England.

[12] One of whom is said to have used it to light a fire. I am indebted to the present (Eighth) Earl of Wicklow for the above information.

[13] The anchor of the ship which took James to France is now to be found at Baron's Court, County Tyrone, having been presented by the King to the Fourth Earl of Abercorn who accompanied him on the voyage.

CHAPTER XI

The Defence of Limerick

THE DEPARTURE of James, following so soon on that of Mountcashel, d'Avaux, and von Rosen, naturally brought to the fore
others who had not hitherto played a very notable part in the
struggle against William of Orange, and prominent among
them were Berwick and Sarsfield.

James FitzJames, the future Duke of Berwick and Marshal
of France, was born on 21 August 1670 at Moulines in the
Bourbonnais, the son of James, Duke of York, and Arabella
Churchill, and it is not uninteresting to note that his birth-
place had also, seventeen years earlier, been that of another
very great soldier, namely Marshal Villars. Arabella was twenty-
one at the time of her son's birth, for she was born on 28
February 1649 and baptized on 16 March of the same year.
She was herself the daughter of Winston Churchill, a decayed
Cavalier who was knighted at the Restoration, and who for a
time represented first Weymouth and then Lyme Regis in the
House of Commons. The Churchills had up to that time played
no great part on the stage of national politics, and outside the
British Isles their name was unknown. This state of affairs,
however, was soon to undergo a change, and the maternal
relatives of the young FitzJames were for a time to be as
prominent as the paternal. The world was a small place, at any
rate where the governing class was concerned, at the end of the
seventeenth century, as Arabella's boy was to find when he
grew to manhood. His uncle was John Churchill, one day to be
Duke of Marlborough and probably the greatest soldier in
British history, and with this uncle he was to cross swords on

more than one occasion, though without any serious disturbance of their personal friendly relations. John Churchill married the formidable Sarah Jennings whose sister, Frances, was the wife of Tyrconnel. As for his Stuart connections, the boy's father was not only heir presumptive to the English throne, but he was first cousin to Louis XIV.

It would be impossible to exaggerate the importance of this background even in the briefest account of Berwick's career. Nationality counted for very little, and nationalism for nothing at all, at that time, and in this respect FitzJames was the child of his age. He entertained feelings of the most devoted loyalty, first to his father, and then to his half-brother, James III, as the successive heads of the House of Stuart; after he entered the French service he was unswervingly loyal to the King of France. On the other hand, there is no evidence that he, or for that matter anyone else, thought it in the least odd that as an Englishman he should have spent many years of his life fighting against the English government and English armies. Fitz-James was by nature a merciful man, and this characteristic was strengthened by the fact that, almost from the beginning of his career, on which ever side he was fighting he had friends and relatives on the other. In effect, his cosmopolitanism, without ever distracting him from what he considered to be the path of duty, rendered him always just and generally considerate where his opponents were concerned. His *Memoirs*, for example, contain many tributes to the constancy and bravery of those against whom he was fighting.

The boy's grandfather, Sir Winston Churchill, was an extremely successful place-hunter, if he was little else, and in due course he followed up the knighthood which had been bestowed upon him at the Restoration by securing the appointment, not only of his son John as a page to the Duke of York, but also of his daughter, Arabella, as a maid of honour to the Duchess of York. She was no great beauty, if contemporary records are to be believed, though the portrait-painters of the day did their best for her; but James was not particular in this respect, and his brother's taunt that his mistresses were so

ugly that they must have been imposed upon him by his con-
fessor as a penance had much truth in it. However this may
be, Arabella became James's mistress in due course.

The circumstances have been racily described by Sir Winston
Churchill of our own time. ' There is a tale of a riding-party
to a greyhound-coursing near York, and of Arabella's horse
running away in a head-long gallop; of a fall and a prostrate
figure on the sward; of the Royal Duke to the rescue, and of a
love born of this incident. Hamilton declares that, while
Arabella's face presented no more than the ordinary feminine
charms, her figure was exceedingly beautiful, and that James
was influenced by the spectacle of beauty in distress and also in
disarray.'[1] In due course four children were born to James
and Arabella, namely the future Duke of Berwick; Henry Fitz-
James, who was created Duke of Albemarle and Grand Prior of
England, whom we have already met in circumstances which
did him no credit; Henriette, who married the first Lord Walde-
grave, and, after his death, the third Viscount of Galmoye;
and Arabella, a nun, who outlived her brothers and sisters,
for she did not die until 1762. In none of her children did
Arabella Churchill appear to take much interest, and over
the most famous of them she never exercised the least influence. In due course she and her royal lover parted, and
shortly after the Revolution she married a Colonel Charles
Godfrey. Through the influence of Marlborough he was
appointed Master of the Jewel Office, and by him Arabella
had two daughters. She herself died in 1730.[2]

The future Duke of Berwick received the greater part of his
education in France, and there he came under influences which
were to affect him for the rest of his life. It was the apogee
of France and her wonderful civilization. Her soldiers were
supreme in the field; her diplomacy was at its most brilliant;
her art and letters had few competitors. The result of this pre-
eminence was felt in all quarters and in all countries, from the
pagodas of China to the cabins of Connacht. The court of Louis
XIV attracted visitors, not only from Europe, but also from
Africa and the East, and the influence of Versailles can still be

traced in the ruins of the Summer Palace of the Manchu Emperors in Peking. There was not a petty German prince but felt impelled to imitate, so far as his resources would permit, the pomp of the King of France. This led at times to extravagances which can only be described as absurd, and the story is told of more than one princeling who provided himself with a French mistress, though rather for ornament than for use; yet what civilization there was in Germany in the century that followed the desolation of the Thirty Years' War owed its inspiration to France.

It was the same in Italy, where French influence early made itself felt, though for long the dominant Power in that peninsula had been Spain: by 1665 Italians had begun to wear wigs in imitation of Louis, and for the rest of his reign his imprint on the manners and customs of the country became even more steadily marked. None of what he was to see during his military career would seem strange to FitzJames, for, apart from the fact that he had been educated in France, his own country of England had no more than the rest of Europe been able to resist the attraction of the French court. ' Into England flowed after 1660 an ever-increasing stream of French ideas and modes of life. Fine Gallic gentlemen surprised simple Englishmen with their quaint airs and graces; French *modistes* appeared with fans and petticoats and " the fashones " to tempt the purse and adorn the persons of our English ladies. Everything now came from Paris, the Mecca of the civilized world, from sedan-chairs and dainty silver brushes for cleaning the teeth to Chatelin's famous fricassees and ragouts.'[3] Even the Highland chieftains aped the manners of the French court,[4] and at the Battle of the Boyne the commands on both sides were given in French. It was a notable achievement, and one of which the echo has not even yet wholly died away.

FitzJames was not destined to remain in the French capital for any great length of time, for in the spring of 1686 he was sent by his father to join the army which the Emperor Leopold I had sent under the command of the Duke of Lorraine to capture Budapest from the Turks, and to drive them out of

P

Hungary. This was to prove a momentous step, and there is no evidence to show why James took it. Recent British sovereigns had given no special proof of military ability, though James himself had proved to be no mean sailor in his earlier days. James IV of Scotland had shown himself a gallant, if unfortunate, commander in the field, and Charles I was by no means so poor a strategist as has been alleged; but none of the other members of the House of Stuart, save possibly Prince Rupert, were distinguished by any sort of military capacity, and the dislike of James I and VI for naked steel is notorious. In these circumstances it would appear to be by no means improbable that FitzJames was embarked on his career at the instigation of his uncle, John Churchill, who had already revealed the genius that was to ensure his place as one of the greatest military commanders in history. Yet the Churchills themselves had been quite undistinguished until the latest generation. Perhaps John detected in his young nephew even at this early age the marks of an ability similar to his own, and therefore advised the King to send him to the wars.

However this may be, there was nothing unusual in the decision. Those who possessed, or whose relatives believed them to possess, military ability had for two centuries been in the habit of seeing a campaign under some distinguished soldier such as Maurice of Nassau or Gustavus Adolphus, and, as has been shown on an earlier page, FitzJames's own father had been no exception, though he was in a slightly different category for when he served in the French and Spanish armies he was an exile from his own country. In this connection it is not uninteresting to note that the only surviving portrait of John Churchill in a regimental uniform is as an ensign in the French service. As the seventeenth century drew to its close there grew up a tendency among the young men of Western Europe to serve in the Imperialist armies against the Turks, in much the same way as the adventurous of an earlier generation had gone on a crusade.

For those who, like FitzJames, were to take up arms as a profession this had a double advantage, for it not only provided them at an early age with a variety of experience which they could not have gained had they remained in the service of their own country, but it also enabled them to meet their contemporaries from other kingdoms, and so to become acquainted with their characters and characteristics. In the seventeenth, and early eighteenth, century there can have been few opposing generals who had not at some time or other in the past fought on the same side, and they had in consequence a pretty shrewd idea of the strategy and tactics which their opponent was likely to employ against them. This personal relationship also made for humanity in the conduct of operations and for a strict adherence to the rules of war: this was particularly noticeable in Ireland where the behaviour of the English generals in 1689-91 represented a marked improvement upon that of their predecessors in the Elizabethan and Cromwellian wars.

The chief event of the campaign of 1686 was the capture of Budapest, and there was little further fighting in Hungary that year, so FitzJames returned to London, and was made colonel of what later became the eighth Foot, which was one of the units that had been raised in the previous year at the time of Monmouth's rebellion. Further honours were, however, in store for the young man, and on 19 March 1687 he was created Duke of Berwick, Earl of Tynemouth, and Baron Bosworth.

Berwick, as he must now be termed, also served in the Imperialist forces in the campaign of 1687 with the rank of colonel, and was given 'command of the regiment of Cuirassiers of Taaffe, who was at that time Lieutenant General of Cavalry, a man of great sense, and favourite of the Duke of Lorraine. He was an Irishman by birth, and brother of the Earl of Carlingford[5] . . . He was one of the most agreeable noblemen in Europe, thorough master of polite literature, and a very able statesman, but not much esteemed in the field.[6] It would, perhaps, not be too fanciful to see in this new-found friendship with Taaffe the origin of that sympathy with Ireland, and attraction to all things Irish, which distinguished Berwick from his father, and in later years caused him to be regarded with some suspicion by the Scottish Jacobites. The campaign of

1687 was mainly notable for the crushing defeat of the Turks at Mohacz, and when Berwick returned to London at the end of it he was made governor of Portsmouth as well as Colonel of the Royal Horse Guards: as the historian of that regiment has written, 'A trusty as well as brilliant successor[7] in the colonelcy of the Blues was forthcoming, however, in the person of James FitzJames, Duke of Berwick. . . The new Colonel, during his brief command, kept well aglow in the Royal Regiment of Horse the sacred fire of his traditional loyalty.[8]

By this time, however, the shadows were beginning to lengthen round his father's throne, so James kept his son at home during 1688. When the Revolution came, and William of Orange landed, Berwick stood by the King, but in spite of the most determined efforts he was unable to restore the situation which, it must be confessed, had only become hopeless in consequence of the incompetence displayed by James himself in the hour of crisis. The victorious Williamites soon blockaded Portsmouth by land and sea, and although Berwick had no doubts about the loyalty of the garrison, which consisted of two thousand, five hundred foot and five hundred dragoons, he was compelled to surrender the place. In December he escaped with his father to France, and in the spring of the following year he accompanied James to Ireland, where his earlier service has already been described.

Patrick Sarsfield is not nearly to well documented as Berwick, who was one day to marry his widow. On his paternal side his background was much the same as that of Tyrconnel, for the family came over to Ireland in the reign of Henry II, and settled in the Pale; from time to time, however, they crossed over to England, for a Sarsfield fought under Edward I against Wallace, and another served in the Scottish wars of Edward III. Patrick's mother, Anne O'More, was of Celtic birth, and could trace her ancestry back into the very dawn of Irish history. The exact date of his birth would appear to be uncertain, but it was probably about 1650, the year in which William of Orange and Marlborough were also born: the place may well have been Lucan in County Dublin where the Sarsfields held the manor. Patrick received his early education in France, and was commissioned by Charles II in 1678; three years later he got himself involved in an incident which recalls Tyrconnel's early career, for in the diary of Narcissus Luttrell we read, under date of 9 December 1681, 'There was a duell fought the sixth between the Lord Newburgh and the Lord Kinsale, as principalls (two striplings under twenty), and Mr. Kirk and Captain Sarsfield, seconds: the principalls had no hurt; but Captain Sarsfield was run through the body, near the shoulder, very dangerously.'[9]

Patrick fought in the Life Guards at the time of Monmouth's rebellion in spite of the fact that his elder brother, William, was married to Monmouth's sister.[10] In a skirmish at Keynsham he had a cut hand, but at Sedgemoor he was much more seriously wounded, was unhorsed, and left for dead.[11] Berwick had no very high opinion of Sarsfield, and he wrote that he was ' a man of an amazing stature, utterly void of sense, very good-natured and very brave '.[12] How much credence should be given to Berwick's views on Sarsfield it is difficult to say, and he may well have been to some extent prejudiced by his wife whose relations with her first husband are said not always to have been of the best. Whatever Sarsfield's merits as a soldier, there can be no question but that he was a patriotic Irishman, and as such he had no sympathy with the Unionist views which were so popular with James and many of his entourage.

Earlier in the war Berwick and Sarsfield would certainly appear to have been on friendly terms as the following letter, from the former to the latter, though of no importance in itself, would seem to testify:

Cavan Park the 31e July

Deare notorious

This is to give you notice that Maréchal Rosen or I will march within three or four days from this place to Balishannon, so that if you looke out sharp this way, you may see us laying on these rebelly and cowring rogues; which may give you also an opportunity of attacking on that side of the water to make a divertion. I am afraid the siege of Derry will be raised, and I

thank god that I have not nor ever will give my consent unto it.
I will say no more this till I meet you at Balishannon. In the
meantime I remain Deare Notorious

Your kind Friend and servant

Berwick.[18]

It was with a rapidly deteriorating situation that these three
men – Tyrconnel, Berwick, and Sarsfield – had to deal on the
morrow of the King's departure for France. The garrison at
Drogheda surrendered the day after the Battle of the Boyne;
they were disarmed, but were allowed to proceed to Athlone.
At Wexford the garrison evacuated the town on William's
approach, leaving behind them a considerable quantity of
stores, arms, and powder. The garrison at Duncannon surrendered after a parley, and were granted permission to march to
Limerick. Waterford also gave in without a fight on condition
that the two regiments there – Kavanagh's and Barrett's –
should be allowed to withdraw to Cork. All these places might
have resisted, and although there is no reason to think that
they could have held out for long their resistance would have
delayed William's plans against Limerick: furthermore, the
surrender of these garrisons, one after another, must have
strengthened his belief that the Irish had no fight left in them.

At only one place did the Williamite army encounter the
opposition which it should have found everywhere, and that
was at Athlone, where Tyrconnel had placed that redoubtable
figure, Colonel Richard Grace, in command. He had with him
his own regiment, which had done well at the Boyne, as well
as the disarmed garrison of Drogheda, and a few other troops,
but there was a serious shortage of munitions of all kinds. Yet
the importance of the place could hardly be exaggerated, for
through it ran the main road to Connacht, and whoever was
in possession of Athlone commanded the middle crossings of
the Shannon. William was under no illusions on this score, so
he sent General Douglas to reduce the town, and for that
purpose he entrusted him with a force of three regiments of
horse, two of dragoons, and ten of foot, together with ten
field-pieces and two mortars. When Douglas summoned Grace

to surrender the Jacobite commander drew a pistol from his belt, fired it over the head of the envoy, and said, ' These are my terms; these only will I give or receive, and when all my provisions are consumed I will eat my old boots.'

The fighting then began, but it was not destined to last for long. Douglas commenced to bombard the town, without making real progress. At the end of a week he found that he was running out of ammunition, and that he had lost between three and four hundred men, so he abandoned the siege, and joined William before Limerick. This failure was a precursor of the greater repulse before the latter town, but at the time its significance was generally ignored.[14]

It is now necessary to turn to the retreat of the Jacobite field army from the Boyne to Limerick, which was a very ill-managed affair except for the French, the cavalry, and one or two regiments of Irish foot. The best contemporary account is probably that of John Stevens, who, as we have seen, was serving with the Grand Prior's Regiment.[15] His unit had been scattered to the winds in the battle, and he tells us that at one time it was reduced to six musketeers, eight pikemen, four ensigns, another lieutenant, and himself, which were all that were left of a strength of eight hundred. At Naas he fell in with an ensign who had a lame horse, and they seem to have shared the poor beast until they reached Kilcullen, in County Kildare, on the night of 2 July, where they found a bed. Next day they were up at dawn, but they had only gone five or six miles, when they ' were overtaken by the Duke of Tyrconnel and his family, some whereof challenged the horse, and indeed he had the King's mark; they being too strong for us to cope with, for then might was the greatest right, they carried him away, leaving us afoot, weary, and without friends or money '.

On the fourth the two travellers reached Kilkenny.

> All the shops and public houses in the town were shut, and neither meat nor drink to be had, though many were fainting through want and weariness. Hunger and thirst put me forward to seek reliefe, where nothing but necessity could have carryed me; but the invincible power of want hides all blushes, so

hearing the stores at the Castle were broken up, and much bread and drink given out, I resolved to try my fortune there and found drink carryed out in pailes, and many of the rabble drunk with what they had got; yet upon my approach I perceived some officers, whom want had carryed thither as well as me but were somewhat more forward, so ill-treated by Brigadier Mackay first, and next by the Duke of Tyrconnel, who gave a Lieut. a thrust on the breast with his cane, that I went away resolved to perish than run the hazard of being ill used.

Tyrconnel reached Limerick on 6 July, the day on which William entered Dublin, and with his old energy set about reconstituting the Jacobite army which to a very large extent was by now little more than a disorganized mob. Stevens represents the condition of his regiment as typical, and when it was inspected on 14 July it was found to consist of no more than a hundred and fifty effectives, of whom fifty were in possession of damaged weapons while the rest had no weapons at all. At first the High Command was desirous of making an example of the men who had thrown away their arms, and, some of the unarmed men for an example to terrify others from throwing away their arms, but the number being so very great it was only declared to them how well they had deserved writes Stevens, ' It was proposed and threatened to shoot to dye.' It was probably a wise decision, for there was already dissension enough in the Jacobite ranks without adding to it by severity of this nature: the immediate task of Tyrconnel and his colleagues was not punishment for past failures but preparation for resistance to the enemy in the immediate future.

Not unnaturally William, ignoring the reverse at Athlone, had decided that the Irish were unlikely to offer any effective resistance whatever he did, and it must be admitted that his experience in the case of so many of the Leinster towns justified him in this belief. He had, too, more than one pressing reason for desiring a speedy end to the struggle in Ireland, and so, taking everything into account, the soundest strategy seemed to be to strike a knock-out blow at the Jacobite forces which were re-grouping at Limerick, so at the beginning of August he moved in the direction of that city. On the way he received news which nearly caused him to abandon the whole enterprise, for he learnt that his army in Flanders had been defeated at Fleurus and that the French had won a victory at sea off Beachy Head; the second piece of news was the more serious because the English sailors had fought in such a manner as to raise doubts with regard to their loyalty to himself. This information brought William back to Dublin, and for a brief space he even thought of returning to England; but the French did not follow up their successes either on land or sea beyond burning Teignmouth, which did the Jacobite cause more harm than good, so the Dutchman resumed his march to Limerick.[16]

When the news of their enemy's decision reached the Jacobite leaders there was at once a difference of opinion amongst them as to the advisability of attempting to defend Limerick. According to Berwick, ' The place had no fortification but a wall without ramparts, and some miserable little towers without ditches.'[17] Lauzun had his instructions from Louvois, and he was not going to risk valuable French lives in the defence of a place the ramparts of which, he declared, ' might be battered down with toasted apples.' So the French troops marched away to Galway on the day on which William's advance-guard appeared before Limerick. Tyrconnel was also opposed to defending the town: his reasons are not obvious, but they were probably strategic. At a lower level there was equal pessimism, for Stevens wrote, ' As for the city of Limerick, which I said was almost defenceless, it had no other than an old stone wall, made against bows and arrows, and a poor covered way made in a month's time.'[18]

Sarsfield took a very different line, being of the opinion that Limerick should be held at all costs, and in the end his advice was taken. Accordingly Tyrconnel appointed Boisseleau, who has been mentioned on an earlier page, to command at Limerick. It was a very happy choice, for this officer of the Gardes Françaises had for some months been training Irish recruits at Cork, so he knew the Irish soldier, and thus was able to get the best out of him. It was indeed fortunate that this should be the case, for the troops under his command were woefully ill-equipped: the MacMahon Regiment, for example, had no arms at all, but it managed all the same to play a prominent part in the repulse of the final Williamite assault by hurling stones on the attacking force. As for numbers, it is once again by no means easy to arrive at any exact estimate. Save for the garrisons at Athlone, Cork, and Kinsale, practically the whole of the available Irish infantry was concentrated at Limerick. Berwick put the Jacobite strength at twenty thousand, of whom not more than half were armed, while Stevens wrote, ' I will not be too exact in affirming what garrison we had. I know, both to encourage us and terrify the enemy, we were given out to be fifteen thousand strong, but I can be positive that to my knowledge we were not in all ten thousand, including the unarmed men, which were a considerable number.' The French reports state that there were twenty-eight Irish infantry regiments at Limerick, one cavalry regiment (Henry Luttrell's), and one dragoon regiment (Maxwell's). The bulk of the cavalry, about 3,500 strong, was encamped about six miles from Limerick on the Clare bank of the Shannon for the purpose of preventing the complete investment of the city, an object which they successfully achieved. This force was commanded by Berwick, and Sarsfield was serving under him.

William arrived before Limerick on 7 August 1690, and at dawn on the following day he summoned the garrison to surrender on the honourable terms which he would be happy to concede. Boisseleau replied to the effect that he was very much surprised by the message that he had received, and that he hoped to deserve a better opinion from the Prince of Orange by a vigorous defence of the place, which he intended to offer with the aid of the troops of the King of Great Britain. The siege then began in earnest.

In spite of these brave words it was clear from the beginning that, unless a diversion of some sort was effected, Limerick could not by itself hold out indefinitely against the force which William could concentrate against it. Berwick certainly was without illusions on this score.

> I had proposed to the Duke of Tyrconnel, as soon as the enemy sat down before Limerick, to pass the Shannon with our three thousand five hundred horse, and destroy all the magazines they had left behind them, especially at Dublin; which would undoubtedly have reduced them to a necessity of decamping. As all the towns in this country were open and without defence, I was morally certain of succeeding in my enterprise; and as to getting back, which was objected to me as being very difficult, the knowledge I had of the country had already suggested to me by what means it might be effected; for besides that we should have had the start of the enemy, I had no doubt of making my way into the North, and returning to our quarters by Sligo. The Duke of Tyrconnel, who was become heavy and fearful, would not agree to my proposal; perhaps too there might be some degree of jealousy at the bottom on his side; for it did not suit with the dignity of Viceroy to become a partisan, and that, besides, neither his age nor bulk were accommodated to such an expedition, the whole conduct of it would have devolved upon me.[19]

It is indeed extraordinary how in Tyrconnel's later years his critics were continually stressing his age and infirmities which the event almost immediately disproved.

Sarsfield was to be more fortunate, for when he heard that William's siege-train was on its way from Cashel he asked Tyrconnel's permission to attack and destroy it, and was given leave to make the attempt. With about five hundred troopers he intercepted the column at Ballyneety, overcame the escort with very little loss, and then rendered the guns useless by the simple process of stuffing them with powder, fixing their mouths to the ground, and then blowing them all up. The explosion was heard in Limerick, where the encouragement it brought to the besieged was only equalled by the dismay which it occasioned to the besiegers. Sarsfield then returned by a different route from that by which he had come, and so eluded a Williamite force which attempted to intercept him. Largely on account of this exploit, worthy of Jeb Stuart in the American Civil War, James created him Earl of Lucan in January 1691. Unfortunately this success seems to have given Sarsfield an exaggerated idea of his own importance, at any rate according to Berwick, always a severe critic where he was concerned, for after paying tribute to the brilliance of the raid, he says that it elated Sarsfield so much ' that he thought himself the greatest general in the world. Henry Luttrell contributed as much as possible to turn his head by incessantly praising him in all companies; not out of any real esteem he had for him, but to make him popular, and by that means render him subservient to his own designs.'[20]

This reverse placed William in a serious quandary. The season was getting late, and with every day that passed his presence was more urgently required elsewhere, so he had no alternative but to put everything he had into one final assault on Limerick; this he did, but owing to Sarsfield's raid the attack had to be made without adequate artillery preparation, and after some extremely heavy fighting it was repulsed with a loss of one thousand, five hundred killed and wounded. William now had no choice save to bow to the inevitable, so on 30 August, he raised the siege, and some days later he returned to England.

It is sad to relate that while the Irish soldiers were so resolutely defending Limerick their leaders were quarrelling among themselves: this, indeed, they had shown a disposition to do ever since the war began, but the presence of James had exercised a restraining influence; now that this was removed their quarrels and intrigues broke out afresh. What it was all about is not easy to discover, and one suspects that the differences were mainly personal, though they were given a political, nationalist, or military colouring as best suited the ' image ' which the particular controversialist wished to assume. Philip Sergeant[21] places considerable reliance upon Stevens, but as he was only a subaltern in a marching regiment it is unlikely that he was directly acquainted with the dissensions in the High Command. The evidence of such always requires to be sifted with care, if not actually regarded with suspicion. Under the stress of war men are inclined to be harsh in their judgments, and a general's reputation with his army is apt to rise or fall like that of a huntsman with his field according to the sport he provides. One moment he is ' the cleverest fellow alive ', and the next he is ' the biggest fool going '. Stevens was a junior officer, quite apart from the fact that he had formed a poor impression of Tyrconnel at Kilkenny, and there is no point in being a junior officer unless one may set the world right, beginning of course, with one's seniors, especially a viceroy. Berwick is a more reliable witness.

> The Duke of Tyrconnel having become again Viceroy of Ireland on the King's retreat, Luttrell[22] ceased not to speak against Tyrconnel and to excite everyone against him. He was now so well able to stir up the chief men of the nation that one day Sarsfield came to me on their behalf, and, after having bound me to secrecy, told me that, being convinced of Tyrconnel's treachery, they had resolved to arrest him, and therefore he proposed to me, on their behalf, that I should take on me the government of the kingdom. My reply was brief: I told him that I was astonished they should make such a proposal to me, that all which might be done against the Viceroy was a crime of high treason, and that in consequence, if they did not cease to cabal, I should be their enemy and should warn the King and Tyrconnel. My words made an impression, and prevented the execution of their plans.[23]

As we have seen, Berwick was by no means uncritical of Tyrconnel, but even in his youth he was essentially fair-minded, and, after all, to quote *The Jacobite Narrative*, ' His Grace (i.e. Tyrconnel) had a discretionary power left him by the King, to make peace or continue war, as he should see it most conducing to his Majesty's interests and his loyal people's welfare. Whether Sarsfield was one of the fomentors of this intrigue, or was the tool of others, is another matter.

William's spectacular failure to take Limerick temporarily roused Jacobite spirits, but nothing could disguise the fact that the general military situation had deteriorated rapidly during the previous six months. It is true that thanks to the successful defence of Athlone and Limerick the line of the Shannon was still intact, and Cork and Kinsale were still held by Jacobite garrisons, but Ulster and Leinster were lost, and William had left a considerable force behind him under the Dutch General Ginkel. Some of what were proving themselves to be the best Irish Regiments were now in the French service, while as for the French themselves, not only had they done nothing to help in the defence of Limerick, but they were waiting at Galway merely for the arrival of the transports which were to take them back to their own country. In these circumstances it was not unreasonable to suppose that another campaign would see the end of organized Jacobite resistance in Ireland altogether, so Tyrconnel determined to go to France to see what assistance could be obtained from Louis XIV. Before he left he paid a brief visit to Limerick, where he handed over the military administration to Berwick, with a council of officers to advise him, while civil affairs were put in the hands of a committee of twelve. The Lord Deputy then returned to Galway whence he sailed to France in the second week of September with Lauzun and the French contingent.

He did not take Frances with him for the simple reason that she had preceded him, nor did she return to Ireland when he did. She was at Saint-Germain when he died, being then aged forty-two, and she lived until 1731. The intervening years she spent in France, England, and Holland, finally settling in Dublin, where she passed the remainder of her days in a house in Paradise Row, Arbour Hill, near Phoenix Park. Accounts vary as to her financial position, but she must have had some money, for she founded a nunnery in King Street for the Order of the Poor Clares. She seems, however, to have been alone at the time of her death, for during the March night it occurred she fell out of bed, and being too feeble to rise or call she was found on the floor in the morning so perished with cold that she died in a few hours. She was buried in a vault in St Patrick's Cathedral.

NOTES

[1] *Marlborough, His Life and Times*, Vol. I, p. 45. London. 1933.

[2] *Cf.* Wilson, C. T.: *James the Second and the Duke of Berwick*, pp. 67-8. London. 1876. Also Fea, Allen: *James II and His Wives*, pp. 66-67.

[3] Bryant, Sir A.: *The England of Charles II*, p. 112. London. 1934.

[4] *Cf.* Burton, J. H.: *Lives of Simon, Lord Lovat, and Duncan Forbes of Culloden*, p. 173. London. 1847.

[5] Who was killed at the Boyne.

[6] Berwick, Duke of: *Memoirs*, Vol. I, pp. 12-13. London. 1779.

[7] To the Earl of Oxford.

[8] Arthur, Sir George: *The Story of the Household Cavalry*, p. 214.

[9] *Cf.* Todhunter, J.: *Life of Patrick Sarsfield, Earl of Lucan*, p. 8. Dublin. 1895.

[10] *Cf.* Scott, Lord George: *Lucy Walter, Wife or Mistress?* pp. 192-3. London. 1947.

[11] *Cf.* Little, Bryan: *The Monmouth Episode*, p. 183. London. 1956.

[12] *Memoirs*, Vol. I, p. 96. London. 1779.

[13] Cox Letters in the National Library of Ireland (MS. No. 990). When or how Sarsfield acquired the nickname of 'Notorious' is obscure.

[14] Grace was killed in the second siege of Athlone in the following year, and according to tradition he was buried in St Mary's church there, but his tomb has never been discovered. It is alleged that earlier in the war Grace had received an offer from Schomberg on behalf of William, and that he wrote his reply indignantly rejecting the proposal, on the back of the Six of Hearts, since when it has been known in Ireland as 'Grace's Card'.

[15] *Journell of my Travels since the Revolution*, p. 85 *et seq.*, B.M. Additional MSS., 36, 298.

[16] The best recent account of the defence of Limerick is that of Dr J. G. Simms in *North Munster Studies*, pp. 308-314. Limerick. 1967.

[17] *Memoirs*, Vol. I, p. 70. London. 1779.

[18] Quoted by Flood, J. M.: *The Sieges of Limerick, 1690-91*, p. 18.

[19] *Memoirs*, Vol. I, pp. 72-73. London. 1779.

[20] *Ibid.*, p. 96.

[21] In *Little Jennings and Fighting Dick Talbot*, Vol. II, pp. 508-521. London. 1913.

[22] Brigadier Henry Luttrell.

[23] *Memoirs*, Vol. I, p. 75. London. 1799.

CHAPTER XII

Aughrim and the End

WITH THE departure of Tyrconnel the war flared up again, for now that he was in supreme command Berwick determined to undertake a limited offensive in the hope of regaining at least some part of Leinster, and of obtaining possession of good strategic points in preparation for the campaign of the following year. Accordingly, with all his cavalry, seven battalions of infantry, and four guns, he marched into County Offaly, by way of Banagher, and attacked Birr Castle. The place, however, was held against him, and his gunners were so raw that they never handled their pieces effectively; moreover, Douglas was known to be advancing with a considerable force. Such being the case, the future conqueror of Nice and Barcelona had to withdraw behind the Shannon once more, but no serious effort was made by the Williamites to interfere with his retreat.

Hardly had he returned to his base from this raid than disturbing news reached him from the South to the effect that his uncle, John Churchill, then Earl of Marlborough, had landed at Cork with the intention of capturing that town and Kinsale. The strategy which this project implied was excellent, for the loss of these ports would seriously compromise the whole Jacobite position in Ireland,[1] since they constituted one of the principal means of communication with the Continent.

Up to this time Marlborough had shown no desire to take part in the Irish war, and various interpretations have been put upon his conduct, not all of them to his credit. To quote Chidsey's biography of him, ' But while James himself was in the field, my Lord Marlborough preferred to remain at home. He wanted to keep his own record technically clear. However, now that James was back in France there was no reason why Churchill should not indulge himself in a little fighting. It was a nice point '.[2] However this may be, in the early days of August he put before Mary II and the Council of Regency the proposal that he should command an expedition against the Munster ports.

The Council decided against the scheme, but Mary insisted on referring it to William, who, in spite of the opposition of his Dutch generals, gave his approval, and from the camp before Limerick wrote, in French incidentally, to Marlborough in the following terms:

> August 14, 1690.
> I have just received your letter of the 7th. I strongly approve of your plan to embark with four thousand infantry and the marines, which together make four thousand nine hundred men, and is a sufficient force to capture Cork and Kinsale. You will have to take enough munitions with you, and use the ships' guns, for we can send you none from here. But for cavalry I will send you enough, and will take good care that the army shall not be a burden upon you. It is only time which must be saved, and you must hasten as quickly as you can, and let me knew when you will be there.[3]

Two points in this letter call for comment. One is William's lack of artillery even before Sarsfield did his work at Bally-neety, and the other is the phrase about taking ' good care that the army shall not be a burden upon you '. This can only refer to the Jacobite field-army, so it must be interpreted as meaning that at that time it was William's intention to remain in Ireland, and cover the sieges of Cork and Kinsale.

It may not be irrelevant to enquire whether Marlborough had not reason to believe that the operation would prove easier than most people, including William, suspected. That the defences of Cork were both out of date and in a dilapidated condition must have been generally known, but there is in the National Library in Dublin a report on Kinsale, compiled in 1680 for Charles II, which concludes, ' It is most certain that

Q

the Fort of Rincoran or Charles Fort can no way be made to resist a considerable force.' At the same time the writer of the report gives it as his opinion that the place could by the expenditure of £11,532 be made safe 'from surprise'. On 5 March 1681 the Farmers of the Revenue of Ireland were authorized to pay up to £20,000 on the fortifications of Kinsale, and it would appear that this amount was also to cover work to be done on the Old Fort across the Bandon River.[4] Now it is at least possible that Marlborough was cognizant of these facts, and thus realized that a spectacular triumph was his for the asking; not, indeed that this consideration in any way detracts from the inherent strategical soundness of the scheme.

This was Marlborough's first independent command, and he realized that, as William had warned him, owing to the lateness of the season time was the most important factor. The expedition and its shipping were concentrated at Portsmouth, where Marlborough arrived on 26 August. He had hoped to sail four days later, but he did not in fact get away until 17 September owing to contrary winds. He gave out that he intended to raid the coast of Normandy as a reprisal for the sack of Teignmouth, but the rumour does not appear to have carried any conviction in France. What did happen, as we have seen, was that in the second week of September the French under Lauzun sailed from Galway, though to what extent this was connected with Marlborough's intended blow in Munster is another matter. Sir Winston Churchill and Captain Cox both hold the view that Lauzun's departure was the direct consequence of this move. It would, of course, have been far sounder strategy for the French general to have marched south, and so to have caught the besiegers of Cork and Kinsale between two fires, but this would not have suited the policy of the French government, which was only desirous of getting rid of its Irish commitment altogether. When Marlborough finally got off from Portsmouth it was with his troops on board eighty-two ships; the crossing was rough and he was very sick, but he soon silenced the outer defences of Cork Harbour, and sailed up to Passage West where, on 22 September he disembarked his force of six thousand three hundred and forty-five men. All this time the French Navy had control of the Channel, but Paris used its sea-power to get Lauzun safely home rather than to prevent Marlborough from crossing to Ireland.

The general strategic position now requires attention. Marlborough had brought over substantially more men than had been mentioned in William's letter, and by the time he arrived at Cork the siege of Limerick had been abandoned, while William had returned to London; Ginkel, however, had been instructed to detach five thousand troops to assist in the operations against the Munster ports. Marlborough had particularly asked for English soldiers with Kirke[5] to command them: what he got was a mixed force of Danes, Dutch, and Huguenots under the Duke of Wurtemburg, for, to quote Sir Winston Churchill, ' It was with all Dutchmen from William downward a maxim that the English were ignorant of war, and must be strongly led by trained foreign officers and upheld by disciplined foreign troops.'

These reinforcements brought the Williamite strength up to twelve thousand, seven hundred and forty-five of all arms; there would not appear to be any record of the artillery available, but very effective use was to be made of the guns of the fleet both at Cork and Kinsale. On the other hand, the Duke of Wurtemburg was at first a very mixed blessing. He was junior in military rank to Marlborough, but he was far superior in birth, and he claimed that this fact entitled him to command the whole force. Marlborough not unnaturally demurred, and after a good deal of dispute a compromise was reached by which the two men were to exercise command on alternate days. Lots were then cast to determine who should command on the first day, and the Englishman won; with his usual tact he chose ' Wurtemburg' as the password, and his rival was so flattered that he chose ' Marlborough' when his turn came. After that there would seem to have been very little trouble, and the Duke tacitly acknowledged the Englishman as the leader of the expedition. Perhaps, as Commandant Cox put it, ' He was made happy by smooth talk, and soon realized that he was in the presence of a real general.'

The Jacobites had very little with which to oppose this great concentration of force. As soon as Berwick was informed of his uncle's landing he took what steps he could to save Cork, but he had only seven or eight thousand men, and they were by no means of the best quality. Furthermore, although liberties might be taken in the case of a general like William, Berwick was well aware that it would be suicide to attempt them when Marlborough was in the field. He moved, indeed, as far as Kilmallock in County Limerick, and the Williamites believed that his intention was to concentrate all the Jacobite forces in that part of Ireland at Newmarket in County Cork.[6] As for the city of Cork itself, not only were the defences in a very dilapidated condition, but the garrison was too small to hold all the necessary works against the vastly superior forces which were to be thrown against them. There were five regiments in all, namely McElligot's, Tyrone's, McCarthy's, Barrett's, and O'Sullivan's, and the total strength of the defence cannot have been more than between four and five thousand men. The Governor of Cork was Colonel Roger McElligot, who seems to have been a Kerry man; he was not a lucky soldier, and he had recently incurred a good deal of criticism for his precipitate surrender of Waterford during the Williamite advance after the Boyne.

Berwick had not been long at Kilmallock before he realized that Cork could not be saved, so he decided to adopt that ' scorched earth ' policy which was so prominent a feature of the fighting on the Eastern Front in the Second World War. In effect, he ordered McElligot to burn the city and fall back into Kerry with the five regiments under his command; he himself advanced as far as Buttevant. McElligot, however, was still smarting under the criticisms of his behaviour at Waterford, and he was determined to save his reputation by making a stand at Cork, untenable though the city might be: he accordingly disregarded Berwick's orders, and returned a disdainful reply to Marlborough's summons to surrender.

To pass from the strategy of the campaign to the tactics of the siege. The city of Cork in those days was little more than an island in the Lee, and it was dominated on all sides by high ground. It would have been a difficult place to defend at the best of times, but, quite apart from the dilapidated state of the fortifications, McElligot had only a limited supply of ammunition, and he was opposed by one of the outstanding generals of history. The Williamite lines were quickly drawn round Cork, and preparations pushed on for the assault; Marlborough then began landing heavy guns from his men-of-war, and their fire was concentrated on the Cat Fort, for Shandon Castle was already in his hands. The Cat fell on 25 September; this accomplished the Williamites started to fire into the city itself, chiefly at Elizabeth Fort, but also raking the Friars' Garden and another battery above it near the Mitre, which was probably a tavern. Some heavy cannon were also landed near the Red Cow by Red Abbey, and a battery of thirty-six pounders was raised. By the following day, 26 September, a breach had been made in the walls, and Marlborough proposed to launch the assault at low tide that evening, when McElligot asked for a parley; this came to nothing, but it did allow the tide to rise and so gained the Jacobites another day: not that this was much use to them, for the garrison was by now down to its last two barrels of powder, and there was no hope of relief from Berwick.

All the same, Marlborough was not taking any risks, and in case the besieged had taken advantage of the respite accorded them to repair the fortifications a terrific fire was opened on the city at dawn on Sunday, 27 September by the Williamite batteries supported by a frigate which came up the river on the flood. By midday the breach had become practicable, and a Danish column, a thousand strong, forded the northern arm of the river, while at one o'clock Charles Churchill, Marlborough's brother, with fifteen hundred English infantry, forded the southern branch of the Lee, and joined the Danes in the Marsh. The combined forces then occupied the counter-scarp and were in the act of re-forming for the assault on the breach, when

McElligot surrendered, being by now without ammunition, reserves, or hope of relief. What was left of the garrison became prisoners of war, and it is to Marlborough's credit that when he entered the city on the following day he sternly repressed the looting which had begun.

Unfortunately the example he set was not followed by his subordinates, and it has to be placed on record that the terms of the surrender of Cork were violated in the same way as the English too often did in the course of their campaigns in Ireland. The articles had expressly stated that the garrison were to be regular ' prisoners of war', and they further stipulated that ' there should be no prejudice to the officers, soldiers, or inhabitants ', while ' the English general should use his endeavour to obtain His Majesty's clemency towards them '. How these terms were interpreted by the victors is described by Charles Leslie:

> The garrison after laying down their arms were stripped and marched to a marshy wet ground, where they were kept with guards for four or five days, and not being sustained were forced by hunger to eat dead horses that lay about them, and several of them died for want even of that when they were removed from thence . . . They were afterwards so crowded in houses, jails, and churches that they could not all lie down at once, and had nothing but the bare floor to lie on, where the want of sustenance, and the lying in their own excrements with the dead carcases lying whole weeks in the same places with them, caused such infection that they died in great numbers daily.[7]

In the following December some two hundred of these unfortunate men were marched to Clonmel under charge of a Captain Launder, who is said to have shot sixteen of them who fell out owing to weakness and hunger; when this officer's brutality became known in official circles the only result was that William gave him a free pardon. The civil inhabitants of Cork, it may be added, fared no better, for the Catholics had their goods seized, and were then turned out of the city. There would appear to be some evidence that William was aware of what was taking place, for in a letter from Kensington, dated 4 October, to Marlborough congratulating him on the capture of Cork, he wrote, ' With regard to the prisoners whom you took at Cork I am told that there is an island where they can be kept in safety, and although this will cost me a great deal in bread, this expense is inevitable, for I have no other means of disposing of them.'[8] To Marlborough's personal credit it must be recorded that in the following January he gave a hundred pounds to be distributed among the ' poor Irish taken at Cork and Kinsale '. As for McElligot, he subsequently entered the Imperial service, and members of his family served the House of Austria until the end of the First World War.

With Cork in his pocket, and mindful of the lateness of the season, Marlborough pushed on without delay to Kinsale. The town itself was by the end of the seventeenth century quite indefensible, and it passed into Williamite hands without resistance. Marlborough then ordered his Danish troops to carry the Old Fort by storm, which they did on 3 October, largely in consequence of the fact that a shot exploded the magazine, and killed the commander of the fort with a number of his officers.

The New, or Charles, Fort remained, and its defender, Sir Edward Scott, who had served under Berwick at Portsmouth two years before, as well as having been an ensign in the First Guards with Marlborough much earlier than that, refused a summons to surrender with the observation that he might be prepared to consider it in a month's time. Accordingly, Marlborough at once opened his trenches, and by 7 October the English and Danes had sapped almost to the counterscarp. Four days later the heavy guns, which had been brought up from Cork, began their bombardment, and by the fifteenth the breach was pronounced ready for assault. The warning in the report to Charles II ten years before was being justified. Berwick had sent Sarsfield with a body of horse to see if any interference with the enemy's operations was practicable, but this proved not to be the case. On the other hand, Marlborough, whose trenches were already half-full of water, and with the number of his sick rapidly increasing, was becoming seriously worried about the approach of winter.

In these circumstances the successful conclusion of negotiations for the surrender of Charles Fort was not difficult. 'He (Scott) hoped in vain to be relieved by the Duke of Berwick; but at length when he saw no likelihood of succour, and that the walls were all battered about his ears, more than two parts of the garrison being cut off, he surrendered the place upon very honourable conditions (his lady riding out in her coach upon the breach), and himself came to Limerick to give the Duke an account of his defence of the town. The garrison, being about one thousand, two hundred men, had liberty to march out, with their arms and baggage, having a party assigned to conduct them to Limerick'.[9] For the rest, Marlborough had retrieved the failure of William before Limerick. 'In twenty-three days,' Lord Wolseley was to write, 'Marlborough had achieved more than all William's Dutch commanders had done both in Ireland and abroad during the whole of the previous year.'[10] As for Scott, he was subsequently to serve with distinction under Marshal Catinat.

The campaigning season thus came to an end with a marked deterioration in the Jacobite military position. The authority of James was for all practical purposes confined to Connacht and the western part of Munster, while Galway and Limerick were the only ports of any size still in Jacobite hands. The line of the Shannon was as yet intact, and, as we shall see, there was to be a good deal of minor activity along it during the winter months, but it was exceedingly doubtful whether it could be held against the Williamite forces by which it was certain to be attacked in the spring. Then again, the nature of the war was changing, and the conflict was degenerating into a social and political revolution. As the polyglot armies of William advanced across the country their march was characterized by every kind of disorder, for the men only too often behaved as if they were at free quarters in enemy territory, and they committed all sorts of atrocities during their marauding. When the peasantry came forward on all sides, as they did in considerable numbers, to claim the benefit of a proclamation by William promising his protection if they surrendered, they found themselves exposed to the violence of his soldiers. This treatment drew many, who would otherwise have remained peaceful, to join the ranks of the tories and rapparees, who were carrying on a guerrilla war against the Williamites. The numbers of these partisans were also greatly increased by the multitudes of Irish soldiers, who had been ordered by their officers to fend for themselves during the winter, after which they were to return to their units in the spring. Atrocity begat atrocity, and mercy of any sort was unknown; such was the deterioration which had taken place in less than two years.

At the same time the rapparees had their uses, as Sarsfield testified when he wrote that they ' take horses from them (the enemy) every day, and if we had a little money to reward them, our cavalry would be very well mounted at the enemy's expense, which would be a double advantage for us, for while accommodating ourselves, there would be as many dismounted men for them. We have already had more than a thousand this winter, and they have brought me thirty-seven from Lanier's quarters, of which twenty-two were out of his stable.'

Military operations were naturally Berwick's preoccupation during the absence of Tyrconnel in France, but he was also called upon to deal with political intrigue upon a scale which taxed the ingenuity of one of his tender years, however useful the experience may have proved in later life. In view of the criticism of Tyrconnel after the departure of James, it is in no way surprising that it should have come to the surface again when he was himself temporarily out of the country, for in politics the absent are always in the wrong. What ensued may, perhaps, best be described in Berwick's own words:

> After the departure of Tyrconnel for France, Simon Luttrell (brother of the Brigadier),[11] and Brigadier Dorrington, came to me at Limerick, from the general assembly of the nation, to tell me they had reason to suspect that Tyrconnel would not represent their wants with sufficient force to the court of France; and therefore they begged of me to take measures for the doing

of it myself. My answer was that I was astonished they dared to hold such assemblies without my permission; that I forbade them to hold any for the future; and that next morning I would acquaint them with my intentions respecting the matter they had spoken to me upon. Accordingly I summoned all the principal Lords, as well of the clergy as of laity, and all the military officers, down to the colonels inclusive, to attend me. I made a speech nearly to the same purpose as I had done the night before; but to show how well I was inclined, I said that to oblige them I was willing to send such persons as they should approve of to France to represent their real condition and necessities. I proposed to them the Bishop of Cork,[12] the two Luttrells, and Colonel Purcell.

My choice was unanimously approved, and a few days after I dispatched my deputies: at the same time I sent Brigadier Maxwell, a Scotsman, to explain to the King my reasons for appointing this deputation, and to beg of him not to suffer either Brigadier Luttrell or Colonel Purcell to return; they were the two most dangerous incendiaries, and I had chosen them on purpose to get them out of the way. When these gentlemen were got on board they conceived a suspicion that Maxwell might be charged with some instructions relating to them, for which reason they proposed to throw him overboard; but were prevented by the Bishop and the elder Luttrell. The first was a prelate of distinguished piety; the other was of an obliging disposition, and always appeared to me to be a man of honour. Notwithstanding Maxwell's representations the King permitted these gentlemen to return to Ireland. Tyrconnel consented to it; but he had reason to repent of it later. As they had apprehensions of being imprisoned, they caused it to be insinuated to the King the Irish would retaliate upon me for whatever treatment they might receive; and this consideration determined the King to let them come back to Ireland.[13]

The fact that Berwick should have included the Bishop of Cork and Cloyne in this mission well illustrates the close connection which existed between the later Stuarts and the Catholic Church in Ireland. On the accession of James II, the first Catholic sovereign since Mary I, it became customary for the Holy See to fill vacancies in Irish bishoprics on Royal

nomination after due consultation with the appropriate
authorities in Rome and in Ireland. This practice was continued
after the flight of James from Ireland, and throughout the life-
time of his son whom the Holy See always recognized as James
III,[14] the last bishop appointed in this way being Philip Mac-
Davitt to the see of Derry. The Bulls of provision issued from
Rome for each new Irish bishop included a clause which made
it plain that the appointment had been made on Royal nomination, and this practice was maintained until the death of James
III in 1766. After his demise the Holy See did not recognize
the titular Charles III as King of England, and the right of
nomination lapsed by disuse, though Stuart influence was still
strong in Rome as long as the Cardinal Duke of York was
alive. An example of an appointment which was felt in Ireland
to be a Stuart nomination against the declared wishes of the
local diocesan chapter and of the bishops of the province of
Dublin, may be found in the appointment of the Dominican
John Troy to be Bishop of Ossory in December 1776.[15]

While the Jacobite cause in Ireland itself was being weakened
by reverses in the field and dissension in the council-chamber
Tyrconnel was able to effect little on its behalf at the court of
the Most Christian King. What he did there has been the subject of much controversy, for he had had many enemies all his
life, and the last months of it were no exception. He certainly
seems to have managed to place the blame for what had gone
wrong in Ireland upon Lauzun, at any rate in the eyes of
Louvois, who was doubtless only too pleased to hear anything
to the discredit of a man whom he disliked anyhow; probably
in consequence of this welcome information Louvois arranged
for Tyrconnel to have an audience of Louis, though he took
care to be present himself. The King was as usual extremely
gracious, but all he would promise were supplies, a little money,
and some officers. At a farewell audience at Versailles on 3
December 1690 Tyrconnel received from Louis the gift of his
own portrait in a magnificent diamond box. Nor was James by
any means unmindful of his services, for he gave him the
Garter, vacant by the death of the Duke of Grafton in the

attack on Cork, and the full title of Lord-Lieutenant, which he had never held before. ' Now Tyrconnel is as great as the King can make him,' remarked the *Jacobite Narrative*.

At this point the emissaries of his enemies reached France, but although their appearance undoubtedly alarmed Tyrconnel, and they wrought all the mischief they could, they effected singularly little. They were received by Louis personally, but they seem on that occasion to have been restrained in their criticisms of the Viceroy: nevertheless, they did receive a promise that the French general who was to be sent to Ireland should be independent of Tyrconnel, though it rested with James to confirm the arrangement. It was probably only the fear of offending Sarsfield, whose friends they were, that prevented Berwick's advice being taken with the result of their incarceration in the Bastille, and this same desire to placate that general at all costs is evident in the fact that Tyrconnel took back to Ireland a patent for Sarsfield to be Earl of Lucan. What he did not take back with him were Frances and his daughters; as has been shown he had sent them on ahead of him, and they remained behind when he left. Ireland in 1691 was not likely to be a suitable place for Jacobite women and children, however exalted their station.

Tyrconnel returned to Ireland in December 1691 to find a situation which was confusing enough at the time, and which is hardly less confusing in restrospect, for the contemporary evidence is extremely conflicting. Berwick says that ' nothing of any consequence passed during the winter ', and John Stevens, who was at Limerick where ' nothing of note happened ', thought the Williamites ' stupefied or wholly devoted to their ease '. Of modern historians, Macaulay asserted pontifically that ' from October, 1690 till May, 1691, no military operation on a large scale was attempted ', and neither Boulger nor Sergeant mention any fighting. More recently, however, the late Henry Mangan found in the French archives two letters, of which Todhunter had earlier published a brief summary,[16] from Sarsfield to Mountcashel which puts the matter in a very different light.[17]

The first letter is dated 24 February 1691 from Limerick, and it begins with a statement to the effect that at the end of the previous campaigning season William's need to finish off the war in Ireland was very pressing in spite of Marlborough's recent victories, while 'he was informed that we were weak, that our horses were on grass and consequently incapable of service, that we had few arms and that our soldiers lacked everything necessary, which was for the most part literally true'. Nevertheless even so it did not appear that the enemy 'would like to try in the heart of the winter an enterprise which they were not capable of carrying out in the finest part of the summer if they were not encouraged by some traitors amongst us'. Sarsfield enumerates these as Lord Riverston, the former Thomas Nugent, whom James had created a peer in 1689; Colonel Alexander Macdonell, the governor of Galway, who had married Riverston's sister; Colonel John Hamilton and Judge Daly. Sarsfield goes on to say that he had seen a letter from the King to Berwick informing him that 'he had received from England the same intelligence concerning the design of those I have just named'. Preparations for a renewed offensive on the part of the Williamites were therefore put in hand.

At the beginning of last December the enemy divided all their army and all their militia into four corps, of which one was of 8,000 men, horse, dragoons, and infantry, was commanded by Douglas. The second, of 6,000 horse, foot, and dragoons was under the command of Kirke and of Lanier; this body which was sometimes divided but hardly separated one from the other, marched to Lanesborough. The third was of 3,500 men and marched towards the county Kerry under the command of Tettan. Ginkel and Scravenmore marched at the head of the fourth which advanced towards the city of Limerick, which they found in good position by the care and vigilance of Colonel Dorrington, who was the governor. They only alarmed the city, and then marched towards Kerry to support the troops they had sent there. As we were warned in advance of their design we did all we could to give them a good reception.

Sarsfield certainly did everything in his power to ensure that the Williamites got ' a good reception ', for he personally visited all the more likely crossing-places of the Shannon, such as Portumna, Banagher, Lanesborough, and Jamestown: in each case he saw that the defending forces were adequate to what might be required of them, and he caused such entrenchments to be thrown up as might be necessary. He stationed himself at Athlone with a strategic reserve of two thousand infantry, horse, and dragoons ' to send help where it should be required '.

The Williamite offensive began with a move in the direction of Lanesborough, but that was apparently too tough a nut to crack, so William's troops contented themselves with ' burning and pillaging a small district of the neighbouring county '. In this operation Kirke had split in two the force under his command, and Sarsfield was going to take advantage of this fact when he was warned by the Jacobite commander at Jamestown that he was himself about to be attacked by Douglas. In these circumstances Sarsfield marched at once to his assistance, considering ' that it was more advisable to preserve what we had than to undertake something against the enemy '. As it happened his presence was unnecessary, for the enemy had been driven off before his arrival; he then prepared to put into operation his plan to attack Kirke's detached corps, but this, too, had been routed without his assistance. Further south Tettau did invade Kerry, but he was unable to effect anything of importance there, and was obliged to withdraw. The result of these various operations was such that Sarsfield was justified in claiming that ' in spite of our enemies we have preserved our quarters on the other side of the Shannon in the county Westmeath, the King's county and around Nenagh for not having succeeded in their attempt on the passages of the Shannon, they hoped at least to oblige all the troops we had on the other side of the river to cross to this side, in order to starve us, but we had secured all the passages so well that their plans have been without effect, and, on the contrary, we have extended our boundaries.'

Corroboration of these reports comes from Williamite sources for in April orders came from William that Douglas and Kirke were posted to Flanders for the ensuing campaign, and that Lanier was to return to England. Their supersession is surely a measure both of Sarsfield's success in defending the line of the Shannon and of their failure to establish the bridgeheads that were required of them.

It is a matter of regret that on the Jacobite side Clifford was not also removed before his negligence or treachery handed Limerick over to the enemy. Sarsfield had little use for him, and in the letter to Mountcashel already quoted he said that Clifford's ' head has been turned, and he has become insupportable because they have not made him a major-general.' A man with a ' chip on his shoulder ' is, indeed, seldom a satisfactory general. In a subsequent letter, also to Mountcashel, from Galway on 23 March 1691, Sarsfield returned to the charge:

> Your friend, Clifford, who is a strong supporter of Tyrconnel, and always as foolish as you knew him, is very discontented. . . His folly was nearly costing us dearly not long ago, for although he was warned in good time that the enemy intended to take his quarters, he continued to spend the preceding night seven miles away, and only arrived in the morning to give his orders at the time when the enemy appeared, and he lost his head so much that he didn't know where he was, so that our fellows were forced to retire in disorder, but also without danger, owing to the weak pursuit by the enemy, who, however, owing to this little appearance of success, did not fail to appear next morning before Ballymore, under General Ginkle, Major-General Kirke, and Lanier, believing that we would abandon the castle to their army, but they deceived themselves, for having advanced to attack a ruin defended by a hundred musketeers, they were so well received that they retired. If Clifford had been believed, the position would have been abandoned, but the governor, who is a man of honour and courage, would not consent, and in fact if we had quitted it we would have lost all that we had beyond the Shannon.

' About the fourteenth of January ', says the *Jacobite Narrative,* ' the Duke of Tyrconnel, accompanied by Sir Richard

Nagle, Sir Stephen Rice and others, returned out of France
into Ireland and landed at Galway, bringing with him a few
thousand pounds in silver and gold. From thence he came to
Limerick, where he was received with the usual respect that is
due to a person in his high station.' The passage from France
was not so easy as it had been, for the loss of Cork and Kinsale
meant that Cape Clear and the coasts of Kerry and Clare had
to be circumnavigated, but whatever the weather Tyrconnel en-
countered on his voyage it can hardly have been as stormy as
the political situation which he found on his arrival at
Limerick.

Following on the intrigues described by Sarsfield in his
letter to Mountcashel firm action had been taken by Berwick,
who had removed from their respective offices Lord Riverston
and Colonel Macdonell, while Judge Daly was put in prison.
Tyrconnel at once restored the first two to favour, while Daly
was released from imprisonment: this last act was at any rate
a mistake, for Daly was very definitely a traitor. In these circumstances Berwick cannot have been sorry that Tyrconnel
had brought with him orders from James that he was himself
to go back to France. He never again served in Ireland in person though he was more than once to be intimately concerned
with events in that country. He has left upon record his criticisms of the campaign after he left, but it must be borne in
mind that he was dependent upon second-hand information for
Irish events in 1691, and prejudiced second-hand evidence at
that, so that his conclusions cannot carry the weight which
they would have done had he taken part in these operations
himself.

Tyrconnel may have failed to persuade Louis to send any
more French troops to Ireland, but the French King did provide some money as well as a general in the person of Lieutenant-General de Saint Ruth,[18] with whom came Major-Generals
d'Usson and the Chevalier de Tassé. To some extent Saint
Ruth seems to have put himself forward to secure the command, for he had praised the valour of the Irish with whom
he had served in Savoy, and he seems to have been very popu-

lar with all ranks in the Mountcashel Brigade. He was essentially a fighting general, but he had fought under the cautious
Catinat, and he had acquired some of that great commander's
skill as a tactician; whether he was equally competent as a
strategist is another matter.[19] Rightly or wrongly Berwick
had no very high opinion of Saint Ruth, either as a man or as
a soldier: 'Saint Ruth was naturally very vain, and though
the Viceroy paid him every attention imaginable, and left the
whole conduct of the campaign to his management, yet having
a superior in the army was a perpetual source of discontent to
him. On this account he had recourse to those turbulent instru-
ments I have already mentioned, and threw out invectives on
all occasions against Tyrconnel, till at last he forced him to
quit the army and retire to Limerick.'[20]

Whether or not Berwick was justified in his attitude towards
Saint Ruth, there can be no doubt that Tyrconnel's supersession by the Frenchman of the command of the army in the
field rankled with the Lord-Lieutenant, and was not the least
of the causes of difference between the two men. Whether
James had acted at the instigation of Louis when he gave to
Saint Ruth the last word in military matters, or whether he was
influenced by Tyrconnel's enemies, is hard to say, but the result
was to create a disastrous division of control, and there were
already dissensions enough in the Jacobite ranks. To make
matters even worse, Saint Ruth contrived to get into the bad
books of Sarsfield as well as those of Tyrconnel, while d'Usson
was on much better terms with the Viceroy than he was with
his own superior officer.

The strategy on both sides in the campaign of 1691 was the
logical outcome of the events of the winter months, and the
Jacobite aim was to repeat the success of Sarsfield in holding
the line of the Shannon, thereby protecting Galway and
Limerick; the focal points were still Limerick and Athlone, for
they both covered crossings of the river. On the Williamite
side no Lord-Lieutenant had been appointed when William
himself left Ireland, and the civil government was in the hands
of the Lords Justices, while the military command was retained

R

by Ginkel, who lay at Mullingar with fifty thousand men. When the campaigning season opened it soon became evident that he had decided on a different strategy from that of William in the previous year. He moved on Athlone, and without any great difficulty obtained possession of the suburbs on the Leinster bank, but even when this had been done his most difficult task lay ahead, for he had to force a passage across a wide river which had only one ford. Here, according to Berwick, the first mistake was made: ' As the fortifications of the town on that side, which was nearest to the King's army, were nothing but mud, it had been proposed to Saint Ruth to level the curtains, so that the army might enter the place in order of battle if there should be occasion; but he payed no attention to it.'[21] Foremost among those who urged this course was Tyrconnel, but his advice was rejected with so bad a grace, and he was personally treated with such gross discourtesy, that, as we have seen, he withdrew to Limerick.

This was bad enough, but worse was to follow, for Ginkel proceeded to open a heavy bombardment of the town, which he continued until a breach was practicable. Major-General Thomas Maxwell, who was in charge of the defence of Athlone, then asked Saint Ruth for reinforcements, only, however, to be told that if he was afraid he would be relieved of his command. Such was the position on 30 June when Ginkel stormed the town, and Saint Ruth found himself reduced to the rôle of a spectator of his opponent's victory; it is true that as soon as he heard what was taking place he had sent two brigades to assist the defenders of Athlone, but it was too late, and they effected nothing. The first result of Saint Ruth's generalship, therefore, was to lose the line of the Shannon which Sarsfield had been at such pains to preserve.

After this disaster the Frenchman immediately broke camp, and retired towards Ballinasloe. There were three main courses then open to him. He could blockade Ginkel in Athlone; he could divide his forces and fall back on Limerick and Galway; or he could risk a pitched battle in the open field. ' Through vexation and shame for his disappointment at Athlone, he resolved at all events to come to a battle,' wrote Berwick. He does not seem to have been under the restraining orders in this matter to which Lauzun had been subject, possibly because his troops were Irish, not French, and so in the eyes of France were the more expendable. However this may be his word in the last resort was law, so having made no attempt to defend the passage over the River Suck, he chose Aughrim as his field of battle.[22] There the greatest pitched battle in Irish history, with the possible exception of Clontarf, was fought on Sunday, 12 July 1691.

The two armies were of approximately equal strength, that is to say about twenty thousand strong, and the Jacobite position was carefully chosen. James's forces occupied the ridge stretching southward from Aughrim village, with their left resting on the ruined castle, and their right on a stream beyond Kilcommodan church. The ground sloped away before their centre to a boggy tract intersected by another stream. A frontal attack by hostile cavalry was impossible, while mounted men could only approach the left by ' an old broken causeway, only large enough for two horses to pass it at a time ', and on the right the ' pass ' of Urachree, being difficult ground, was easily defended. On neither wing was the ground on the Jacobite side of the approach sufficiently extended for a large force to deploy. On the left the causeway opened into a flat cornfield in front of the castle, where not more than four battalions could form a front; on the right there was more space, but still not enough for any great force. The Jacobites were drawn up in two lines of infantry regiments along the brow of the hill, with the cavalry on either wing. Further back, in the left rear, Sarsfield was posted with a reserve of horse – a mere six squadrons according to Berwick – out of sight of the field of battle and with instructions from Saint Ruth, with whom his relations would not appear to have improved, not to move without orders.

The Jacobites remained on the defensive – it will be remembered that different tactics had cost the Scots dear at Dunbar in 1650 – and thus forced their opponents to attack in peculiarly difficult circumstances. A ding-dong struggle produced something like stalemate. The Irish right wing held, and the Irish foot in the centre behaved so well that Saint Ruth declared he would beat the enemy back to the gates of Dublin. Only on the Jacobite left had the Williamites won any success, but this meant that they could now bring their cavalry to bear against the Irish foot, and that in a flank attack. Saint Ruth realized the threat, and resolved to meet it before it could develop. He had plenty of horse for the purpose, but for some reason, probably personal, he omitted even to acquaint Sarsfield with the course of events. As Saint Ruth rode over to take command of the charge he stopped for a moment to direct the fire of a battery, and he was just moving on when a ball from the Williamite lines at the extreme range of eight hundred yards struck him dead.

There are two schools of thought in respect of the consequences of Saint Ruth's death. Some maintain that it converted what might have been a Jacobite victory into a Jacobite defeat, while others assert that the battle was already lost in any event – Berwick held the latter view. No one seemed able to take the dead man's place at such short notice, so the projected counter-attack was never made, and the Williamites pressed their advantage. As for Sarsfield, his first knowledge of what had taken place is said to have been conveyed by the spectacle of the fugitives streaming over the hill.

Tyrconnel was at Limerick when the news of Aughrim reached him. According to the *Jacobite Narrative,*

> He was struck with a deep wound of sorrow, and the more because the battle was lost so unexpectedly. However, he roused his courage and kept hope alive, resolving to continue the war since he found the excellent magnanimity of the army and that the loss of that day was not very considerable. Upon which, in the first place, he despatches away into France three expresses, one after the other, the Earl of Abercorn, the Lord Thomas Howard of Norfolk, and Mr. Doran, his own secretary, that if one or two should fail in the journey, the third might arrive safe at St. Germain's to give the King a true account of

the combat at Aughrim. Secondly, he requests by these couriers a reinforcement of trained men out of France at the farthest by the next spring, and in the interim provisions and ammunition for the army; for he did not doubt to preserve Limerick. . . Thirdly, he goes out of Limerick on the fourth morning after the battle to receive the cavalry six miles off the town, which he cantoned near Limerick . . . while he was expecting the foot to come in, and then he will enter upon a consultation upon what is best to be done in this straitness of time.

Ginkel for his part followed up his victory by marching straight on Galway, which capitulated on 22 July after a mere show of resistance, and then moved on to Limerick. From William's point of view it was of the utmost importance to prevent the Irish from lasting over another winter, for he wanted his troops back on the mainland of Europe, where he and his allies were being hard pressed by the generals of Louis XIV. Hoping as he did to thwart William's purpose, Tyrconnel was the mainstay of the defence, and he spared no effort in the uphill task of reconciling the Irish and French standpoints.[23]

Unhappily he found himself concerned with treason on his own side as well as with activity on the enemy's, and the chief traitor was Henry Luttrell, who had got in touch with Ginkel immediately after the fall of Galway, and discussed what could be granted in case of submission. In making this approach Luttrell seems to have had the support of a section of the army, but not of Sarsfield, through whom, in fact, his treachery was discovered in the shape of a letter from the Williamite headquarters. Sarsfield took it to Tyrconnel, and Luttrell was arrested and tried, but he had too much influence to receive a more severe sentence than imprisonment during the King's pleasure. It may be added that when the Jacobite cause finally went down after the surrender of Limerick he was set at liberty and received a pension from William.

By this time Tyrconnel's life was drawing to a close. On 10 August he was the chief guest at a dinner party given by his friend d'Usson, and 'he and the company were very merry,' says the *Jacobite Narrative,* 'but at night, upon his preparing to go to bed, he found himself indisposed. The next day his malady increased. Remedies were applied yet to no effect. On the third day, observing his weakness to be great, he settled his wordly affairs and took care for his conscience. . . On the following day His Excellency grew speechless, and on Friday the four-teenth, being the fifth day of his sickness, he expired.' It need hardly be said that the rumour at once went round that he had been poisoned by an extremist on his own side, and mention was made of a cup of ratafia, but Mr Sergeant was probably nearer to the truth when he wrote that ' the combined effect of his unceasing toil and anxiety, his excessive bulk and weak heart – and, no doubt, also the over-merry party at d'Usson's – were sufficient to account for the sudden collapse of a man of sixty-one, without recourse to the horrible idea that someone in his own party brought him to an unnatural end.'[24]

On his death-bed Tyrconnel appointed three Lords Justices to carry on the government of that part of Ireland which still remained in Jacobite hands: they were Alexander Fitton, Lord Gosworth; Sir Richard Nagle; and Francis Plowden, an English-man who had recently arrived from Saint Germain, and who was later one of the governors of the Prince of Wales. By their instructions Tyrconnel was buried in Limerick cathedral ' not with that pomp his merits exacted,' says the *Jacobite Narrative,* ' but with that decency which the present state of affairs admitted '.

NOTES

[1] The best recent account of this operation is by Cox, Captain, G. S.: *Marlborough in Ireland, An Cosantoir,* Vol. VIII, no. 6, pp. 287-293.

[2] Chidsey, D. B.: *Marlborough, Portrait of a Conqueror,* pp. 140-141. London. 1930.

[3] Quoted by Churchill, W. S.: *Marlborough, His Life and Times,* Vol. I, pp. 326-327. London. 1933.

[4] *Cf. Calendar of Treasury Books,* 1681-85, p. 69. Particulars of the artillery to be furnished are given in the *Calendar of State Papers, Domestic,* 1679-80, p. 244.

[5] Five years earlier he had earned an unenviable reputation in the suppression of Monmouth's rising, and more recently he had relieved Derry.

[6] *Cf.* Davies, Very Rev. R.: *Journal,* p. 149.

[7] *Answer to King's State of the Protestants.*

[8] Quoted by Churchill, W. S.: *Marlborough: His Life and Times,* Vol. I, p. 330. London. 1933.

[9] *King James's Irish Army List,* Vol. II, p. 663.

[10] *Life of Marlborough,* Vol. II, p. 216. London. 1894.

[11] *I.e.* Henry Luttrell. After the battle of Aughrim he was suspected of intrigue with the enemy, and was put under arrest by Sarsfield. There would appear to have been some ground for the suspicion, since William subsequently gave him a pension. Henry Luttrell was murdered in Dublin in 1717, but the identity of the assassin was never discovered.

[12] Peter Creagh, Catholic Bishop of Cork and Cloyne, later translated to Dublin.

[13] *Memoirs,* Vol. I, pp. 78-83. London. 1779.

[14] *Cf.* Renehan, L.: *Collections of Irish Church History,* pp. 297-8. Dublin. 1861.

[15] *Cf.* Carrigan: *History and Antiquities of the Diocese of Ossory,* Vol. I, pp. 180-2.

[16] *Life of Patrick Sarsfield, Earl of Lucan,* pp. 125 and 129-132. Dublin. 1895.

[17] *Ministere de la Guerre,* A 1066 *(Irlande VI),* No. 187. Also *The Irish Sword,* Vol. I, pp. 24-32. Dublin. 1953.

[18] His real name was Charles Chalmot, Marquis de St Rhue.

[19] *Cf.* Boulger, D. C.: *The Battle of the Boyne,* p. 225. London. 1911.

[20] *Memoirs,* Vol. I, p. 91. London. 1779.

[21] *Ibid.* p. 89.

[22] *Cf.* Dr G. A. Hayes-McCoy in *The Journal of the Galway Archaeological and Historical Society,* Vol. XX, Nos. I and II.

[23] *Cf.* J. G. Simms in *The Irish Sword,* No. 5, pp. 23-28. Dublin. 1956.

[24] *Little Jennings and Fighting Dick Talbot,* Vol. II, p. 562. London. 1913.

EPILOGUE

As HAS been shown, Galway capitulated to the Williamites on 22 July after a mere show of resistance, and Ginkel then moved on Limerick, which might well have proved a very difficult nut to crack in view of what had happened there in the previous year, but the heart had gone out of the Jacobites; Tyrconnel was no longer there to animate them, and the French assistance was delayed until it was useless. In these circumstances it is impossible not to agree with Dr Simms that Ginkel's victory ' was psychological rather than military '.[1]

On 16 September he managed to throw a bridge of tin boats across the Shannon above Limerick, and on the 22nd he passed over it with a large part of his army, approaching the Thomond bridge, which joins Clare to the English town of Limerick. This move did not, indeed, put him in any better position for an assault on the city, as he still had the river between him and the town, but it cut the garrison off from the Irish cavalry and dragoons on the Clare side. By this time Sarsfield and Wauchope were weary of waiting for French help that never came, nor did they see much point in conducting a long guerrilla war in Connacht. On the other hand the author of the *Jacobite Narrative* says that Tyrconnel would never have surrendered Limerick ' because he expected to retrieve the country by spinning out the war.[2] So a council of war was held, and it was decided to capitulate, not only on behalf of the garrison at Limerick, but for all the Jacobite forces still under arms in Ireland. Over a fortnight later Châteaurenard arrived with a fleet consisting of eighteen men-of-war and twenty cargo vessels well supplied with food and ammunition.

The terms of the military capitulation were relatively easy

to arrange, and, as in Cromwell's time, it was agreed that those Irish soldiers who were desirous of entering the French service should be transported to France, for William was no more desirous than had been the Lord Protector of leaving large numbers of fighting-men at large in Ireland. The articles of the civil treaty were more complicated to arrange, and hostilities were suspended until the arrival of the Williamite Lords Justices from Dublin. By the Treaty of Limerick, as ultimately arranged, Catholics were to exercise their religion as in the reign of Charles II; a Parliament was to be summoned as soon as possible, and endeavours made to obtain for its members such further security as would preserve them from disturbance on account of their religion; and no extra oath was to be extracted from Catholics who submitted other than that of allegiance. All persons within Limerick and other garrison towns at the time of the capitulation, and all officers and men in the counties of Limerick, Clare, Kerry, Cork, and Mayo, were to be restored to their estates as in the time of Charles II: such persons were to receive a full amnesty, and were not to be molested by lawsuits for acts committed during the war.

Whether the victors signed this treaty with the deliberate intention of breaking it, or whether the idea occurred to them when Sarsfield and his soldiers had been safely transported to France, is not easy to determine, but there can surely be little doubt that had Tyrconnel lived, and the advice with which he is credited been taken, the results of the war might have been very different. Ginkel and William were eager to bring hostilities to an end, and the Irish were still more dangerous than many historians have supposed. Limerick was indeed hard-pressed, but its powers of resistance were far from exhausted, and even if it had been taken it would have been possible to carry on a guerrilla type of war, for which both the country and the people were by no means unsuited. Such a war would have prevented England from employing its full force on the mainland of Europe, and might at any moment have been rendered formidable by the arrival of help from France.

The greater the necessity for making terms on the Williamite side the stronger was the moral obligation to adhere to them with strict fidelity, and there were strong arguments for leniency. It was in particular monstrous to treat the Irish as rebels. James had neither deserted nor abdicated the Irish throne: on the contrary, he had been driven by the Revolution to pay his first visit to Ireland, and he had been more truly *de facto* King of Ireland during the past two years than in any other period of his reign. In any event, as far back as the end of the fifteenth century it had been held that no person assisting a *de facto* monarch should be liable to impeachment or attainder.

It was the English Parliament, always a foe to Irish liberty, which set the example of intolerance, and with the failure of James 'an opportunity was missed of founding an Irish nation'.[3] When it is asked why the Irish, having fought so valiantly for three long years, made no move on their own soil in 1715 and 1745, the answer must be the numbing effect of the Penal Laws. In spite of the promises solemnly made at the surrender of Limerick, no Catholic was allowed to play a part in the national life. In 1759 a Catholic girl of considerable fortune was urged by a suitor to change her faith, and to avoid him she fled to the house of a friend. The latter was denounced to the authorities, and at his trial the Chancellor very aptly summed up the existing state of affairs by declaring that the 'law does not presume a Papist to exist in the kingdom, nor can they as much as breathe here without the connivance of the Government.'

A Catholic was excluded both from voting and from taking a seat in Parliament. He might not aspire to the Bench or the Bar, act as sheriff, or hold any office under the Crown. No Catholic might buy land, inherit it, or receive it as a gift from a Protestant. No lease might be held for more than thirty-one years, or on such terms that the profits exceeded one-third of the rent. On a man's death his estate was divided among his sons, but if the eldest became a Protestant the whole was settled on him. All bishops and priests who refused to take the Oath of Allegiance were ordered to leave the country. Only registered priests might celebrate Mass; all others were subject to the penalties of High Treason. Catholics were forbidden to teach in a school or to enter a university, while they were not allowed to send their children abroad to be educated. No such vindictive treatment was meted out to the opponents of the Revolution in the other two kingdoms, and after their betrayal at Limerick the Irish had as much hope of successfully resisting their conquerors by force of arms as had the Jews in more recent times of overthrowing the not dissimilar tyranny of Hitler.

NOTES

[1] *The Irish Sword*, Vol. II, pp. 23-28. Dublin. 1954.
[2] P. 175. ed. J. T. Gilbert. Dublin. 1892.
[3] Maxwell, C.: *Dublin under the Georges, 1714-1830*. Dublin. 1964.

SHORT BIBLIOGRAPHY

Belloc, H.: *James the Second.* (London. 1928)

Boulger, D. C.: *The Battle of the Boyne.* (London. 1911)

Churchill, Sir Winston: *Marlborough, His Life and Times.* (London. 1933-1938)

D'Avaux, Comte: *Négociations en Irlande, 1689-1690.* (Dublin. 1934)

Franciscan Fathers: *Father Luke Wadding.* (Dublin. 1957)

Haswell, Jock: *James II.* (London. 1972)

MacLysaght, Edward: *Irish Life in the Seventeenth Century.* (Cork. 1950)

Milligan, C. D.: *History of the Siege of Londonderry.* (Belfast. 1951)

Petrie, Sir Charles: *The Marshal Duke of Berwick.* (London. 1953)

Petrie, Sir Charles: *The Jacobite Movement.* (London. 1959)

Sergeant, P. W.: *Little Jennings and Fighting Dick Talbot.* (London. 1913)

Simms, J. G.: *The Williamite Confiscation in Ireland, 1690-1703.* (London. 1956)

Simms, J. G.: *Jacobite Ireland, 1685-1691.* (London. 1969)

INDEX